Business Glossary
English-Italian/Italian-English

Titles in the series

Business Glossaries in:

English-French/French-English	ISBN 0-948549-52-1
English-German/German-English	ISBN 0-948549-53-X
English-Spanish/Spanish-English	ISBN 0-948549-54-8
English-Italian/Italian-English	ISBN 0-948549-55-6

Also available

Bilingual Business Dictionaries:

Business French (French-English/English-French)
600pp 50,000 terms   ISBN 0-948549-64-5
Business German (German-English/English-German)
650pp 50,000 terms   ISBN 0-948549-50-5
Business Spanish (English-Spanish/Spanish-English)
736pp 50,000 terms   ISBN 0-948549-30-0

Multilingual Menu Dictionary   ISBN 0-948549-86-6
(English/Italian/French/German/Spanish/Japanese)

For our complete catalogue with over 40 specialist English and
bilingual dictionaries, use the order form at the back of this book.

Business Glossary
English-Italian/Italian-English

General Editor
PH Collin

Italian Editors
Peter Blanchard
Sylvia Berlincioni

PETER COLLIN PUBLISHING

First Published in Great Britain 1995

published by
Peter Collin Publishing Ltd
1 Cambridge Road, Teddington, Middlesex, TW11 8DT

Business Glossary Text
© Copyright P.H. Collin 1995

British Library Cataloguing in Publications Data

A Catalogue record for this book is available from the British Library

ISBN 0-948549-55-6

Text computer typeset by PCP
Printed and bound in Finland by WSOY

Cover illustration by Gary Weston

Preface

This glossary is for any business person or traveller who needs to deal with a foreign business language. It contains over 5,000 essential business terms with clear and accurate translations.

How to use this glossary

This glossary is arranged in two main sections. The first lists English terms with a French translation, the second half lists Spanish terms with equivalent English translation.

Throughout the Business Glossary we have used a number of abbreviations:

adj	adjective	aggetivo
adv	adverb	avverbio
f	feminine	femminile
fpl	feminine plural	femminile plurale
m	masculine	maschile
mf	masculine or feminine	maschile o femminile
mpl	masculine plural	maschile plurale
n	noun	sostantivo
v	verb	verbo

Prefazione

Questo glossario è rivolto a qualsiasi viaggiatore o persona di affari che abbia necessità di usare una lingua straniera a livello di business. Contiene piu di 5000 termini commerciali indispensabili con traduzioni chiare e accurate.

Come usare questo glossario

Questo glossario è organizzato in due sezioni principali. La prima elenca le parole inglesi con le traduzioni italiane, mentre la seconda elenca le parole italiane con la traduzione inglese equivalente. In tutto il Glossario Commerciale abbiamo usato un certo numero di abbreviazioni:

adj	adjective	aggetivo
adv	adverb	avverbio
f	feminine	femminile
fpl	feminine plural	femminile plurale
m	masculine	maschile
mf	masculine or feminine	maschile o femminile
mpl	masculine plural	maschile plurale
n	noun	sostantivo
v	verb	verbo

English-Italian
Inglese-Italiano

Aa

A1 di prima classe

abandon abbandonare *o* lasciare

abandon an action rinunciare ad un'azione (f)

abatement riduzione (f)

abroad all'estero

absence assenza (f) *o* mancanza (f)

absent assente

absolute monopoly monopolio (m) perfetto

accelerated depreciation ammortamento (m) accelerato

accept (v) *[agree]* accettare

accept (v) *[take something]* accettare

accept a bill accettare una cambiale

accept delivery of a shipment prendere in consegna un carico di merce

accept liability for something assumersi la responsabilità di qualcosa

acceptable accettabile *o* soddisfacente

acceptance accettazione (f)

acceptance of an offer accettazione (f) di un'offerta

acceptance sampling campionatura (f) per accettazione

accommodation address indirizzo (m) di comodo

accommodation bill cambiale (f) di favore *o* effetto (m) di comodo

according to conformemente a

account conto (m)

account executive direttore (m) del servizio marketing *o* direttore delle vendite

account for rendere conto

account in credit conto (m) in credito

account on stop conto (m) bloccato

account: on account in acconto

accountant ragioniere (m) *o* ragioniera (f) *o* contabile (m)

accounting contabilità (f)

accounts department reparto (m) contabilità

accounts payable conti (mpl) passivi

accounts receivable conti (mpl) attivi

accrual importo (m) maturato

accrual of interest maturazione (f) degli interessi

accrue maturare *o* accumularsi

accrued interest interesse (m) maturato

accumulate accumulare *o* accantonare

accurate accurato *o* preciso

acknowledge receipt of a letter accusare ricevuta di una lettera

acknowledgement conferma (f)

acquire a company entrare in possesso di una società

acquisition acquisizione (f) *o* acquisto (m)

across-the-board uniforme *o* indiscriminato

act (v) *[do something]* agire

act (v) *[work]* funzionare

act of God causa (f) di forza maggiore

acting facente funzione di *o* sostituto

acting manager direttore (m) facente funzione

action *[lawsuit]* azione (f) *o* causa (f)

action *[thing done]* azione (f)

action for damages causa (f) per risarcimento

actual effettivo *o* reale

actuals prezzi effettivi (mpl) di vendita

actuarial tables tavole (fpl) attuariali

actuary attuario (m)

ad valorem ad valorem *o* in base al valore di

ad valorem tax tassa (f) ad valorem

add aggiungere *o* sommare

add on 10% for service aggiungere il 10% per il servizio

add up a column of figures sommare una colonna di cifre

addition *[calculation]* addizione (f) *o* somma (f)

addition *[thing added]* aggiunta (f)

additional addizionale *o* supplementare

additional charges spese (fpl) supplementari

additional premium premio (m) addizionale

address (n) indirizzo (m) *o* recapito (m)

address (v) indirizzare *o* rivolgere la parola a qualcuno

address a letter *or* **a parcel** indirizzare una lettera *o* un pacco

address label etichetta (f) indirizzata

address list lista (f) di indirizzi

addressee destinatario (m)

adequate adeguato *o* sufficiente

adjourn aggiornare *o* rimandare

adjourn a meeting aggiornare una riunione

adjudicate in a dispute pronunciarsi in una vertenza

adjudication aggiudicazione (f) *o* giudizio (m)

adjudication tribunal tribunale (m) di arbitrato

adjudicator giudice (m)

adjust adattare *o* adeguare

adjustment accomodamento (m) *o* accordo (m)

administration amministrazione (f) *o* gestione (f)

administrative amministrativo

administrative expenses spese (fpl) di amministrazione

admission ammissione (f)

admission charge spese (fpl) d'ammissione *o* spese d'entrata

admit *[confess]* ammettere

admit *[let in]* far entrare

advance (adj) anticipato

advance (n) *[increase]* aumento (m)

advance (n) *[loan]* anticipo (m)

advance (v) *[increase]* aumentare

advance (v) *[lend]* prestare

advance booking prenotazione (f) anticipata

advance on account anticipazione (f) su un conto

advance payment pagamento (m) anticipato

advertise fare pubblicità *o* reclamizzare

advertise a new product reclamizzare un nuovo prodotto

advertise a vacancy pubblicare un'inserzione (f) per un impiego disponibile

advertisement annuncio (m) pubblicitario *o* pubblicità (f)

advertiser inserzionista (m) *o* chi fa pubblicità

advertising pubblicità (f) *o* reclame (f)

advertising agency agenzia (f) di pubblicità

advertising budget budget (m) pubblicitario

advertising campaign campagna (f) pubblicitaria

advertising manager direttore (m) della pubblicità

advertising rates tariffe (f) delle inserzioni pubblicitarie

advertising space spazio (m) pubblicitario

advice note bolletta (f) d'avviso

advise *[tell what happened]* informare *o* avvisare

advise *[what should be done]* consigliare *o* raccomandare

adviser *or* **advisor** consulente (m)

affidavit attestazione (f) ufficiale

affiliated affiliato *o* associato

affirmative affermativo

afford permettersi *o* avere i mezzi economici

after-sales service assistenza (f) post-vendita alla clientela

after-tax profit utile (m) al netto delle imposte

agency agenzia (f)

agenda ordine (m) del giorno

agent *[representative]* agente (m) *o* rappresentante (m)

agent *[working in an agency]* agente (m)

AGM (= annual general meeting) Assemblea (f) Generale degli Azionisti

agree *[accept]* accettare

agree *[approve]* approvare

agree *[be same as]* concordare *o* corrispondere a

agree to do something acconsentire a fare qualcosa *o* accettare di fare qualcosa

agree with *[be same as]* concordare *o* corrispondere a

agree with *[of same opinion]* essere d'accordo con

agreed convenuto *o* concordato

agreed price prezzo (m) concordato

agreement accordo (m)

agricultural agricolo *o* agrario

aim (n) scopo (m) *o* proposito (m)

aim (v) avere lo scopo di

air aria (f)

air freight trasporto (m) merci via aerea

air freight charges *or* **rates** spese trasporto merci via aerea

air letter lettera (f) aerea

air terminal terminal (m) della compagnia aerea

airfreight (v) trasportare merci via aerea

airline linea (f) aerea *o* compagnia (f) aerea

airmail (n) posta (f) aerea

airmail (v) spedire per posta aerea

airmail sticker etichetta (f) di posta aerea

airport aeroporto (m)

airport bus autobus (m) dell'aeroporto

airport tax tasse (fpl) aeroportuali

airport terminal terminal (m)

airtight packaging imballaggio (m) ermetico

all expenses paid tutte le spese pagate

all-in totale *o* globale

all-in price prezzo (m) tutto compreso

all-risks policy polizza (f) contro tutti i rischi

allocate stanziare

allow *[agree]* accettare *o* ammettere

allow *[give]* accordare *o* cedere

allow *[permit]* permettere

allow 10% for carriage calcolare 10% per il trasporto

allow for calcolare *o* dedurre

allowance for depreciation accantonamento (m) al fondo di ammortamento

alphabetical order ordine (m) alfabetico

alter modificare *o* cambiare

alteration modifica (f) *o* cambiamento (m)

alternative (adj) alternativo

alternative (n) alternativa (f)

amend correggere

amendment emendamento (m) *o* rettifica (f)

American (adj) americano

American (n) Americano, -ana

amortization ammortamento (m)

amortize ammortare *o* ammortizzare

amount *[of money]* ammontare (m) *o* importo (m)

amount owing importo (m) dovuto

amount paid importo (m) pagato

amount to ammontare a

analyse *or* **analyze** analizzare

analyse the market potential analizzare il potenziale del mercato

analysis analisi (f)

announce annunciare

announcement annuncio (m)

annual annuale *o* annuo

annual accounts rendiconti (mpl) annuali

annual general meeting (AGM) Assemblea (f) Generale degli Azionisti

annual report relazione (f) annuale al bilancio

annually annualmente

answer (n) risposta (f)

answer (v) rispondere

answer a letter rispondere a una lettera

answer the telephone rispondere al telefono

answering machine segreteria (f) telefonica

answering service servizio (m) segreteria telefonica

antedate retrodatare

apologize scusarsi

apology scusa (f)

appeal (n) *[against a decision]* ricorso (m) *o* appello (m)

appeal (n) *[attraction]* richiamo (m)

appeal (v) *[against a decision]* ricorrere in appello *o* appellare

appeal to (v) *[attract]* attirare

appear sembrare

appendix appendice (f)

applicant for a job candidato (m) a un posto di lavoro

application domanda (f) *o* istanza (f)

application for a job domanda (f) d'impiego

application form modulo (m) per domanda di assunzione

apply for *[ask for]* chiedere

apply for a job fare domanda d'impiego

apply in writing fare domanda scritta

apply to *[affect]* riguardare

appoint nominare

appointment *[job]* impiego (m) *o* posto (m)

appointment *[meeting]* appuntamento (m)

appointment *[to a job]* nomina (f)

appointments book agenda (f)

appointments vacant impieghi (mpl) disponibili

appreciate *[how good something is]* apprezzare

appreciate *[increase in value]* aumentare di valore

appreciation *[how good something is]* apprezzamento (m)

appreciation *[in value]* rivalutazione (f)

appropriate (v) *[funds]* destinare

approval benestare (m)

approval: on approval in prova *o* in esame

approve the terms of a contract approvare i termini di un contratto

approximate approssimativo

approximately approssimativamente

arbitrate in a dispute arbitrare una vertenza

arbitration arbitrato (m)

arbitration board *or* **arbitration tribunal** tribunale (m) arbitrale

arbitrator arbitro (m)

area *[of town]* zona (f) *o* quartiere (m)

area *[region]* area (f) *o* regione (f)

area *[subject]* campo (m)

area *[surface]* superficie (f)

area code codice (m) di zona

area manager direttore (m) di zona

argument discussione (f) *o* disputa (f)

arrange *[meeting]* stabilire *o* organizzare

arrange *[set out]* sistemare *o* disporre

arrangement *[compromise]* intesa (f) *o* accordo (m)

arrangement *[system]* sistemazione (f) *o* disposizione (m)

arrears arretrati (mpl)

arrival arrivo (m)

arrivals arrivi (mpl)

arrive arrivare

article *[clause]* clausola (f)

article *[item]* articolo (m) *o* prodotto (m)

articles of association atto (m) costitutivo di società *o* statuto (m) societario

articulated lorry *or* **articulated vehicle** camion/autocarro (m) articolato *o* veicolo articolato

as per advice come consigliato

as per invoice come da fattura

as per sample come da campione

asap (= **as soon as possible**) al più presto possibile *o* nel più breve termine

ask *[someone to do something]* chiedere (a qualcuno di fare qualcosa)

ask for *[ask a price]* chiedere (un prezzo)

ask for *[something]* chiedere *o* domandare

ask for a refund chiedere un rimborso

ask for further details *or* **particulars** chiedere ulteriori dettagli *o* particolari

assembly *[meeting]* assemblea (f)

assembly *[putting together]* assemblaggio (m) *o* montaggio (m)

assembly line catena (f) di montaggio

assess accertare *o* stabilire il valore

assess damages accertare i danni

assessment of damages accertamento (m) dei danni

asset bene (m) *o* cespite (m)

asset value valore (m) patrimoniale (di imprese)

assets and liabilities attività (fpl) e passività (fpl)

assign a right to someone attribuire un diritto a qualcuno

assignee assegnatario (m)

assignment *[cession]* cessione (f) *o* trasferimento (m)

assignment *[work]* incarico (m)

assignor cedente (m) *o* parte venditrice (f)

assist assistere

assistance aiuto (m) *o* assistenza (f)

assistant assistente (mf) *o* collaboratore (m)

assistant manager vice direttore

associate (adj) associato

associate (n) associato (m) *o* socio (m)

associate company società (f) collegata

association associazione (f)

assurance assicurazione (f)

assurance company compagnia (f) di assicurazione

assurance policy polizza (f) di assicurazione

assure someone's life assicurare la vita di qualcuno

attach attaccare *o* unire

attack attaccare *o* assalire

attend (meeting) assistere a

attend to occuparsi di

attention attenzione (f)

attorney procuratore (m)

attract attrarre

attractive salary stipendio (m) interessante

auction (n) asta (f)

auction (v) vendere all'asta

auction rooms sala (f) di vendita all'asta

audit (n) revisione (f) contabile

audit (v) verificare

audit the accounts verificare i conti

auditing revisione contabile (f) *o* certificazione (f)

auditor revisore (m) ufficiale dei conti

authenticate autenticare *o* legalizzare

authority autorità (f)

authorization autorizzazione (f)

authorize *[give permission]* autorizzare

authorize payment autorizzare un pagamento

authorized autorizzato

availability disponibilità (f)

available disponibile

available capital capitale (m) disponibile

average (adj) medio

average (n) media (f)

average (n) *[insurance]* avaria (f)

average (v) calcolare una media

average price prezzo (m) medio

avoid evitare

await instructions attendere istruzioni

award (n) giudizio (m) arbitrale

award (v) assegnare

award a contract to someone aggiudicare un contratto a qualcuno

Bb

back (n) dorso (m) *o* retro (m)

back orders ordinazioni (fpl) inevase

back payment pagamento (m) degli arretrati

back tax imposta (f) arretrata

backdate retrodatare

backer sostenitore (m) *o* avallante (m)

backhander bustarella (f)

backing appoggio (m) *o* aiuto (m)

backlog lavoro (m) arretrato

backup (adj) *[computer]* di salvaguardia

backup copy copia (f) di riserva

backwardation deporto (m)

bad buy cattivo acquisto (m)

bad debt credito (m) inesigibile

bag borsa (f)

bail someone out ottenere la liberazione (su cauzione) di qualcuno

balance (n) bilancio (m) *o* bilancia (f)

balance (v) bilanciare

balance (v) *[a budget]* pareggiare un budget

balance brought down *or* **brought forward** saldo (m) da riportare

balance carried down *or* **carried forward** saldo (m) riportato

balance due to us saldo (m) dovuto

balance of payments bilancia (f) dei pagamenti

balance of trade bilancia (f) commerciale

balance sheet bilancio (m) d'esercizio

ban (n) interdizione (f)

ban (v) interdire *o* vietare

bank (n) banca (f)

bank (v) depositare in banca *o* avere un conto in banca

bank account conto (m) bancario

bank balance saldo (m) in banca

bank base rate tasso (m) ufficiale di sconto

bank bill *[GB]* effetto (m) bancario

bank bill *[US]* banconota (f)

bank book libretto (m) di versamento

bank borrowings prestiti (mpl) bancari

bank charges spese (fpl) bancarie

bank credit credito (m) bancario

bank deposits depositi (mpl) bancari

bank draft assegno (m) circolare

bank holiday giorno (m) di chiusura degli sportelli bancari *o* festa (f) nazionale

bank loan prestito (m) bancario

bank manager direttore (m) di banca

bank statement estratto (m) conto bancario

bank transfer bonifico (m)

bankable paper effetti (mpl) bancabili *o* strumenti (mpl) scontabili

banker banchiere (m) *o* funzionario (m) di banca

banker's draft assegno (m) circolare

banker's order ordine (m) bancario

banking attività (f) bancaria

banking hours orario (m) di banca

banknote banconota (f)

bankrupt (adj) fallito

bankrupt (n) fallito (m)

bankrupt (v) fare fallire

bankruptcy fallimento (m)

bar chart diagramma (m) a barre

bar code codice (m) a barre

bargain (n) *[cheaper than usual]* affare (m) *o* occasione (f)

bargain (n) *[deal]* affare (m)

bargain (n) *[stock exchange]* vendita (f) di realizzo

bargain (v) contrattare *o* tirare sul prezzo

bargain offer offerta (f) d'occasione

bargain price prezzo (m) d'occasione

bargaining contrattazione (f)

bargaining position situazione (f) contrattuale

bargaining power potere (m) contrattuale

barrier barriera (f)

barter (n) baratto (m) *o* scambio (m)

barter (v) barattare

bartering scambio (m) di merci e prodotti

base (n) *[initial position]* base (f)

base (n) *[place]* base (f)

base (v) *[in a place]* essere di base a *o* avere la propria sede in

base (v) *[start to calculate from]* basarsi

base year anno (m) di base

basic (adj) *[most important]* di base *o* fondamentale

basic (adj) *[simple]* di base *o* basilare

basic discount sconto (m) di base

basic tax tassa (f) di base

basis base (f) *o* fondamento (m)

batch (n) *[of orders]* gruppo (m)

batch (n) *[of products]* partita (f) di merci

batch (v) mettere insieme

batch number numero (m) di partita

batch processing elaborazione (f) di massa

bear (n) *[Stock Exchange]* ribassista (m)

bear (v) *[carry]* portare

bear (v) *[interest]* fruttare

bear (v) *[pay for]* sostenere

bear market mercato (m) al ribasso

bearer portatore (m) *o* portatrice (f)

bearer bond obbligazione (f) al portatore

begin cominciare *o* iniziare

beginning inizio (m)

behalf: on behalf of a nome di *o* per conto di

belong to appartenere a

below-the-line expenditure spese (f) straordinarie

benchmark punto (m) di riferimento

beneficiary beneficiario (m)

benefit (n) beneficio (m) *o* utilità (f)

benefit from (v) trarre vantaggio da

berth (n) ormeggio (m)

berth (v) ormeggiare

best (adj) migliore

best (n) il meglio

best-selling car automobile (f) di grande successo

bid (n) *[at an auction]* offerta (f)

bid (n) *[offer to buy]* offerta (f)

bid (n) *[offer to do work]* offerta (f) d'appalto

bidder offerente (m)

bidding offerta (f)

bilateral bilaterale

bill (n) *[US]* banconota (f)

bill (n) *[in a restaurant]* conto (m)

bill (n) *[in Parliament]* progetto (m) di legge

bill (n) *[list of charges]* fattura (f) *o* bolletta (f)

bill (n) *[written promise to pay]* effetto (m) *o* cambiale (f)

bill (v) fatturare

bill of exchange cambiale (f)

bill of lading polizza (f) di carico

bill of sale fattura (f) *o* atto (m) di vendita

billing fatturazione (f)

billion *[UK]* bilione (m)

billion *[US]* miliardo (m)

bills for collection effetti (mpl) all'incasso

bills payable effetti (mpl) passivi *o* cambiali (fpl) da pagare

bills receivable effetti (mpl) attivi *o* cambiali (fpl) da incassare

binding vincolante

black economy economia (f) nera

black list (n) lista (f) nera

blacklist (v) inserire in una lista (f) di proscrizione

black market mercato (m) nero

blame (n) biasimo (m) *o* colpa (f)

blame (v) biasimare

blank (adj) in bianco *o* vuoto

blank (n) spazio (m) *o* vuoto (m)

blank cheque assegno (m) in bianco

blister pack pacco (m) con confezione 'blister' (in plastica trasparente con personalizzazione)

block (n) *[building]* palazzo (m)

block (n) *[of shares]* pacchetto (m) (azionistico)

block (v) bloccare

block booking noleggio (m) in blocco

blocked currency valuta (f) bloccata

blue chip titolo (m) di prim'ordine

blue-chip investments investimenti (mpl) in titoli di prim'ordine

board (n) *[group of people]* Consiglio (m) di Amministrazione

board (v) imbarcarsi

board meeting riunione (f) del consiglio di amministrazione

board of directors Consiglio (m) di Amministrazione

board: on board a bordo

boarding card *or* **boarding pass** carta (f) d'imbarco

boardroom sala (f) riunioni

bona fide in buona fede

bond *[borrowing by government]* obbligazione (f)

bonded warehouse magazzino (m) doganale

bonus gratifica (f) *o* premio (m)

bonus issue emissione (f) gratuita di azioni *o* aumento (m) gratuito di capitale

book (n) libro (m)

book (v) prenotare

book sales vendite (fpl) registrate

book value valore (m) contabile

booking registrazione (f) *o* prenotazione (f)

booking clerk impiegato (m) alla biglietteria

booking office ufficio (m) prenotazioni

bookkeeper contabile (mf) *o* ragioniere (m)

bookkeeping contabilità (f)

boom (n) sviluppo (m) favorevole dell'economia *o* boom (m)

boom (v) prosperare

boom industry industria (f) che si è sviluppata rapidamente

booming fiorente

boost (n) spinta (f)

boost (v) lanciare

border frontiera (f)

borrow prendere a prestito *o* mutuare

borrower mutuatario (m)

borrowing mutuo (m)

borrowing power potere (m) per ricorrere al prestito

boss (informal) capo (m)

bottleneck strozzatura (f) (nel processo aziendale)

bottom fondo (m)

bottom line nodo (m) della questione

bought ledger mastro (m) dei conti dei creditori

bought ledger clerk responsabile (m) del mastro dei conti dei creditori

bounce *[cheque]* respingere

box number casella (f) postale

boxed set presentazione (f) in cofanetto

boycott (n) boicottaggio (m)

boycott (v) boicottare

bracket (n) *[tax]* fascia (f)

bracket together raggruppare

branch settore (m)

branch manager direttore (m) di filiale

branch office filiale (f)

brand marchio (m) *o* marca (f)

brand image immagine (f) del prodotto

brand loyalty fedeltà (f) alla marca

brand name marca (f) *o* nome del prodotto

brand new nuovo di zecca

breach of contract inadempimento (m) del contratto

breach of warranty violazione (f) di garanzia

break (n) pausa (f)

break (v) *[contract]* rompere

break an agreement infrangere un accordo

break down (v) *[itemize]* dettagliare

break down (v) *[machine]* rompersi

break down (v) *[talks]* arenarsi *[di trattative]*

break even (v) giungere al punto di pareggio

break off negotiations sospendere le trattative

break the law violare la legge

breakages rotture (fpl) *o* danni (mpl)

breakdown (n) *[items]* ripartizione (f)

breakdown (n) *[machine]* guasto (m)

breakdown (n) *[talks]* rottura (f)

breakeven point punto (m) di pareggio fra costi e ricavi

bribe (n) tangente (f) *o* bustarella (f)

bribe (v) corrompere (con denaro *o* doni)

brief (v) dare istruzioni

briefcase borsa (f) *o* cartella (f)

bring portare

bring a civil action intentare causa civile

bring in apportare *o* rendere

bring out lanciare

British britannico *o* inglese

brochure fascicolo (m)

broke (informal) al verde

broker broker (m)

brokerage *or* **broker's commission** commissione (f) di mediazione

brown paper carta (f) da pacco

bubble pack confezione (f) a bolla di plastica trasparente

budget (n) *[government]* bilancio (m) dello Stato

budget (n) *[personal, company]* bilancio (m) preventivo *o* budget (m)

budget (v) budgettare

budget account *[in bank]* contabilità (f) di bilancio

budgetary budgetario *o* relativo al budget

budgetary control controllo (m) budgetario

budgetary policy politica (f) di budget

budgeting preparazione (f) del budget

building society istituto (m) di credito fondiario

built-in incorporato *o* inserito

bulk volume (m) *o* grande quantità (f)

bulk buying acquisto (m) in massa

bulk shipments spedizione (f) in massa

bulky voluminoso

bull *[stock exchange]* speculatore al rialzo

bull market mercato (m) al rialzo

bulletin bollettino (m)

bullion oro (m) in verghe

bureau de change ufficio (m) cambio

bus autobus (m)

business *[commerce]* affari (mpl)

business *[company]* impresa (f)

business *[discussion]* affare (m)

business address indirizzo (m) d'ufficio

business call telefonata (f) d'affari

business card biglietto (m) da visita

business centre centro (m) d'affari

business class classe (f) business

business equipment apparecchiatura (f) d'ufficio

business hours ore (f) d'ufficio

business letter lettera (f) d'affari

business lunch pranzo (m) d'affari

business premises locali (mpl) d'azienda *o* locali commerciali

business strategy strategia (f) commerciale

business transaction transazione (f) commerciale

business trip viaggio (m) d'affari

business: on business per affari

businessman *or* **businesswoman** uomo (m) d'affari *o* donna (f) d'affari

busy occupato

buy (v) comperare

buy back riacquistare

buy for cash comperare in contanti

buy forward comperare a termine

buyer *[for a store]* responsabile (m) di un ufficio acquisti

buyer *[person]* compratore (m)

buyer's market mercato (m) al ribasso

buying acquisto (m)

buying department ufficio (m) acquisti

by-product prodotto (m) derivato

Cc

cable address indirizzo (m) cablografico

calculate calcolare

calculation calcolo (m)

calculator calcolatore (m)

calendar month mese (m) solare

calendar year anno (m) solare

call (n) *[for money]* richiesta (f) di pagamento

call (n) *[phone]* chiamata (f)

call (n) *[stock exchange]* opzione (f) d'acquisto

call (n) *[visit]* visita (f)

call (v) *[ask to do something]* invitare

call (v) *[meeting]* convocare

call (v) *[phone]* chiamare

call off a deal disdire un affare

call rate tasso (m) su prestiti a breve

callable bond obbligazione (f) redimibile

campaign campagna (f)

cancel cancellare *o* annullare

cancel a cheque annullare un assegno

cancel a contract annullare un contratto

cancellation cancellazione (f) *o* disdetta (f)

cancellation clause clausola (f) di rescissione

cancellation of an appointment revoca (f) di una nomina

candidate candidato (m)

canvass procacciare

canvasser piazzista (m) *o* propagandista (m)

canvassing propaganda (f)

canvassing techniques tecniche (f) di propaganda

capable of capace di

capacity *[ability]* abilità (f) *o* capacità (f)

capacity *[production]* capacità (f) produttiva

capacity *[space]* capacità (f)

capacity utilization utilizzo (m) della capacità produttiva

capital capitale (m) *o* capitali (mpl)

capital account conto (m) capitale

capital assets immobilizzazioni (fpl)

capital equipment immobilizzi (mpl) tecnici

capital expenditure spese (fpl) conto capitali

capital gains plusvalenza (f)

capital gains tax imposta (f) sulle plusvalenze

capital goods beni (mpl) strumentali

capital loss perdita (f) di capitale

capital-intensive industry industria (f) a forte assorbimento di capitali

capitalization capitalizzazione (f)

capitalization of reserves capitalizzazione delle riserve

capitalize capitalizzare

capitalize on trarre vantaggio da

captive market mercato (m) controllato da un solo fornitore

capture impadronirsi

carbon copy copia (f) carbone

carbon paper carta (f) carbone

carbonless autocopiante

card *[business card]* biglietto (m)

card *[material]* cartoncino (m)

card *[membership]* tessera (f)

card *[postcard]* cartolina (f) postale

card index (n) schedario (m)

card phone telefono (m) a schede

card-index (v) schedare

card-index file fascicolo (m) dello schedario

card-indexing schedatura (f)

cardboard cartone (m)

cardboard box scatola (f) di cartone

care of (c/o) presso

cargo carico (m)

cargo ship nave (f) da carico

carnet *[document]* carnet (m)

carriage trasporto (m)

carriage forward porto (m) assegnato

carriage free franco di porto

carriage paid porto (m) pagato

carrier *[company]* trasportatore (m) *o* impresa (f) di trasporti

carrier *[vehicle]* camion (m)

carry *[approve in a vote]* far approvare

carry *[have in stock]* avere

carry *[produce]* produrre

carry *[transport]* portare *o* trasportare

carry forward riportare a nuovo

carry on a business svolgere esercizio d'impresa

carry over a balance riportare un pareggio

cartel cartello (m)

carton *[box]* cartone (m) *o* imballo (m) di cartone

carton *[material]* cartone (m)

case (n) *[box]* cassa (f)

case (n) *[suitcase]* valigia (f)

case (v) *[put in boxes]* imballare

cash (adv) in contanti

cash (n) *[money]* denaro (m) contante

cash a cheque incassare un assegno

cash account conto (m) di cassa

cash advance anticipo (m) in contanti

cash and carry supermercato (m) all'ingrosso

cash balance saldo (m) di cassa

cash book libro (m) cassa

cash card tessera (f) prelievo contanti

cash deal transazione (f) sul disponibile

cash deposit deposito (m) in contanti

cash desk sportello (m) di cassa

cash discount sconto (m) cassa *o* sconto per pagamento in contanti

cash dispenser cassa (f) automatica prelievi

cash float fondo (m) di cassa

cash flow flusso (m) di cassa

cash flow forecast previsioni (fpl) del flusso di cassa

cash flow statement rendiconto (m) del flusso di cassa

cash in hand fondo (m) di cassa

cash offer offerta (f) reale *o* offerta per contanti

cash on delivery (c.o.d.) pagamento (m) alla consegna

cash payment pagamento (m) in contanti

cash price prezzo (m) per contanti *o* condizioni (fpl) per pagamento in contanti

cash purchase acquisto (m) per contanti

cash register registratore (f) di cassa

cash reserves riserva (f) di cassa

cash sale vendita (f) per contanti

cash terms condizioni (fpl) per pagamento in contanti

cash till contenitore (m) di contanti

cash transaction transazione (f) sul disponibile

cash voucher pezza (f) giustificativa di cassa

cashable incassabile

cashier cassiere (m) *o* cassiera (f)

cashier's check *[US]* assegno (m) di cassa (spiccato dalla banca su se stessa in favore di terzi)

casting vote voto (m) decisivo

casual work lavoro (m) saltuario

casual worker lavoratore (m) saltuario

catalogue catalogo (m)

catalogue price prezzo (m) di catalogo

category categoria (f)

cater for provvedere di generi alimentari

caveat emptor 'l'acquirente presti la dovuta attenzione'

ceiling limite (m) massimo

ceiling price prezzo (m) massimo

cellular phone telefono (m) cellulare

central centrale

central bank banca (f) centrale

central purchasing acquisto (m) centralizzato

centralization centralizzazione (f)

centralize centralizzare

centre centro (m)

CEO (= chief executive officer) Direttore Generale (m)

certificate certificato (m)

certificate of approval certificato (m) di accettazione

certificate of deposit certificato (m) di deposito

certificate of guarantee certificato (m) di garanzia

certificate of origin certificato (m) d'origine

certificate of registration certificato (m) d'iscrizione

certificated certificato

certificated bankrupt debitore (m) autorizzato al concordato preventivo

certified accountant revisore (m) ufficiale dei conti *o* (in US) ragioniere (m) iscritto all'albo

certified cheque assegno (m) a copertura garantita

certified copy copia (f) autentica

certify certificare *o* autenticare

cession cessione (f)

chain *[of stores]* catena (f)

chain store negozio (m) che fa parte di una catena

chairman *[of committee]* presidente (m)

chairman *[of company]* presidente (m)

chairman and managing director presidente e amministratore delegato

Chamber of Commerce Camera (f) di Commercio

change (n) *[cash]* spiccioli (mpl)

change (n) *[difference]* cambiamento (m)

change (v) *[money]* cambiare

change hands essere venduto

change machine macchina (f) che cambia denaro in spiccioli

channel (n) canale (m)

channel (v) canalizzare

channels of distribution canali (mpl) di distribuzione

charge (n) *[in court]* accusa (f)

charge (n) *[money]* carico (m)

charge (n) *[on account]* addebito (m)

charge (v) *[money]* far pagare

charge a purchase addebitare un acquisto

charge account conto (m) personale

charge card carta (f) di credito

chargeable caricabile

charges forward pagamento (m) a carico del destinatario

charter (n) noleggio (m)

charter (v) noleggiare

charter an aircraft noleggiare un aeroplano

charter flight volo (m) charter

charter plane aeroplano (m) a noleggio

charterer noleggiatore (m) (di navi, aerei)

chartering noleggio (m)

chase *[an order]* dare la caccia a

chase *[follow]* inseguire

cheap economico *o* a basso prezzo

cheap labour manodopera (m) a basso prezzo

cheap money denaro (m) a buon mercato

cheap rate tariffa (f) ridotta

check (n) *[examination]* controllo (m)

check (n) *[stop]* arresto (m)

check (v) *[examine]* esaminare *o* controllare

check (v) *[stop]* arrestare

check in *[at airport]* presentarsi al check in

check in *[at hotel]* firmare il registro

check out *[of hotel]* lasciare libera la camera dell'albergo

check sample campione (m) (statistico) di controllo

check-in *[at airport]* controllo (m) passeggeri

check-in counter check in (m)

check-in time ora (f) di accettazione

checkout *[in supermarket]* cassa (f)

cheque assegno (m)

cheque (guarantee) card carta (f) assegni

cheque account conto (m) assegni

cheque book libretto (m) assegni

cheque number numero (m) dell'assegno

cheque stub matrice (f) dell'assegno

cheque to bearer assegno (m) al portatore

chief (adj) principale

chief clerk capo (m) ufficio

chief executive (officer) direttore (m) generale

choice (adj) di prima qualità

choice (n) *[choosing]* scelta (f)

choice (n) *[items to choose from]* scelta (f)

choice (n) *[thing chosen]* scelta (f)

choose scegliere

Christmas bonus gratifica (f) natalizia *o* tredicesima (f)

chronic cronico

chronological order ordine (m) cronologico

c.i.f. (= cost, insurance and freight) costo (m), assicurazione (f) e nolo (m)

circular (n) lettera (f) circolare

circular letter lettera (f) circolare

circular letter of credit lettera (f) di credito circolare

circulation *[money]* circolazione (f)

circulation *[newspaper]* tiratura (f)

civil law diritto (m) civile

claim (n) domanda (f) d'indennizzo *o* reclamo (m)

claim (v) *[insurance]* rivendicare *o* presentare una domanda d'indennizzo

claim (v) *[right]* rivendicare

claim (v) *[suggest]* affermare

claimant ricorrente *o* chi fa ricorso

claims department ufficio (m) indennità

claims manager responsabile (m) dei reclami

class classe (f) *o* categoria (f)

classification classificazione (f)

classified ads annunci (mpl) economici (su giornale) *o* inserzioni (fpl)

classified advertisements annunci economici

classified directory elenco (m) classificato

classify classificare

clause clausola (f)

clawback ricuperare mediante tassazione

clear (adj) *[complete]* libero

clear (adj) *[easy to understand]* chiaro

clear (v) *[stock]* liquidare

clear a cheque compensare un assegno

clear a debt estinguere un debito

clear profit utile (m) netto

clearance certificate certificato (m) di sdoganamento

clearance of a cheque compensazione (f) di un assegno

clearing *[paying]* saldo (m) di un debito

clearing bank banca (f) di compensazione

clerical impiegatizio *o* d'ufficio

clerical error errore (m) di trascrizione

clerical staff personale (m) impiegatizio

clerical work lavoro (m) d'ufficio

clerk impiegato (m)

client cliente (mf)

clientele clientela (f)

climb salire *o* ascendere

clinch concludere definitivamente

clipping service servizio (m) stralci giornalistici

close (n) *[end]* chiusura (f)

close (v) *[after work]* chiudere *o* finire

close a bank account chiudere un conto bancario

close a meeting togliere la seduta

close an account chiudere un conto

close down chiudere *o* sospendere un'attività

close to vicino a

closed chiuso

closed market mercato (m) chiuso

closing (adj) di chiusura finale

closing (n) chiusura (f)

closing balance bilancio (m) di chiusura

closing bid ultima offerta (f) (di licitazione)

closing date termine (m) ultimo *o* data di chiusura

closing price prezzo (m) di chiusura

closing stock giacenze (fpl) finali alla chiusura dell'esercizio

closing time ora (f) di chiusura

closing-down sale svendita (f) per chiusura d'esercizio

closure chiusura (f) *o* termine (m)

c/o (= care of) presso

co-creditor creditore (m) in solido

co-director condirettore (m)

co-insurance coassicurazione (f)

co-operate cooperare

co-operation cooperazione (m) *o* collaborazione (f)

co-operative (adj) cooperativo *o* cooperativa

co-operative (n) cooperativa (f)

co-opt someone cooptare qualcuno

co-owner comproprietario (m)

co-ownership comproprietà (f)

COD *or* **c.o.d.** (= cash on delivery) pagamento (m) alla consegna

code codice (m)

code of practice codice (m) di etica professionale

coding codifica (f) *o* codificazione (f)

coin moneta (f) (metallica)

cold call visita (f) a freddo

cold start partenza (f) fredda

cold storage conservazione (f) in ambiente frigorifero

cold store magazzino (m) frigorifero

collaborate collaborare

collaboration collaborazione (f)

collapse (n) crollo (m)

collapse (v) crollare *o* cadere

collateral (adj) collaterale

collateral (n) garanzia (f) collaterale

collect (v) *[fetch]* cogliere *o* raccogliere

collect (v) *[money]* recuperare

collect a debt recuperare un debito

collect call *[US]* telefonata (f) a carico del ricevente

collection *[of goods]* ritiro (m)

collection *[of money]* recupero (m)

collection *[postal]* levata (f)

collection charges *or* **collection rates** spese (fpl) d'incasso

collective collettivo

collective ownership proprietà (f) collettiva

collective wage agreement contratto (m) salariale collettivo

collector raccoglitore (m)

commerce commercio (m)

commercial (adj) commerciale

commercial (n) *[TV]* pubblicità (f) *o* spot (m)

commercial attaché addetto (m) commerciale

commercial college scuola (m) superiore di commercio

commercial course corso (m) a indirizzo commerciale

commercial directory annuario (m) commerciale

commercial district distretto (m) commerciale

commercial failure insuccesso (m) commerciale

commercial law diritto (m) commerciale

commercial traveller commesso (m) viaggiatore

commercial undertaking iniziativa (f) commerciale

commercialization commercializzazione (f)

commercialize commercializzare

commission *[committee]* comitato (m)

commission *[money]* commissione (f) *o* percentuale (f)

commission agent agente (m) commissionario

commission rep rappresentante (m) commissionario

commit *[crime]* commettere

commit funds to a project affidare fondi ad un progetto

commitments impegni (mpl)

commodity merce (f) *o* bene (m)

commodity exchange Borsa (f) Merci

commodity futures contratti (mpl) a termine su materie prime

commodity market mercato (m) delle materie prime

common *[frequent]* comune *o* usuale

common *[to more than one]* comune

common carrier vettore (m)

common ownership proprietà (f) comune

common pricing prezzi (mpl) correnti

communicate comunicare

communication *[general]* comunicazione (f)

communication *[message]* comunicazione (f)

communications comunicazioni (fpl)

community comunità (f)

commute *[exchange]* scambiare

commute *[travel]* fare il pendolare

commuter pendolare (m)

companies' register Registro (m) delle SPA

company compagnia (f) *o* società (di capitali)

company director amministratore (m) di società

company law diritto (m) societario

company secretary segretario (m) del consiglio d'amministrazione

comparability comparabilità (f)

comparable paragonabile

compare confrontare *o* paragonare

compare with essere paragonabile

comparison confronto (m)

compensate compensare

compensation compenso (m) *o* ricompensa (f)

compensation for damage risarcimento (m) di danni

compete with someone *or* **with a company** competere con qualcuno *o* con un'azienda

competing (adj) in concorrenza

competing firms aziende (f) in concorrenza

competing products prodotti (mpl) che si fanno concorrenza

competition concorrenza (f) *o* competizione (f)

competitive competitivo

competitive price prezzo (m) allineato

competitive pricing determinazione (f) del prezzo di concorrenza

competitive products prodotti (mpl) competitivi

competitively priced con prezzo competitivo

competitiveness competitività (f)

competitor concorrente (m)

complain (about) protestare *o* reclamare

complaint protesta (f) *o* reclamo (m)

complaints department ufficio (m) reclami

complementary complementare

complete (adj) completo

complete (v) finire *o* portare a termine

completion completamento (m)

completion date data (f) di ultimazione

completion of a contract adempimento (m) di un contratto

compliance adempimento (m)

complimentary in omaggio

complimentary ticket biglietto (m) omaggio

compliments slip cartoncino (m) della società

comply with conformarsi a *o* osservare

composition *[with creditors]* accomodamento (m)

compound interest interesse (m) composto

comprehensive comprensivo

comprehensive insurance assicurazione (f) globale

compromise (n) compromesso (m)

compromise (v) venire a un compromesso

compulsory obbligatorio

compulsory liquidation liquidazione (f) coatta

compulsory purchase espropriazione (f) per pubblica utilità

computer computer (m)

computer bureau ufficio (m) computer

computer department ufficio (m) computer

computer error errore (m) di computer

computer file archivio (m) (di un computer)

computer language linguaggio (m) di computer

computer listing registrazione (f) sul computer

computer printer stampante (f) lineare

computer printout tabulato (m)

computer program programma (m) di computer

computer programmer programmatore (m) di computer

computer programming programmazione (f) di computer

computer services servizi (mpl) di elaborazione elettronica

computer system sistema (m) elettronico di elaborazione

computer terminal terminale (m) di computer

computer time tempo (m) di elaborazione

computer-readable leggibile dal computer

computer-readable codes codici (mpl) leggibili dal computer

computerize computerizzare

computerized elaborato a mezzo computer

concealment of assets occultamento (m) di beni

concern (n) *[business]* azienda (f) *o* ditta (f)

concern (n) *[worry]* preoccupazione (f)

concern (v) *[deal with]* interessarsi di

concession *[reduction]* agevolazione (f)

concession *[right]* concessione (f)

concessionaire concessionario (m)

conciliation conciliazione (f)

conclude *[agreement]* concludere

condition *[state]* condizione (f)

condition *[terms]* condizione (f)

condition: on condition that a condizione che

conditional soggetto a condizioni

conditions of employment condizioni (fpl) di assunzione

conditions of sale condizioni (fpl) di vendita

conduct negotiations condurre una trattativa

conference *[large]* conferenza (f) *o* congresso (m)

conference *[small]* riunione (f)

conference phone telefono (m) per conferenze

conference room sala (f) riunioni

confidence fiducia (f)

confidential riservato

confidential report rapporto (m) riservato

confidentiality riservatezza (f)

confirm confermare

confirm a booking confermare una prenotazione

confirm someone in a job confermare l'assunzione di una persona

confirmation conferma (f)

conflict of interest conflitto (m) di interessi

conglomerate conglomerato (m)

connect collegare

connecting flight volo (m) di coincidenza

connection coincidenza (f)

consider considerare

consign consegnare

consignee consegnatario (m)

consignment *[sending]* spedizione (f)

consignment *[things sent, received]* invio (m)

consignment note lettera (f) di vettura

consignor mittente (m)

consist of consistere in

consolidate consolidare

consolidate *[shipments]* consolidare spedizioni

consolidated consolidato

consolidated shipment spedizione (f) consolidata

consolidation consolidamento (m)

consortium consorzio (m)

constant costante

consult consultarsi

consultancy consulenza (f)

consultancy firm ditta (f) di consulenza

consultant consulente (m)

consulting engineer consulente (m) tecnico

consumables generi (mpl) di consumo

consumer consumatore (m)

consumer credit credito (m) al consumatore

consumer durables beni (mpl) di consumo durevoli

consumer goods beni (mpl) di consumo

consumer panel gruppo (m) selezionato di consumatori

consumer price index indice (m) dei prezzi al consumo

consumer protection protezione (f) del consumatore

consumer research ricerca (f) di mercato sui bisogni dei consumatori

consumer spending spese (fpl) di consumo

consumption consumo (m)

contact (n) *[general]* contatto (m)

contact (n) *[person]* contatto (m)

contact (v) mettersi in contatto con

contain contenere

container *[box, tin]* contenitore (m)

container *[for shipping]* container (m)

container port scalo (m) per container

container ship nave (f) per trasporto di container

container terminal terminal (m) per container

containerization *[putting into containers]* containerizzazione (f)

containerization *[shipping in containers]* trasporto (m) in container

containerize *[put into containers]* containerizzare

containerize *[ship in containers]* spedire merce in container

contents contenuto (m)

contested takeover acquisizione (f) di controllo contestata

contingency contingenza (f)

contingency fund fondo (m) di previdenza

contingency plan piano (m) di contingenza

continual continuo

continually continuamente

continuation continuazione (f)

continue continuare

continuous continuo

continuous feed alimentazione (f) continua

continuous stationery moduli (mpl) a striscia continua

contra account conto (m) di contropartita

contra an entry stornare una registrazione

contra entry registrazione (f) di storno

contract (n) contratto (m)

contract (v) contrarre

contract law diritto (m) contrattuale

contract note fissato (m) bollato

contract of employment contratto (m) di lavoro

contract work lavoro (m) a contratto

contracting party parte (f) contraente

contractor imprenditore (m)

contractual contrattuale

contractual liability responsabilità (f) contrattuale

contractually contrattualmente

contrary contrario

contrast (n) contrasto (m)

contribute contribuire

contribution contributo (m)

contribution of capital apporto (m) di capitali

contributor sottoscrittore (m)

control (n) *[check]* controllo (m) *o* verifica (f)

control (n) *[power]* controllo (m) *o* potere (m)

control (v) controllare

control a business detenere il controllo azionario

control key tasto (m) di comando

control systems sistema (m) di controllo

controlled economy economia (f) controllata

controller *[US]* revisore (m) dei conti

controller *[who checks]* controllore (m)

controlling (adj) controllante

convene convocare

convenient comodo

conversion conversione (f)

conversion of funds conversione (f) di fondi

conversion price *or* **conversion rate** tasso (m) di conversione

convert convertire

convertibility convertibilità (f)

convertible currency valuta (f) convertibile

convertible loan stock obbligazioni (fpl) convertibili

conveyance trasmissione (f)

conveyancer notaio (m) *o* legale (m) che si occupa dei trapassi di proprietà

conveyancing esame (m) dei documenti e stesura degli atti necessari per il trasferimento di proprietà

cooling off period (after purchase) periodo (m) che permette un ripensamento (da parte dell'acquirente)

cooperative society società (f) cooperativa

copartner consocio (m)

copartnership associazione (f) in compartecipazione

cope essere all'altezza

copier copiatrice (f)

copy (n) *[a document]* copia (f)

copy (n) *[book, newspaper]* copia (f) *o* esemplare (m)

copy (n) *[of document]* copia (f)

copy (v) copiare *o* riprodurre

copying machine copiatrice (f)

corner (n) *[angle]* angolo (m)

corner (n) *[monopoly]* accaparramento (m) *o* monopolio (m)

corner shop negozio (m) d'angolo

corner the market accaparrarsi il mercato (m)

corporate image immagine (f) aziendale

corporate name ragione (f) sociale

corporate plan programma (m) aziendale

corporate planning programmazione (f) aziendale

corporate profits utili (mpl) societari

corporation corporazione (f)

corporation tax imposta (f) sulla società

correct (adj) corretto

correct (v) correggere

correction correzione (f)

correspond with someone essere in corrispondenza con qualcuno

correspond with something equivalere a qualcosa

correspondence corrispondenza (f)

correspondent *[journalist]* inviato (m)

correspondent *[who writes letters]* corrispondente (mf)

cost (n) costo (m)

cost (v) costare

cost accountant analista (m) dei costi

cost accounting contabilità (f) basata sui conti

cost analysis analisi (f) dei costi

cost centre centro (m) di costi

cost factor fattore (m) costo

cost of living costo (m) della vita *o* carovita (m)

cost of sales costo (m) delle vendite

cost plus costo (m) più una percentuale

cost price prezzo (m) sotto costo

cost, insurance and freight (c.i.f.) costo (m), assicurazione (f) e nolo (m)

cost-benefit analysis analisi (f) preventiva della convenienza dei costi

cost-cutting riduzione (f) dei costi

cost-effective redditizio

cost-effectiveness redditività (f) dei costi

cost-of-living allowance indennità (f) di contingenza

cost-of-living bonus contingenza (f)

cost-of-living increase aumento (m) del costo della vita

cost-of-living index indice (m) del costo della vita

cost-push inflation inflazione (f) da costi

costing valutazione (f) dei costi

costly costoso

costs spese (fpl)

counsel avvocato (mf)

count (v) *[add]* contare

count (v) *[include]* includere

counter banco (m)

counter staff personale (m) al banco

counter-claim (n) controrichiesta (f)

counter-claim (v) presentare una controrichiesta

counter-offer controfferta (f)

counterbid controfferta (f)

counterfeit (adj) contraffatto *o* falso

counterfeit (v) contraffare

counterfoil matrice (f)

countermand fermare

countersign contrassegno (m)

country *[not town]* campagna (f)

country *[state]* paese (m) *o* nazione (f)

country of origin paese (m) d'origine

coupon buono (m)

coupon ad materiale pubblicitario con buono

courier *[guide]* guida (f) (turistica)

courier *[messenger]* messaggero (m) *o* corriere (m)

court corte (f) di Giustizia

court case causa (f) legale

covenant (n) convenzione (f)

covenant (v) convenire

cover (n) *[insurance]* copertura (f) assicurativa

cover (n) *[top]* copertura (f)

cover (v) *[expenses]* coprire *o* pagare

cover (v) *[put on top]* coprire

cover a risk assicurarsi contro un rischio

cover charge prezzo (m) del coperto

cover costs coprire i costi

cover note polizza (f) provvisoria

covering letter lettera (f) di accompagnamento

covering note polizza (f) provvisoria

crane gru (f)

crash (n) *[accident]* incidente (m)

crash (n) *[financial]* crollo (m)

crash (v) *[fail]* crollare

crash (v) *[hit]* scontrarsi con

crate (n) cassa (f)

crate (v) imballare (merce) in casse

credit (n) credito (m)

credit (v) accreditare (un conto)

credit account conto (m) creditori

credit agency agenzia (f) per reperimento di referenze

credit balance differenza (f) a credito

credit bank istituto (m) di credito

credit card carta (f) di credito

credit card sale vendita (f) con carta di credito

credit ceiling massimale (m) di credito *o* tetto (m) salariale

credit column colonna (f) dell'avere

credit control controllo (m) del credito

credit entry registrazione (f) contabile a credito

credit facilities agevolazioni (fpl) creditizie

credit freeze blocco (m) del credito

credit limit limite (m) di credito

credit note nota (f) di accredito

credit policy politica (f) creditizia

credit rating grado (m) di solvibilità

credit side avere (m) *o* lato (m) dell'attivo

credit-worthy solvibile

credit: on credit a credito

creditor creditore (m)

cross a cheque sbarrare un assegno

cross off depennare

cross out cancellare

cross rate cambio (m) incrociato

crossed cheque assegno (m) sbarrato

cubic cubico

cubic measure misure (fpl) cubiche

cum con

cum coupon con coupon (m)

cum dividend con dividendo (m)

cumulative cumulativo

cumulative interest interesse (m) composto

cumulative preference shares azioni (fpl) privilegiate cumulative

currency moneta (f) legale

currency conversion conversione (f) della valuta

currency note banconota (f)

currency reserves riserve (fpl) valutarie

current corrente

current account conto (m) corrente

current assets attività (fpl) liquide

current cost accounting contabilità (f) a costi correnti

current liabilities passività (fpl) correnti

current price prezzo (m) corrente

current rate of exchange tasso (m) di cambio corrente

current yield rendimento (m) immediato

curriculum vitae (CV) curriculum (m) vitae

curve curva (f)

custom clientela (f)

custom-built or **custom-made** fatto appositamente

customer cliente (mf)

customer appeal richiamo (m) per i clienti

customer loyalty fedeltà (f) dei clienti

customer satisfaction soddisfazione (f) dei clienti

customer service department ufficio (m) assistenza ai clienti

customs dogana (f)

Customs and Excise Ufficio Dazio e Dogana

customs barrier barriera (f) doganale

customs broker agente (m) doganale

customs clearance svincolo (m) doganale

customs declaration dichiarazione (f) doganale

customs declaration form modulo (m) di dichiarazione doganale

customs duty dazio (m) doganale

customs entry point punto (m) per la dichiarazine doganale d'entrata

customs examination controllo (m) doganale

customs formalities formalità (fpl) doganali

customs officer doganiere (m)

customs official ufficiale (m) di dogana

customs receipt avviso (m) di ricevimento doganale

customs seal sigillo (m) doganale

customs tariff tariffa (f) doganale

customs union unione (f) doganale

cut (n) taglio (m)

cut (v) tagliare

cut down on expenses ridurre le spese

cut price (n) prezzo (m) ridotto

cut-price (adj) a prezzo ridotto

cut-price goods merce (f) a prezzo ridotto

cut-price petrol benzina (f) a prezzo ridotto

cut-price store negozio con merce a prezzi ridotti

cut-throat competition concorrenza (f) spietata

CV (= curriculum vitae) Curriculum (m) Vitae

cycle ciclo (m)

cyclical ciclico

cyclical factors elementi (mpl) ciclici

Dd

daily quotidiano

daisy-wheel printer stampante (f) con testina a margherita

damage (n) danno (m)

damage (v) danneggiare

damage survey perizia (f) d'avaria

damage to property danno (m) alla proprietà

damaged danneggiato

damages risarcimento (m) dei danni

data dati (mpl)

data processing elaborazione (f) dei dati

data retrieval ricerca (f) automatica dell'informazione

database base (f) di dati

date (n) data (f)

date (v) datare

date of receipt data (f) di ricevimento

date stamp datario (m)

dated datato

day *[24 hours]* giorno (m)

day *[working day]* giorno (m)

day shift turno (m) di giorno

day-to-day giorno per giorno

dead (adj) *[person]* morto

dead account conto (m) chiuso

dead loss perdita (f) secca

deadline termine (m) ultimo

deadlock (n) punto (m) morto

deadlock (v) essere a un punto morto

deadweight peso (m) morto

deadweight cargo carico (m) lordo

deadweight tonnage portata (f) lorda

deal (n) operazione (f) *o* affare (m)

deal in (v) commerciare *o* negoziare

deal with an order dare corso ad un'ordinazione

deal with someone trattare con qualcuno

dealer commerciante (m)

dealing *[commerce]* commercio (m)

dealing *[stock exchange]* transazioni (fpl) *o* operazioni (fpl)

dear caro

debenture obbligazione (f) (di società private)

debenture holder obbligazionista (m)

debit (n) addebito (m)

debit an account addebitare un conto

debit balance saldo (m) debitore

debit column colonna (f) del dare

debit entry registrazione (f) a debito

debit note nota (f) di addebito

debits and credits dare e avere

debt debito (m)

debt collection recupero (m) di crediti

debt collection agency agenzia (f) per il recupero dei crediti

debt collector esattore (m) dei crediti

debtor debitore (m)

debtor side colonna (f) del dare

debts due credito (m) esigibile

decentralization decentramento (m)

decentralize decentrare

decide decidere

decide on a course of action decidere una linea di condotta

deciding decisivo

deciding factor elemento (m) decisivo

decimal (n) decimale (m)

decimal point virgola (f) decimale

decision decisione (f)

decision maker persona (f) che prende decisioni

decision making processo (m) decisionale

decision-making processes processo (m) di decisione

deck piano (m)

deck cargo carico (m) di coperta

declaration dichiarazione (f)

declaration of bankruptcy dichiarazione (f) di fallimento

declaration of income dichiarazione (f) dei redditi

declare dichiarare

declare goods to customs dichiarare le merci alla dogana

declare someone bankrupt dichiarare qualcuno fallito

declared dichiarato

declared value valore (m) dichiarato

decline (n) declino (m)

decline (v) *[fall]* rifiutare

decontrol abolire i controlli (mpl)

decrease (n) diminuzione (f)

decrease (v) diminuire

decrease in price diminuzione (f) dei prezzi

decrease in value diminuzione (f) del valore

decreasing (adj) decrescente

deduct dedurre

deductible detraibile

deduction detrazione (f)

deed atto (m)

deed of assignment atto (m) di cessione

deed of covenant atto (m) di donazione

deed of partnership atto (m) costitutivo

deed of transfer atto (m) di trasferimento

default (n) inadempienza (f)

default (v) essere contumace

default on payments inadempienza (f) nel pagamento

defaulter inadempiente (m)

defect difetto (m)

defective *[faulty]* difettoso

defective *[not valid]* privo di validità *o* viziato

defence *[legal]* difesa (f)

defence *[protection]* difesa (f)

defence counsel avvocato (m) difensore

defend difendere

defend a lawsuit difendere una causa

defendant accusato (m)

defer differire

defer payment differire un pagamento

deferment rinvio (m)

deferment of payment rinvio (m) di pagamento

deferred differito

deferred creditor creditore (m) differito

deferred payment pagamento (m) differito

deficit deficit (m) *o* disavanzo (m)

deficit financing finanziamento (m) del disavanzo (m)

deflation deflazione (f)

deflationary deflazionistico

defray *[costs]* pagare

defray someone's expenses sostenere le spese di qualcuno

del credere star del credere

del credere agent agente (m) del credere

delay (n) ritardo (m)

delay (v) ritardare

delegate (n) delegato (m)

delegate (v) delegare

delegation *[action]* delega (f) *o* delegazione (f)

delegation *[people]* delegazione (f)

delete eliminare

deliver consegnare

delivered price prezzo (m) franco

delivery *[bill of exchange]* cessione (f) di una cambiale

delivery *[goods]* consegna (f) di merce

delivery date data (f) di consegna

delivery note bolla (f) di spedizione

delivery order ordine (m) di consegna

delivery time data (f) di consegna

delivery van furgone (m) per le consegne

deliveryman uomo (m) delle consegne *o* fattorino (m)

demand (n) *[for payment]* domanda (f) *o* richiesta (f)

demand (n) *[need]* domanda (f)

demand (v) domandare

demand deposit deposito (m) a vista

demonstrate dimostrare

demonstration dimostrazione (f)

demonstration model campione (m) per dimostrazione

demonstrator dimostratore (m)

demurrage ritardo (m)

department *[in government]* ministero (m)

department *[in office]* reparto (m) *o* sezione (f)

department *[in shop]* reparto (m)

department store grande magazzino (m)

departmental dipartimentale

departmental manager capo (m) servizio

departure *[going away]* partenza (f)

departure *[new venture]* nuovo orientamento (m)

departure lounge salone (m) delle partenze

departures partenze (fpl)

depend on contare su

depending on a condizione che

deposit (n) *[in bank]* deposito (m)

deposit (n) *[paid in advance]* acconto (m)

deposit (v) versare denaro

deposit account conto (m) di deposito

deposit slip distinta (f) di versamento

depositor depositante (m)

depository *[place]* deposito (m)

depot magazzino (m)

depreciate *[amortize]* ammortizzare

depreciate *[lose value]* svalutare

depreciation *[amortizing]* ammortamento (m)

depreciation *[loss of value]* svalutazione (f)

depreciation rate quota (f) d'ammortamento

depression depressione (f)

deputize for someone rappresentare qualcuno

deputy delegato (m) *o* sostituto (m)

deputy manager vice direttore (m)

deputy managing director vice amministratore (m) delegato

deregulation deregolamentazione (f) *o* abolizione (f) della regolamentazione

describe descrivere

description descrizione (f)

design (n) design (m) *o* progettazione (f)

design (v) progettare

design department dipartimento *o* ufficio design

desk scrivania (f)

desk diary agenda (f) da tavolo

desk-top publishing (DTP) desktop publishing (m)

destination destinazione (f)

detail (n) dettaglio (m)

detail (v) dettagliare

detailed dettagliato

detailed account resoconto (m) dettagliato

determine determinare

Deutschmark marco (m) tedesco

devaluation svalutazione (f)

devalue svalutare

develop *[build]* costruire *o* sviluppare

develop *[plan]* sviluppare

developing country paese (m) in via di sviluppo

development sviluppo (m) *o* progresso (m)

device congegno (m)

diagram diagramma (m)

dial (v) a number formare *o* comporre un numero telefonico

dial direct teleselezione (f)

dialling chiamata (f) (telefonica)

dialling code prefisso (m) telefonico

dialling tone segnale (m) di linea libera

diary diario

dictate dettare

dictating machine dittafono (m)

dictation dettatura (f)

differ dissentire

difference differenza (f)

differences in price differenze (fpl) di prezzo

different diverso

differential (adj) differenziale

differential tariffs tariffe (fpl) differenziali

digit cifra (f) *o* numero (m)

dilution of equity diluizione (f) della partecipazione azionaria

direct (adj) diretto

direct (adv) direttamente

direct (v) dirigere *o* guidare

direct cost costo (m) diretto

direct debit addebito (m) diretto

direct mail vendita (f) diretta tramite corrispondenza

direct mailing pubblicità (f) a mezzo posta

direct selling vendita (f) diretta

direct tax imposta (f) diretta

direct taxation tassazione (f) diretta

direct-mail advertising pubblicità (f) a mezzo posta

direction direzione (f) *o* istruzione (f)

directions for use istruzioni (fpl) per l'uso

directive direttiva (f)

director amministratore (m)

directory annuario (m)

disburse pagare

disbursement esborso (m) *o* pagamento (m)

discharge (n) *[of debt]* pagamento (m) di un debito

discharge (v) *[employee]* licenziare

discharge a debt estinguere un debito

disclaimer smentita (f)

disclose rivelare *o* divulgare

disclose a piece of information divulgare un'informazione

disclosure rivelazione (f) *o* divulgazione (f)

disclosure of confidential information divulgazione (f) di un'informazione riservata

discontinue interrrompere

discount (n) sconto (m)

discount (v) vendere sotto costo

discount house *[bank]* banca (f) di sconto

discount house *[shop]* negozio (m) di vendita a prezzi ridotti

discount price prezzo (m) scontato

discount rate tasso (m) di sconto

discount store magazzino (m) a prezzi scontati

discountable scontabile

discounted cash flow (DCF) sconto (m) del valore attuale

discounter scontista (m)

discrepancy discrepanza (f)

discuss discutere

discussion discussione (f)

dishonour non onorare

dishonour a bill non onorare un effetto

disk disco (m)

disk drive unità (f) a dischi magnetici

diskette dischetto (m)

dismiss an employee licenziare un dipendente

dismissal licenziamento (m)

dispatch (n) *[sending]* spedizione (f)

dispatch (v) *[send]* spedire

dispatch department servizio (m) spedizioni

dispatch note bolla (f) di spedizione

display (n) esposizione (f) *o* mostra (f)

display (v) esporre

display case vetrinetta (f)

display material materiale (m) da esposizione

display pack confezione (f) per esposizione

display stand banco (m) di esposizione

display unit video-unità

disposable da non restituire *o* da gettare

disposal vendita (f)

dispose of excess stock eliminare le scorte in eccesso

dissolve risolvere *o* dissolvere

dissolve a partnership sciogliere una società di persone

distress merchandise merci (fpl) vendute sottocosto

distress sale vendita (f) di merce sottocosto

distributable profit utili (mpl) distribuibili

distribute *[goods]* distribuire

distribute *[share]* distribuire

distribution distribuzione (f)

distribution channels canali (mpl) di distribuzione

distribution costs costi (mpl) di distribuzione

distribution manager direttore (m) delle distribuzioni

distribution network rete (f) di distribuzione

distributor distributore (m)

distributorship concessione (f) di vendita

diversification diversificazione (f)

diversify diversificare

dividend dividendo (m)

dividend cover rapporto (m) fra utile e dividendo

dividend warrant cedola (f) di dividendo

dividend yield reddito (m) da dividendi

division *[part of a company]* reparto (m)

division *[part of a group]* divisione (f)

dock (n) bacino (m)

dock (v) *[remove money]* decurtare

dock (v) *[ship]* entrare in porto *o* attraccare

docket elenco (m) delle cause

doctor's certificate certificato (m) medico

document documento (m)

documentary documentario (m)

documentary evidence documentazione (f)

documentary proof prova (f) documentata

documentation documentazione (f)

documents documenti (mpl)

dollar dollaro (m)

dollar area area (f) del dollaro

dollar balance bilancia (f) commerciale in dollari

dollar crisis crisi (f) del dollaro

domestic domestico

domestic market mercato (m) interno

domestic production produzione (f) nazionale

domestic sales vendite (fpl) interne

domestic trade commercio (m) interno

domicile domicilio (m)

door porta (f)

door-to-door a domicilio (m)

door-to-door salesman venditore (m) a domicilio

door-to-door selling vendita (f) porta a porta

dossier dossier (m) o pratica (f)

dot-matrix printer stampante (f) a matrice d'aghi

double (adj) doppio

double (v) raddoppiare

double taxation doppia tassazione (f)

double taxation agreement sgravio (m) per doppia tassazione

double-book riservare una camera a due clienti

double-booking prenotazione (f) di una camera a due clienti

down discendente o giù

down payment versamento (m) d'acconto

down time tempo (m) improduttivo

down-market mercato (m) in ribasso

downside factor fattore (m) negativo

downtown (adv) in centro

downtown (n) centro (m) (di città)

downturn regresso (m)

downward discendente o giù

dozen dozzina (f)

drachma [Greek currency] dracma (f)

draft (n) [money] tratta (f)

draft (n) [rough plan] bozza (f)

draft (v) abbozzare o redigere

draft a contract preparare lo schema di un contratto

draft a letter stendere la minuta (f) di una lettera

draft plan bozza (f) di un piano

draft project bozza (f) di un progetto

draw [a cheque] emettere un assegno

draw [money] prelevare

draw up redigere

draw up a contract stipulare un contratto

drawee trattario (m)

drawer traente (m)

drawing account conto (m) corrente

drive (n) [campaign] campagna (f)

drive (n) [energy] grinta (f)

drive (n) [part of machine] trasmissione (f)

drive (v) [a car] condurre o guidare

driver conducente (m)

drop (n) caduta (f) o ribasso (m)

drop (v) cadere o calare

drop in sales ribasso (m) delle vendite

due [awaited] atteso

due [owing] dovuto

dues [orders] ordinazioni (fpl) inevase

duly [in time] come previsto

duly [legally] regolarmente o dovutamente

dummy fittizio o falso

dummy pack confezione (f) finta

dump bin scaffale (m) per esposizione (in negozi)

dump goods on a market svendere merci sul mercato

dumping vendita (f) sottocosto

duplicate (n) duplicato (m)

duplicate (v) duplicare

duplicate an invoice fare il duplicato di una fattura

duplicate receipt or **duplicate of a receipt** ricevuta (f) in duplicato

duplication duplicazione (f)

durable goods beni (mpl) durevoli

duty [tax] dazio (m)

duty-free esente da dazio

duty-free shop 'duty free shop' o negozio (m) esente da tasse

duty-paid goods merce (f) con dazio pagato

Ee

e. & o.e. (errors and omissions excepted) Salvo errori e omissioni (S. E. & O)

early prossimo

earmark funds for a project accantonare fondi (mpl) per un progetto

earn *[interest]* fruttare

earn *[money]* guadagnare

earning capacity capacità (f) di guadagno

earnings *[profit]* utile (m) *o* profitto (m)

earnings *[salary]* guadagni (mpl)

earnings per share *or* **earnings yield** utile (m) per azione

easy facile

easy terms condizioni (fpl) moderate

economic *[general]* economico

economic *[profitable]* vantaggioso

economic cycle ciclo (m) economico

economic development sviluppo (m) economico

economic growth crescita (f) economica

economic indicators indicatori (mpl) economici

economic model modello (m) economico

economic planning programmazione (f) economica

economic trends congiuntura (f)

economical economico

economics *[profitability]* redditività (f)

economics *[study]* economia (f) *o* scienze (fpl) economiche

economies of scale economia (f) di massa

economist economista (mf)

economize economizzare

economy *[saving]* economia (f)

economy *[system]* economia (f)

economy class classe (f) turistica

ecu *or* **ECU (= European currency unit)** ecu (m) (Unità di Conto Europea)

effect (n) effetto (m)

effect (v) effettuare

effective effettivo

effective date data (f) di entrata in vigore

effective demand domanda (f) effettiva

effective yield rendimento (m) effettivo

effectiveness efficacia (f)

efficiency efficienza (f)

efficient efficiente

effort sforzo (m)

elasticity elasticità (f)

elect eleggere

election elezione (f)

electronic mail posta (f) elettronica

electronic point of sale (EPOS) punto (m) di vendita elettronico

elevator *[goods]* montacarichi (m)

elevator *[grain]* silo (m)

email (= electronic mail) posta (f) elettronica

embargo (n) embargo (m)

embargo (v) mettere l'embargo su

embark imbarcare *o* imbarcarsi

embark on imbarcarsi in

embarkation imbarco (m)

embarkation card carta (f) d'imbarco

embezzle appropriarsi indebitamente

embezzlement appropriazione (f) indebita

embezzler colpevole (m) di appropriazione indebita

emergency emergenza (f)

emergency reserves riserve (fpl) d'emergenza

employ impiegare *o* assumere

employed *[in job]* impiegato

employed *[money]* investito

employed *[used]* impiegato

employee dipendente (m)

employer datore (m) di lavoro

employment impiego (m)

employment agency agenzia (f) di lavoro

employment bureau agenzia (f) di lavoro

empty (adj) vuoto

empty (v) vuotare

EMS (= European Monetary System) SME (Sistema Monetario Europeo)

encash incassare

encashment incasso (m)

enclose allegare

enclosure allegato (m)

end (n) fine (f) *o* termine (m)

end (v) finire *o* concludere

end of season sale svendite (fpl) di fine stagione

end product prodotto (m) finito

end user utente (m) finale

endorse a cheque girare un assegno

endorsee giratario (m)

endorsement *[action]* girata (f)

endorsement *[on insurance]* restrizione (f)

endorser girante (m)

energy *[electricity]* energia (f)

energy *[human]* energia (f) *o* dinamismo (m)

energy-saving (adj) che risparmia energia

enforce applicare

enforcement imposizione (f)

engaged *[telephone]* occupato

engaged tone segnale (m) di linea occupata

enquire (= inquire) chiedere informazioni

enquiry (= inquiry) richiesta (f) di informazioni

enter *[go in]* entrare

enter *[write in]* registrare

enter into *[discussion]* prendere parte in

entering annotazione (f)

enterprise impresa (f)

entitle conferire il diritto

entitlement diritto (m)

entrepot port porto (m) di transito

entrepreneur imprenditore (m)

entrepreneurial imprenditoriale

entrust affidare

entry *[going in]* entrata (f)

entry *[writing]* scrittura (f) contabile

entry visa visto (m) d'ingresso

epos *or* **EPOS (= electronic point of sale)** punto (m) di vendita elettronico

equal (adj) uguale

equal (v) uguagliare

equalization equalizzazione (f)

equip equipaggiare

equipment apparecchiatura (f)

equities azioni (fpl) ordinarie

equity passivo (m) patrimoniale

equity capital capitale (m) effettivo

erode erodere

error errore (m)

error rate percentuale (f) d'errore

errors and omissions excepted (e. & o.e.) salvo errori e omissioni (S.E & O)

escalate intensificare

escape clause clausola (f) di salvaguardia

escrow account conto (m) a garanzia

escudo *[Portuguese currency]* escudo (m)

essential indispensabile

establish stabilire *o* istituire

establishment *[business]* azienda (f) commerciale

establishment *[staff]* personale (m)

estimate (n) *[calculation]* valutazione (f)

estimate (n) *[quote]* preventivo (m)

estimate (v) stimare *o* valutare

estimated valutato

estimated figure cifra (f) preventivata

estimated sales vendite (fpl) presunte

estimation opinione (f)

EU (= European Union) UE (Unione (f) Europea)

Eurocheque euroassegno (m)

Eurocurrency euromoneta (f)

Eurodollar eurodollaro (m)

Euromarket euromercato (m)

European europeo

European Investment Bank (EIB) Banca (f) Europea per gli Investimenti (BEI)

European Monetary System (EMS) Sistema (m) Monetario Europeo (SME)

European Union (EU) Unione (f) Europea (UE)

evade evadere

evade tax sottrarsi al pagamento delle tasse

evaluate valutare

evaluate costs valutare i costi

evaluation valutazione (f)

evasion evasione (f) d'imposta

ex coupon ex cedola (f)

ex dividend ex dividendo (m)

ex-directory che non compare nell'elenco telefonico

exact (adj) esatto

exact (v) esigere

exactly esattamente

examination *[inspection]* esame (f)

examination *[test]* esame (f)

examine esaminare

exceed sorpassare *o* superare

excellent eccellente

except eccetto *o* tranne

exceptional eccezionale *o* straordinario

exceptional items voci (fpl) straordinarie

excess eccesso

excess baggage bagaglio (m) in eccesso

excess capacity capacità (f) produttiva in eccesso

excess profits sovrapprofitti (mpl)

excessive eccessivo

excessive costs costi (mpl) eccessivi

exchange (n) *[currency]* cambio (m)

exchange (v) *[currency]* cambiare

exchange (v) *[one thing for another]* scambiare con

exchange control controlli (mpl) valutari

exchange rate tasso (m) di cambio

exchangeable scambiabile

Exchequer Ministero del Tesoro

excise (v) *[cut out]* tagliare

excise duty imposta (f) indiretta

Excise officer daziere (m)

exclude escludere

excluding escluso

exclusion esclusione (f)

exclusion clause clausola (f) di esclusione

exclusive agreement accordo (m) in esclusiva

exclusive of escluso

exclusive of tax tassa (f) esclusa

exclusivity esclusività (f)

execute eseguire

execution esecuzione (f)

executive (adj) esecutivo

executive (n) dirigente (m)

executive director direttore (m) esecutivo

exempt (adj) esente

exempt (v) esentare

exempt from tax esente da tassa

exemption esenzione (f)

exemption from tax esenzione (f) da tassa

exercise (n) esercizio (m)

exercise (v) esercitare

exercise an option esercitare un'opzione

exercise of an option esercizio (m) di un'opzione

exhibit (v) esibire

exhibition esposizione (f) *o* mostra (f)

exhibition hall sala (f) esposizioni

exhibitor espositore (m) *o* standista (m)

expand ampliare

expansion allargamento (m)

expenditure spese (fpl)

expense spesa (f) *o* conto (m)

expense account conto (m) spese

expenses spese (fpl)

expensive costoso

experienced esperto

expertise 'expertise' (f) *o* perizia (f)

expiration termine (m)

expire terminare *o* scadere

expiry fine (f) *o* scadenza (f)

expiry date data (f) di scadenza

explain spiegare

explanation spiegazione (f)

exploit sfruttare

explore esplorare

export (n) esportazione (f)

export (v) esportare

export department reparto (m) esportazioni

export duty dazio (m) d'esportazione

export licence *or* **export permit** licenza (f) d'esportazione

export manager direttore (m) del reparto esportazioni

export trade commercio (m) d'esportazione

exporter esportatore (m)

exporting (adj) esportatore

exports esportazioni (fpl)

exposure rischio (m) finanziario

express (adj) *[fast]* espresso

express (adj) *[stated clearly]* espresso

express (v) *[send fast]* spedire per espresso

express (v) *[state]* esprimere

express delivery spedizione (f) per espresso

express letter lettera (f) espresso

extend *[grant]* accordare

extend *[make longer]* prolungare

extended credit credito (m) prorogato

extension *[making longer]* prolungamento (m)

extension *[telephone]* interno (m)

external *[foreign]* estero *o* straniero

external *[outside a company]* esterno

external account conto (m) estero (fuori l'area di sterlina)

external audit revisione (f) esterna

external auditor revisore (m) esterno

external trade commercio (m) estero

extra extra

extra charges spese (fpl) extra

extraordinary straordinario

extraordinary items voci (fpl) straordinarie

extras spese (fpl) supplementari

Ff

FAO (= for the attention of) all'attenzione di

face value valore (m) nominale

facilities servizi (mpl) *o* mezzi (mpl)

facility *[building]* edificio (m)

facility *[credit]* agevolazione (f)

facility *[ease]* agevolazione (f)

factor (n) *[influence]* fattore (m)

factor (n) *[person, company]* agente (m) di factoring *o* società di factoring

factor (v) fare del factoring

factoring factoring (m)

factoring charges costi (mpl) di factoring

factors of production fattori (mpl) di produzione

factory fabbrica (f)

factory inspector ispettore (m) aziendale

factory outlet punto (m) di vendita diretta della fabbrica

factory price prezzo (m) di fabbrica

fail *[go bust]* fallire

fail *[not to do something]* non riuscire *o* non fare

fail *[not to succeed]* fallire

failing that se non è possibile

failure insuccesso (m)

fair (adj) giusto *o* equo

fair dealing trattamento (f) equo

fair price prezzi (mpl) equi

fair trade commercio (m) libero

fair trading commercio (m) libero

fair wear and tear normale usura (f) e degrado (m)

fake (n) imitazione (f)

fake (v) falsificare

faked documents documenti (mpl) falsi

fall (n) caduta (f) *o* crollo (m)

fall (v) *[go lower]* cadere

fall (v) *[on a date]* scadere

fall behind *[be in a worse position]* rimanere indietro

fall behind *[be late]* essere in ritardo (nel fare una cosa)

fall due essere dovuto

fall off scendere *o* diminuire

fall through fallire *o* non arrivare a compimento

falling in ribasso

false falso

false pretences millantato credito (m)

false weight peso (m) contraffatto

falsification falsificazione (f)

falsify falsificare

family company ditta (f) a conduzione familiare

fare tariffa (f)

farm out work appaltare del lavoro

fast (adj) veloce

fast (adv) velocemente *o* rapidamente

fast-selling items articoli (mpl) che vendono rapidamente

fault *[blame]* colpa (f)

fault *[mechanical]* difetto (m)

faulty equipment apparecchiatura (f) difettosa

favourable favorevole

favourable balance of trade bilancia (f) commerciale attiva

fax (n) fax (m)

fax (v) inviare per fax

feasibility fattibilità (f)

feasibility report studio (m) della fattibilità

fee *[admission]* quota (f) d'iscrizione

fee *[for services]* emolumento (m) *o* compenso (m)

feedback controreazione (f)

ferry traghetto (m)

fiddle (n) imbroglio (m) *o* truffa (f)

fiddle (v) imbrogliare

field campo (m) *o* area (f)

field sales manager direttore (m) vendite esterne

field work attività (f) esterna di ricerca e di studio

FIFO (= first in first out) primo ad entrare primo ad uscire

figure cifra (f)

figures cifre (fpl) *o* numeri (mpl)

file (n) *[computer]* file (m) *o* archivio (m)

file (n) *[documents]* fascicolo (m)

file (v) *[request]* inoltrare

file a patent application inoltrare una domanda di brevetto

file documents depositare documenti

filing *[action]* schedatura (f)

filing cabinet schedario (m)

filing card scheda (f)

fill a gap colmare una lacuna (f)

final finale

final demand domanda (f) finale

final discharge quietanza (f) finale

final dividend dividendo (m) finale

finalize completare

finance (n) finanza (f) *o* attività (f) finanziaria

finance (v) finanziare

finance an operation finanziare un'operazione

finance company società (f) finanziaria

finance director direttore (m) delle finanze

finances finanze (fpl)

financial finanziario *o* economico

financial assets disponibilità (fpl) finanziarie

financial crisis crisi (f) finanziaria

financial institution Istituto (m) finanziario

financial position posizione (f) finanziaria

financial resources risorse (fpl) finanziarie

financial risk rischio (m) finanziario

financial settlement regolamento (m) finanziario

financial year esercizio (m) finanziario

financially finanziariamente

financing finanziamento (m)

fine (adv) *[very good]* molto bene

fine (adv) *[very small]* fine

fine (n) multa (f)

fine (v) multare

fine tuning perfetta sintonia (f)

finished finito

finished goods prodotti (mpl) finiti

fire (n) fuoco (m) *o* incendio (m)

fire damage danno (m) causato da un incendio

fire insurance assicurazione (f) contro gli incendi

fire regulations norme (fpl) antincendio

fire risk rischio (m) d'incendio

fire-damaged goods merce (f) danneggiata da incendio

firm (adj) stabile *o* solido

firm (n) ditta (f) *o* azienda (f) *o* impresa (f)

firm (v) consolidarsi

firm price prezzo (m) stabile

first primo

first in first out (FIFO) primo ad entrare primo ad uscire

first option prima opzione (f)

first quarter primo trimestre (m)

first-class prima classe

fiscal fiscale

fiscal measures provvedimenti (mpl) fiscali

fittings accessori (mpl)

fix *[arrange]* fissare

fix *[mend]* riparare

fix a meeting for 3 p.m. fissare una riunione per le 3 del pomeriggio

fixed fisso *o* fissato

fixed assets immobilizzi (mpl)

fixed costs costi (mpl) fissi

fixed deposit deposito (m) vincolato

fixed exchange rate tasso (m) fisso di cambio

fixed income reddito (m) fisso

fixed interest interesse (m) fisso

fixed scale of charges tabella (f) fissa dei prezzi

fixed-interest investments investimenti (mpl) ad interessi fissi

fixed-price agreement contratto (m) a prezzo fisso

fixing fissaggio (m)

flat (adj) *[dull]* piatto

flat (adj) *[fixed]* fisso

flat (n) appartamento (m)

flat rate importo (m) fisso

flexibility flessibilità (f)

flexible flessibile

flexible prices prezzi (mpl) flessibili

flexible pricing policy politica (f) dei prezzi flessibile

flight *[of money]* fuga (f) (di denaro)

flight *[of plane]* volo (m)

flight information informazioni (fpl) di volo

flight of capital capitale (m) in fuga

flip chart blocco (m) di fogli per lavagna

float (n) *[money]* anticipo (m)

float (n) *[of company]* lancio (m) di una società

float (v) *[a currency]* far fluttuare

float a company lanciare una società

floating fluttuante

floating exchange rates tasso fluttuante di cambio

floating of a company lancio (m) di una società

flood (n) inondazione (f)

flood (v) inondare

floor *[level]* piano (m)

floor *[surface]* pavimento (m)

floor manager capo (m) reparto

floor plan planimetria (f)

floor space superficie (f) di pavimento

flop (n) insuccesso (m)

flop (v) fare fiasco

flotation lancio (m) di una società

flourish prosperare

flourishing fiorente

flourishing trade attività (f) commerciale fiorente

flow (n) flusso (m)

flow (v) fluire

flow chart schema (m) del ciclo

flow diagram diagramma (m) del ciclo di lavorazione

fluctuate fluttuare *o* oscillare

fluctuating fluttuante

fluctuation fluttuazione (f)

FOB *or* **f.o.b. (free on board)** franco a bordo

follow seguire *o* fare seguito

follow up aggiornamento (m) *o* sollecito (m)

follow-up letter lettera (f) di sollecito

for sale in vendita

forbid proibire

force majeure causa (f) di forza maggiore

force prices down provocare la diminuzione dei prezzi

force prices up far salire i prezzi

forced forzato

forced sale vendita (f) coatta

forecast (n) previsione (f)

forecast (v) prevedere

forecasting attività (f) previsionale

foreign straniero *o* estero

foreign currency divise (fpl) *o* moneta (f) straniera

foreign exchange *[changing money]* mercato (m) dei cambi

foreign exchange *[currency]* divise (fpl) *o* valuta (f) estera

foreign exchange broker agente (m) in cambi

foreign exchange dealer operatore (m) in cambi

foreign exchange market mercato (m) dei cambi

foreign investments investimenti (mpl) esteri

foreign money order ordine (m) di pagamento di valuta estera

foreign trade commercio (m) estero

forfeit (n) multa (f) *o* penalità (f)

forfeit (v) perdere (un diritto)

forfeit a deposit perdere un deposito

forfeiture perdita (f) (di un diritto)

forge falsificare

forgery *[action]* contraffazione (f)

forgery *[copy]* falso (m)

fork-lift truck carrello (m) elevatore (a forche)

form (n) modulo (m)

form (v) formare *o* comporre

form of words formulazione (f)

formal formale

formality formalità (f)

forward spedire

forward buying acquisto (m) a termine

forward contract contratto (m) a termine

forward market mercato (m) a termine

forward rate corso (m) per operazioni a termine

forward sales vendite (fpl) a termine

forwarding spedizione (f) *o* inoltro (m)

forwarding address indirizzo (m) d'inoltro

forwarding agent spedizioniere (m) (per via terra)

forwarding instructions istruzioni (fpl) per la spedizione

fourth quarter quarto trimestre (m)

fragile fragile

franc franco (m)

franchise (n) concessione (f)

franchise (v) concedere il diritto di esclusiva

franchisee concessionario (m)

franchiser concedente (m)

franchising concessione (f) di vendita

franco senza spese (fpl) *o* franco

frank (v) affrancare

franking machine macchina (f) affrancatrice

fraud frode (f)

fraudulent fraudolento *o* disonesto

fraudulent transaction operazione (f) disonesta

fraudulently disonestamente

free (adj) *[no payment]* gratis

free (adj) *[no restrictions]* libero

free (adj) *[not busy]* libero

free (adj) *[not occupied]* libero

free (adv) *[no payment]* gratis *o* gratuitamente

free (v) liberare

free delivery consegna (f) gratuita

free gift omaggio (m) *o* dono (m)

free market economy economia (f) di mercato libero

free of charge gratuito *o* franco di spese

free of duty franco dogana (f)

free of tax esente da tasse

free on board (f.o.b.) franco a bordo

free on rail franco su rotaia

free port porto (m) franco

free sample campione (m) gratuito

free trade libero scambio (m)

free trade area zona (f) di libero scambio

free trade zone zona (f) di libero scambio

free trial prova (f) gratuita

free zone zona (f) franca

freelance (n) "freelance" *o* libero professionista (m)

freeze (n) blocco (m) (commerciale)

freeze (v) *[prices]* congelare

freeze credits congelare un credito

freeze wages and prices bloccare i salari e i prezzi

freight *[carriage]* trasporto (m) (via mare)

freight costs spese (fpl) di trasporto

freight depot scalo (m) merci

freight forward porto (m) assegnato

freight plane aereo (m) da carico

freight rates tariffe (fpl) di nolo

freight train treno (m) merci

freightage trasporto (m) di merci

freighter *[plane]* aereo (m) da carico

freighter *[ship]* nave (f) da carico

freightliner treno (m) merci

frequent frequente

frozen congelato *o* bloccato

frozen account conto (m) congelato

frozen assets cespiti (mpl) congelati

frozen credits crediti (mpl) congelati

fulfil an order evadere un'ordinazione

fulfilment adempimento (m)

full pieno *o* intero

full discharge of a debt pieno scarico (m) di un debito

full payment pagamento (m) a saldo *o* pagamento totale

full price prezzo (m) intero

full refund rimborso (m) totale

full-scale **(adj)** in scala (f) naturale

full-time orario (m) pieno

full-time employment impiego (m) a tempo pieno

fund (n) fondo (m) *o* fondi (mpl)

fund (v) finanziare

funding (financing) finanziamento (m)

funding *[of debt]* consolidamento (m)

further to in seguito a

future delivery futura consegna (f)

futures contratti (mpl) a termine e a premio

Gg

gain (n) *[getting bigger]* aumento (m)

gain (n) *[increase in value]* guadagno (m)

gain (v) *[become bigger]* aumentare

gain (v) *[get]* ottenere

gap divario (m)

gap in the market apertura (f) sul mercato

GDP (= gross domestic product) prodotto (m) interno lordo (PIL)

gear ingranaggio (m)

gearing rapporto (m) di indebitamento

general generale

general audit revisione (f) contabile periodica

general average avaria (f) generale

general manager direttore (m) generale

general meeting assemblea (f) generale

general office ufficio (m) pubblico

general post office Amministrazione Centrale delle Poste (UK)

general strike sciopero (m) generale

gentleman's agreement accordo (m) sulla parola (f)

genuine vero *o* autentico

genuine purchaser acquirente (m) genuino

get procurarsi

get along cavarsela

get back *[something lost]* avere indietro

get into debt indebitarsi

get rid of something liberarsi di qualcosa

get round *[a problem]* aggirare

get the sack essere licenziato

gift regalo (m)

gift coupon buono (m) premio

gift shop negozio (m) per articoli da regalo

gift voucher buono (m) premio

gilt-edged securities titoli (mpl) di prim'ordine

gilts titoli (mpl) di prim'ordine

giro account conto corrente di corrispondenza

giro account number numero (m) di conto corrente di corrispondenza

giro system (sistema di) giroconto (m)

give *[as gift]* regalare

give *[pass]* dare

give away regalare

glut (n) saturazione (f)

glut (v) saturare

GNP (= gross national product) prodotto (m) nazionale lordo (PNL)

go andare

go into business mettersi in affari

go-ahead (adj) intraprendente

go-slow sciopero (m) bianco

going andamento (m)

going rate tariffa (f) in vigore

gold card carta (f) di credito d'oro

good buono

good buy buon affare (m)

good management buona gestione (f)

good quality buona qualità (f)

good value (for money) conveniente

goods merce (f)

goods depot deposito (m) merci

goods in transit merce (f) in transito

goods train treno (m) merci

goodwill avviamento (m) commerciale

government (adj) governativo *o* del governo

government (n) governo (m)

government bonds titoli (mpl) di stato

government contractor fornitore (m) allo stato *o* statale

government stock titoli (mpl) di stato

government-backed con l'appoggio del governo

government-controlled a controllo statale

government-regulated a controllo statale

government-sponsored sponsorizzato dal governo

graded advertising rates tariffe (fpl) pubblicitarie differenziali

graded hotel albergo (m) selezionato

graded tax imposta (f) progressiva

gradual graduale

graduate trainee laureato (m) che fa tirocinio come dirigente

graduated graduato

graduated income tax imposta (f) progressiva sul reddito

gram *or* **gramme** grammo (m)

grand total totale (m) generale

grant (n) concessione (f) *o* borsa (f) di studio

grant (v) concedere *o* accordare

gratis gratis

grid griglia (f) *o* reticolo (m)

grid structure struttura a rete

gross (adj) lordo

gross (n) (= 144) grossa (f) (dodici dozzine)

gross (v) avere un ricavo lordo *o* incassare

gross domestic product (GDP) prodotto (m) interno lordo (PIL)

gross earnings guadagno (m) lordo

gross income reddito (m) lordo

gross margin margine (m) lordo

gross national product (GNP) prodotto (m) nazionale lordo (PNL)

gross profit utile (m) lordo

gross salary stipendio (m) lordo

gross tonnage tonnellaggio (m) lordo

gross weight peso (m) lordo

gross yield rendimento (m) lordo

group *[of businesses]* gruppo (m) industriale

group *[of people]* gruppo (m)

growth crescita (f)

growth index indice (m) di crescita

growth rate percentuale (f) di crescita

guarantee (n) garanzia (f)

guarantee (v) garantire

guarantee a debt garantire un debito

guaranteed minimum wage salario (m) minimo garantito

guarantor avallante (m)

guideline direttiva (f)

guild gilda (f) *o* corporazione (f)

guilder *[Dutch currency]* fiorino (m) (olandese)

Hh

haggle mercanteggiare

half (adj) mezzo

half (n) metà (f)

half a dozen *or* a half-dozen mezza dozzina (f)

half-price sale saldo (m) a metà prezzo

half-year semestre (m)

half-yearly accounts contabilità (f) semestrale

half-yearly payment pagamento (m) semestrale

half-yearly statement resoconto (m) semestrale

hand in consegnare *o* restituire

hand luggage bagaglio (m) a mano

hand over passaggio (m) delle consegne

handle (v) *[deal with]* occuparsi di

handle (v) *[sell]* commerciare

handling maneggio (m) *o* gestione (f)

handling charge spese (fpl) di confezione, spedizione

handwriting calligrafia (f)

handwritten scritto a mano

handy maneggevole *o* pratico

harbour porto (m)

harbour dues diritti (mpl) portuali

harbour facilities impianti (mpl) portuali

hard bargain affare (m) poco vantaggioso

hard bargaining trattative (fpl) difficili

hard copy copia (f) in chiaro

hard currency valuta (f) solida

hard disk hard disk (m)

hard selling campagna (di vendita, di pubblicità) aggressiva

harmonization armonizzazione (f)

haulage trasporto (m)

haulage contractor trasportatore (m)

haulage costs *or* haulage rates prezzo (m) del trasporto

head of department capo (m) reparto

head office sede (f)

headquarters (HQ) sede (f) centrale

heads of agreement capi (mpl) d'intesa

health salute (f) *o* sanità (f)

health insurance assicurazione (f) malattie

healthy profit buon guadagno (m)

heavy *[important]* grave

heavy *[weight]* pesante

heavy costs *or* heavy expenditure forti costi (mpl) *o* spese (fpl)

heavy equipment apparecchiatura (f) pesante

heavy goods vehicle (HGV) veicolo (m) per merci pesanti

heavy industry industria (f) pesante

heavy machinery macchinario (m) pesante

hectare ettaro (m)

hedge (n) barriera (f) *o* protezione (f)

hedging copertura (f)

HGV (= heavy goods vehicle) veicolo (m) per merci pesanti

hidden asset attività (fpl) occulte

hidden reserves riserve (fpl) occulte

high interest interesse (m) alto

high rent affitto (m) alto

high taxation tassazione (f) alta

high-quality di qualità superiore

high-quality goods prodotti (mpl) di alta qualità

highest bidder migliore offerente (m)

highly motivated sales staff personale (m) di vendita molto motivato

highly qualified altamente qualificato

highly-geared company azienda (f) con forte indebitamento

highly-paid altamente retribuito

highly-priced ad alto prezzo

hire (n) noleggio (m)

hire a car noleggiare un'automobile

hire car automobile (f) a noleggio

hire purchase (HP) acquisto (m) rateale

hire staff assumere personale

hire-purchase company ditta (f) di vendita a rate

historic(al) cost costo (m) effettivo

historical figures cifre (fpl) effettive

hive off assegnare la produzione di qualcosa ad un'azienda consociata

hoard ammasso (m)

hoarding *[for posters]* tabellone (m)

hoarding *[of goods]* accaparramento (m)

hold (n) *[ship]* stiva (f)

hold (v) *[contain]* contenere

hold (v) *[keep]* tenere

hold a meeting *or* **a discussion** tenere una seduta

hold out for fare il braccio di ferro per

hold over posporre

hold the line please *or* **please hold** resti in linea per favore

hold up (v) *[delay]* trattenere

hold-up (n) *[delay]* ritardo (m)

holder *[person]* titolare (m)

holder *[thing]* contenitore (m) *o* sostegno (m)

holding company 'holding' (f) *o* società (f) controllante

holiday pay retribuzione (f) ferie

home address indirizzo (m) personale

home consumption consumo (m) interno *o* nazionale

home market mercato (m) nazionale

home sales vendite (fpl) nazionali *o* vendite sul mercato interno

homeward freight carico (m) di ritorno

homeward journey viaggio (m) di ritorno

homeworker lavoratore (m) a domicilio

honorarium onorario (m)

honour a bill onorare una cambiale

honour a signature onorare una firma

horizontal communication comunicazione (f) orizzontale

horizontal integration integrazione (f) orizzontale

hotel hotel (m) *o* albergo (m)

hotel accommodation ricettività (f) alberghi

hotel bill conto dell'albergo

hotel manager direttore (m) d'albergo

hotel staff personale (m) alberghiero

hour ora (f)

hourly orario

hourly rate retribuzione (f) a ore

hourly wage salario (m) orario

hourly-paid workers dipendenti (mpl) pagati a ore

house *[company]* ditta (f) *o* impresa (f)

house *[for family]* casa (f)

house insurance assicurazione (f) sulla casa

house magazine rivista (f) aziendale

house-to-house a domicilio *o* di casa in casa

house-to-house selling vendita (f) a domicilio

HP (= hire purchase) sistema (m) di acquisti a rate

HQ (= headquarters) sede centrale

hurry up affrettarsi

hype (n) montatura (f) giornalistica

hype (v) fare un grosso lancio pubblicitario di

hypermarket ipermercato (m)

Ii

illegal illegale

illegality illegalità (f)

illegally illegalmente

illicit illecito

ILO (= International Labour Organization) Organizzazione Internazionale del Lavoro (OIL)

IMF (= International Monetary Fund) Fondo Monetario Internazionale

imitation imitazione (f)

immediate immediato

immediately immediatamente

imperfect imperfetto

imperfection imperfezione (f)

implement (n) strumento (m)

implement (v) attuare *o* realizzare

implement an agreement rendere effettivo un accordo

implementation attuazione (f)

import (n) importazione (f)

import (v) importare

import ban divieto (m) di importazione

import duty dazio (m) doganale

import levy prelievo (m) sulle importazioni

import licence *or* **import permit** licenza (f) di importazione

import quota contingente (m) di importazione

import restrictions restrizioni (fpl) alle importazioni

import surcharge soprattassa (f) di importazione

import-export (adj) importazioni-esportazioni

importance importanza (f)

important importante

importation importazione (f)

importer importatore (m)

importing (adj) importatore, importatrice

importing (n) importazione (f)

imports importazioni (fpl)

impose imporre

impulse impulso (m)

impulse buyer acquirente (mf) che compra per impulso

impulse purchase acquisto (m) fatto per impulso

in-house interno (alla ditta, allo stabilimento)

in-house training addestramento (m) interno (alla ditta)

incentive incentivo (m)

incentive bonus gratifica (f) di bilancio

incentive payments premio (m) d'operosità

incidental expenses spese (fpl) impreviste

include includere

inclusive incluso

inclusive charge spesa (f) compresa

inclusive of tax comprese tasse (fpl)

income reddito (m)

income tax imposta (f) sul reddito

incoming call telefonata (f) in arrivo

incoming mail posta (f) in arrivo

incompetent incapace

incorporate *[a company]* costituire

incorporation costituzione (f)

incorrect scorretto

incorrectly scorrettamente

increase (n) aumento (m)

increase (n) *[higher salary]* aumento (m)

increase (v) aumentare

increase (v) in price aumentare di prezzo

increasing crescente

increasing profits utile (m) in aumento

increment incremento (m)

incremental incrementativo

incremental cost costo (m) marginale

incremental scale scala (f) incrementale

incur incorrere (in)

incur *[costs]* sostenere spese

incur debts contrarre debiti

indebted indebitato

indebtedness indebitamento (m)

indemnification indennità (f) *o* indennizzo (m)

indemnify risarcire *o* indennizzare

indemnify someone for a loss risarcire qualcuno per una perdita

indemnity garanzia (f) *o* assicurazione (f)

independent indipendente

independent company azienda (f) autonoma

index (n) *[alphabetical]* indice (m)

index (n) *[of prices]* indice (m)

index (v) elencare

index card scheda (f)

index number indice (m) economico

index-linked indicizzato

indexation *or* **index-linking** indicizzazione (f)

indicator indicatore (m)

indirect indiretto

indirect labour costs costi (mpl) indiretti del lavoro

indirect tax imposte (fpl) indirette

indirect taxation tassazione (f) indiretta

induction inserimento (m) in un nuovo lavoro

induction course or induction training corso (m) introduttivo

industrial industriale

industrial accident infortunio (m) sul lavoro

industrial arbitration tribunal tribunale (m) di arbitrato industriale

industrial capacity capacità (f) industriale

industrial centre centro (m) industriale

industrial design disegno (m) industriale

industrial disputes vertenza (f) operaia

industrial espionage spionaggio (m) industriale

industrial estate zona (f) industriale

industrial expansion espansione (f) industriale

industrial processes processi (mpl) industriali

industrial relations relazioni (fpl) industriali

industrial tribunal tribunale (m) del lavoro

industrialist industriale (m)

industrialization industrializzazione (f)

industrialize industrializzare

industrialized societies paesi (mpl) industrializzati

industry [companies] industria (f)

industry [general] industria (f)

inefficiency inefficienza (f)

inefficient inefficiente

inflated currency moneta (f) inflazionata

inflated prices prezzi (mpl) inflazionati

inflation inflazione (f)

inflationary inflazionistico

influence (n) influenza (f)

influence (v) influenzare

inform informare

information informazione (f)

information bureau ufficio (m) informazioni

information officer impiegato (m) addetto alle informazioni

infrastructure infrastruttura (f)

infringe infrangere

infringe a patent usurpare un brevetto

infringement of customs regulations violazione (f) dei regolamenti doganali

infringement of patent usurpazione (f) di brevetto

initial (adj) iniziale

initial (v) siglare

initial capital capitale (m) d'apporto

initiate iniziare

initiate discussions iniziare un dibattito (m)

initiative iniziativa (f)

inland interno o del territorio nazionale

innovate innovare

innovation innovazione (f)

innovative innovativo

innovator innovatore (m)

input (v) information immettere informazioni nel computer

input tax IVA (Imposta sul Valore Aggiunto)

inquire chiedere informazioni

inquiry richiesta (f)

insider persona (f) che dispone di informazioni riservate

insider dealing compravendita (f) di azioni da parte degli stessi amministratori della Società

insolvency insolvenza (f)

insolvent insolvente

inspect esaminare

inspection ispezione (f)

instalment rata (f)

instant (adj) [current] corrente

instant (adj) [immediate] immediato o istantaneo

instant credit credito (m) immediato

institute (n) istituto (m)

institute (v) istituire

institution istituzione (f)

institutional istituzionale

institutional investors investitori (mpl) istituzionali

instruction istruzione (f)

instrument [device] strumento (m)

instrument *[document]* documento (m) *o* strumento (m)

insufficient funds *[US]* fondi (mpl) insufficienti

insurable assicurabile

insurance assicurazione (f)

insurance agent agente (m) di assicurazione

insurance broker mediatore (m) assicurativo

insurance claim richiesta (f) di indennizzo assicurativo

insurance company compagnia (f) di assicurazione

insurance contract contratto (m) di assicurazione

insurance cover copertura (f) assicurativa

insurance policy polizza (f) di assicurazione

insurance premium premio (m) di assicurazione

insurance rates tariffe (fpl) di assicurazione

insurance salesman venditore (m) di assicurazioni

insure assicurare

insurer assicuratore (m)

intangible intangibile

intangible assets attività (fpl) immateriali

interest (n) *[investment]* partecipazione (f)

interest (n) *[paid on investment]* interesse (m)

interest (v) interessare

interest charges addebiti (mpl) per interessi

interest rate tasso (m) d'interesse

interest-bearing deposits depositi (mpl) fruttiferi

interest-free credit credito (m) esente da interessi

interface (n) interfaccia (f)

interface (v) fungere da interfaccia

interim dividend dividendo (m) in acconto

interim payment pagamento (m) provvisorio

interim report relazione (f) provvisoria

intermediary intermediario (m)

internal *[inside a company]* interno

internal *[inside a country]* interno

internal audit revisione (f) interna

internal auditor revisore (m) interno

internal telephone telefono (m) interno

international internazionale

international call telefonata (f) internazionale

international direct dialling teleselezione (f) internazionale

International Labour Organization (ILO) Organizzazione Internazionale del Lavoro (OIL)

international law diritto (m) internazionale

International Monetary Fund (IMF) Fondo Monetario Internazionale (FMI)

international trade commercio (m) internazionale

interpret interpretare

interpreter interprete (mf)

intervention price prezzo (m) d'intervento

interview (n) intervista (f)

interview (n) *[for a job]* intervista (f) *o* colloquio (m)

interview (v) intervistare

interview (v) *[for a job]* avere un colloquio con

interviewee intervistato (m)

interviewer intervistatore (m)

introduce introdurre *o* presentare

introduction *[bringing into use]* introduzione (m)

introduction *[letter]* lettera (f) di presentazione

introductory offer offerta (f) di propaganda

invalid inabile *o* privo di validità

invalidate invalidare

invalidation annullamento (m)

invalidity inabilità (f) *o* invalidità (f)

inventory (n) *[list of contents]* inventario (m)

inventory (n) *[stock]* inventario (m) *o* scorte (fpl) *o* stock (m)

inventory (v) inventariare *o* fare l'inventario

inventory control controllo (m) di magazzino

invest investire

investigate investigare

investigation analisi (f) *o* indagine (f)

investment investimento (m)

investment income reddito (m) da investimenti

investor investitore (m)

invisible assets beni (mpl) invisibili

invisible earnings proventi (mpl) da partite invisibili

invisible trade commercio (m) invisibile

invitation invito (m)

invite invitare

invoice (n) fattura (f)

invoice (v) fatturare

invoice number numero (m) di fattura

invoice value prezzo (m) di fattura

invoicing fatturazione (f)

invoicing department ufficio (m) addetto alla fatturazione

IOU (= I owe you) riconoscimento (m) scritto di un debito *o* pagherò (m)

irrecoverable debt debito (m) inesigibile

irredeemable bond obbligazione (f) irredimibile

irregular irregolare

irregularities irregolarità (fpl)

irrevocable irrevocabile

irrevocable acceptance effetto (m) accettato irrevocabilmente

irrevocable letter of credit lettera (f) di credito irrevocabile

issue (n) *[magazine]* numero (m)

issue (n) *[of shares]* rilascio (m) *o* emissione (f)

issue (v) *[shares]* emettere

issue a letter of credit aprire una lettera di credito

issue instructions diramare istruzioni

issuing bank banca (f) d'emissione

item *[information]* voce (f)

item *[on agenda]* argomento (m) *o* questione (f)

item *[thing for sale]* articolo (m)

itemize specificare *o* dettagliare

itemized account conto (m) dettagliato

itemized invoice fattura (f) dettagliata

itinerary itinerario (m)

Jj

job *[employment]* impiego (m) *o* lavoro (m)

job *[piece of work]* lavoro (m)

job analysis analisi (f) delle mansioni

job application domanda (f) di lavoro

job cuts riduzione (f) di posti lavorativi

job description descrizione (f) dei compiti

job satisfaction soddisfazione (f) sul lavoro

job security sicurezza (f) del posto di lavoro

job specification specificazione (f) delle mansioni

job title denominazione (f) della mansione

join unire

joint congiunto *o* unito

joint account conto (m) congiunto

joint discussions discussione (f) collettiva

joint management condirezione (f)

joint managing director condirettore (m)

joint owner comproprietario (m)

joint ownership comproprietà (f)

joint signatory firmatario (m) congiunto

joint venture 'joint venture' (f) *o* associazione (f) in partecipazione

jointly in comune

journal *[accounts book]* libro (m) giornale

journal *[magazine]* rivista (f) *o* periodico (m)

journey order ordine trasmesso dal

dettagliante al fornitore tramite commesso viaggiatore

judge (n) giudice (m) *o* magistrato (m)

judge (v) giudicare

judgement *or* **judgment** verdetto (m) *o* decisione (f)

judgment debtor debitore (m) riconosciuto da tribunale

judicial processes procedimenti (mpl) legali

jump the queue passare in testa ad una coda

junior (adj) junior *o* giovane

junior clerk apprendista (m)

junior executive *or* **junior manager** dirigente (m) di grado inferiore

junior partner socio di minore importanza (più recente)

junk bonds obbligazioni (fpl) 'cartastraccia'

junk mail opuscoli (mpl) pubblicitari

jurisdiction giurisdizione (f)

Kk

keen competition concorrenza (f) accanita

keen demand forte richiesta (f)

keen prices prezzi (mpl) concorrenziali

keep a promise mantenere una promessa

keep back trattenere

keep up tenere su

keep up with the demand stare al passo con la richiesta

key (adj) *[important]* chiave

key *[on keyboard]* tasto (m)

key *[to door]* chiave (f)

key industry industria (f) chiave/di base

key personnel *or* **key staff** personale-chiave

key post posto (m) chiave

keyboard (n) tastiera (f)

keyboard (v) digitare

keyboarder operatore (m) su tastiera

keyboarding immissione (f) mediante tastiera

kilo *or* **kilogram** chilo (m) *o* chilogrammo (m)

knock down (v) *[price]* ridurre *o* abbassare

knock off *[reduce price]* abbassare *o* ridurre il prezzo di

knock off *[stop work]* cessare di lavorare

knock-on effect effetto (m) a catena

knockdown prices riduzione (f) di prezzi

krona *[currency used in Sweden and Iceland]* corona (f) (svedese)

krone *[currency used in Denmark and Norway]* corona (danese, norvegese)

Ll

label (n) etichetta (f)

label (v) etichettare

labelling etichettatura (f)

labour lavoro (m)

labour costs costo (m) della manodopera

labour disputes vertenza (f) di lavoro

labour force forza (f) lavoro

lack of funds mancanza (f) di fondi

land (n) terra (f) *o* terreno (m)

land (v) *[of plane]* atterrare

land (v) *[passengers, cargo]* sbarcare

land goods at a port scaricare merce in un porto

landed costs costi (mpl) fondiari

landing card carta (f) di sbarco

landing charges spese (fpl) di scarico (da nave)

landlord locatore (m)

lapse (v) scadere

laser printer stampante (f) laser

last in first out (LIFO) ultimo a entrare, primo a uscire

last quarter ultimo trimestre (m)

late (adv) tardi *o* in ritardo

late-night opening aprire fino a notte tarda

latest recentissimo

launch (n) lancio (m)

launch (v) lanciare

launching lancio (m)

launching costs costi (mpl) di lancio

launching date data (f) del lancio

launder (money) riciclare

law *[rule]* legge (f)

law *[study]* diritto (m)

law courts tribunale (m)

law of diminishing returns legge (f) del rendimento decrescente

law of supply and demand legge (f) dell'offerta e della domanda

lawful legittimo

lawful trade commercio (m) legittimo

lawsuit causa (f)

lawyer avvocato (m)

lay off workers licenziare personale (per mancanza di attività)

LBO (= leveraged buyout) finanziamento (m) per l'acquisto del pacchetto azionario contro garanzia delle attività finanziarie

L/C (= letter of credit) lettera (f) di credito

lead time intervallo (m) (fra ordinazione e consegna)

leaflet volantino (m)

leakage dispersione (f)

lease (n) affitto (m)

lease (v) *[of landlord]* affittare *o* dare in affitto

lease (v) *[of tenant]* affittare *o* tenere in affitto

lease back praticare il leasing (m) immobiliare

lease equipment affittare *[impianti]*

lease-back leasing (m) immobiliare

leasing 'leasing' (m)

leave (n) congedo (m)

leave (v) *[go away]* partire *o* lasciare

leave (v) *[resign]* abbandonare *o* lasciare

leave of absence aspettativa (f) *o* congedo (m) autorizzato

ledger libro (m) mastro

left *[not right]* sinistro

left luggage office ufficio (m) deposito bagagli

legal *[according to law]* legale

legal *[referring to law]* giuridico

legal advice consulenza (f) legale

legal adviser consulente (m) legale

legal costs *or* **legal charges** spese (fpl) legali

legal currency moneta (f) legale

legal department ufficio (m) legale

legal expenses spese (fpl) legali

legal proceedings vie (fpl) legali

legal status stato (m) giuridico

legal tender moneta (f) a corso legale

legislation legislazione (f)

lend prestare

lender prestatore (m)

lending prestito (m)

lending limit limite (m) del prestito

lessee affittuario (m)

lessor locatore (m)

let (n) affitto (m)

let (v) affittare

let an office affittare un negozio

letter lettera (f)

letter of application richiesta (f) di iscrizione

letter of appointment lettera (f) di assunzione

letter of complaint lettera (f) di reclamo

letter of credit (L/C) lettera (f) di credito

letter of intent lettera (f) di intenti

letter of reference lettera (f) di referenze

letters of administration nomina (f) di amministratratore giudiziario

letters patent brevetto (m)

letting agency agenzia (f) immobiliare

level (n) livello (m)

level off *or* **level out** stabilizzarsi

leverage leva (f) finanziaria

leveraged buyout (LBO) finanziamento (m) per l'acquisto del pacchetto azionario contro garanzia delle attività societarie

levy (n) imposta (f)

levy (v) imporre (una tassa)

liabilities passività (fpl)

liability responsabilità (f) *o* obbligo (m)

liable for responsabile per

liable to passibile di

licence licenza (f)

license autorizzare

licensee concessionario (m)

licensing concessione (f) di licenze

lien privilegio (m)

life assurance assicurazione (f) sulla vita

life insurance assicurazione (f) sulla vita

life interest usufrutto (m) *o* rendita (f) vitalizia

LIFO (= last in first out) metodo (m) LIFO (ultimo a entrare, primo a uscire)

lift (n) ascensore (m)

lift (v) *[remove]* togliere

lift an embargo togliere l'embargo

limit (n) limite (m)

limit (v) limitare

limitation restrizione (f)

limited limitato

limited (liability) company (Ltd) società (f) di capitali a responsabilità limitata

limited liability responsabilità (f) limitata

limited market mercato (m) limitato

limited partnership società (f) in accomandita semplice

line (n) linea (f)

line management linea (f) gerarchica

line organization organizzazione (f) gerarchica

line printer stampante (f) lineare

liquid assets liquidità (fpl)

liquidate a company mettere in liquidazione una società

liquidate stock mettere in liquidazione scorte di magazzino

liquidation liquidazione (f)

liquidator liquidatore (m)

liquidity liquidità (f)

liquidity crisis crisi (f) di mancanza di liquidità

lira *[currency used in Italy and Turkey]* lira (f) (italiana, turca)

list (n) lista (f)

list (n) *[catalogue]* listino (m) *o* catalogo (m)

list (v) elencare

list price prezzo (m) di listino

litre litro (m)

Lloyd's register Registro (m) dei Lloyd (di classificazione delle navi)

load (n) carico (m)

load (v) caricare

load (v) *[computer program]* caricare

load a lorry *or* **a ship** caricare un camion *o* una nave

load factor coefficiente (m) di carico

load line linea (f) di carico

loading bay area (f) di carico

loading ramp rampa (f) di carico

loan (n) prestito (m) *o* mutuo (m)

loan (v) prestare *o* dare in prestito

loan capital capitale (m) mutuato

loan stock capitale (m) obbligazionario

local locale/del luogo

local call telefonata (f) urbana

local government ente (m) locale

local labour manodopera (m) locale

lock (n) serratura (f)

lock (v) chiudere a chiave

lock up a shop *or* **an office** chiudere a chiave un negozio *o* un ufficio

lock up capital investire capitali

lock-up premises immobile (m) con chiusura di sicurezza

log (v) registrare

log calls registrare chiamate

logo logogramma (m)

long lungo *o* per molto tempo

long credit credito (m) a lungo termine

long-dated bill effetto (m) a lunga scadenza

long-distance flight volo (m) a lunga percorrenza

long-haul flight volo (m) a lungo raggio

long-range a lunga scadenza

long-standing di vecchia data

long-standing agreement accordo (m) di lunga data

long-term a lungo termine

long-term debts debiti (mpl) a lungo termine

long-term forecast previsione (f) a lungo termine

long-term liabilities passività (fpl) a lungo termine

long-term loan mutuo (m) a lunga scadenza

long-term planning pianificazione (f) a lunga scadenza

loose sciolto

lorry camion (m)

lorry driver camionista (m)

lorry-load carico (di camion)

lose *[fall to a lower level]* cadere

lose an order perdere un'ordinazione

lose money perdere denaro

loss *[not a profit]* perdita (f)

loss *[of something]* perdita (f)

loss of an order perdita (f) di un'ordinazione

loss of customers perdita (f) di clientela

loss-leader articolo (m) di richiamo per la clientela

lot *[of items]* partita (f) (di merci)

low (adj) basso *o* scadente

low (n) basso livello (m)

low sales vendite (fpl) basse

low-grade di qualità inferiore

low-level di livello inferiore

low-quality di qualità inferiore

lower (adj) inferiore *o* più basso

lower (v) abbassare

lower prices abbassare i prezzi

lowering calo (m)

Ltd (= limited company) a responsabilità limitata

luggage bagaglio (m)

lump sum importo (m) forfettario

luxury goods articoli (mpl) di lusso

Mm

machine macchina (f)

macro-economics macroeconomia (f)

magazine rivista (f)

magazine insert fascicolo (m) supplementare (in una rivista)

magazine mailing invio (m) di riviste per posta

magnetic tape *or* **mag tape** nastro (m) magnetico

mail (n) *[letters sent or received]* posta (f)

mail (n) *[postal system]* posta (f)

mail (v) spedire per posta

mail shot campagna (f) promozionale a mezzo posta

mail-order ordinazioni (fpl) per corrispondenza

mail-order business *or* **mail-order firm** *or* **mail-order** società (f) di vendita per corrispondenza

mail-order catalogue catalogo (m) di vendita per corrispondenza

mailing invio (m) (per posta)

mailing list elenco (m) di indirizzi

mailing piece materiale (m) promozionale preparato specificatamente per l'invio (per posta)

mailing shot campagna (f) promozionale a mezzo posta

main principale

main building edificio (m) principale

main office sede (f) centrale *o* direzione (f) centrale

maintain *[keep at same level]* mantenere

maintain *[keep going]* tenere in efficienza

maintenance *[keeping in working order]* manutenzione (f)

maintenance *[keeping things going]* mantenimento (m)

maintenance of contacts mantenimento (m) di contatti

maintenance of supplies mantenimento (m) delle provvigioni

major maggiore *o* importante

major shareholder azionista (m) principale

majority maggioranza (f)

majority shareholder azionista (m) di maggioranza

make good *[a defect or loss]* indennizzare *o* risarcire

make money fare soldi

make out *[invoice]* compilare

make provision for provvedere a

make up for compensare

make-ready time periodo (m) di avviamento

maladministration cattiva amministrazione (f)

man (n) uomo (m)

man (v) fornire il personale (necessario)

man-hour ora (f) lavorativa

manage amministrare *o* gestire

manage property amministrare un patrimonio

manage to riuscire a

manageable trattabile *o* controllabile

management *[action]* gestione (f)

management *[managers]* direzione (f)

management accounts conti (mpl) gestione

management buyout (MBO) acquisto (m) di una società da parte dei suoi stessi dirigenti

management consultant consulente (m) di direzione aziendale

management course corso (m) in amministrazione

management team quadri (mpl) direttivi

management techniques tecniche (fpl) gestionali

management trainee apprendista (m) in direzione aziendale

management training addestramento (m) dei dirigenti

manager *[of branch or shop]* direttore (m), direttrice (f)

manager *[of department]* direttore (m), direttrice (f)

managerial direttivo *o* gestionale

managerial staff personale (m) dirigente

managing director (MD) amministratore delegato

mandate mandato (m)

manifest manifesto (m)

manned aperto

manning organico (m)

manning levels livello (m) di organico

manpower manodopera (f)

manpower forecasting previsione (f) della necessità di manodopera

manpower planning programmazione (f) delle assunzioni di manodopera

manpower requirements esigenza (f) di manodopera

manpower shortage carenza (f) di manodopera

manual (adj) manuale

manual (n) manuale (m)

manual work lavoro (m) manuale

manual worker manovale (m)

manufacture (n) lavorazione (f) *o* fabbricazione (f)

manufacture (v) produrre *o* fabbricare

manufactured goods manufatti (mpl)

manufacturer produttore (m) *o* fabbricante (m)

manufacturer's recommended price (MRP) prezzo (m) di fabbrica consigliato

manufacturing manifatturiero

manufacturing capacity capacità (f) di produzione

manufacturing costs costi (mpl) di produzione

manufacturing overheads spese (fpl) generali di produzione

margin *[profit]* margine (m)

margin of error margine (m) di errore

marginal marginale

marginal cost costo (m) marginale

marginal pricing determinazione (f) marginale del prezzo

marine marittimo

marine insurance assicurazione (f) marittima

marine underwriter assicuratore (m) marittimo

maritime marittimo *o* navale

maritime law diritto (m) della navigazione

maritime lawyer avvocato (m) che si occupa del diritto della navigazione

maritime trade commercio (m) marittimo

mark (n) impronta (f)

mark (n) *[currency used in Germany]* marco (m) tedesco

mark (v) notare

mark down abbassare il prezzo (di articoli)

mark up aumentare il prezzo (di articoli)

mark-down diminuzione (f) di prezzo

mark-up *[action]* aumento (m) di prezzo

mark-up *[profit margin]* margine (m) *o* utile lordo

marker pen evidenziatore (m)

market (n) *[place]* mercato (m)

market (n) *[possible sales]* mercato (m)

market (n) *[where a product might sell]* mercato (m)

market (v) vendere *o* commercializzare

market analysis analisi (f) di mercato

market analyst analista (m) di mercato

market capitalization capitalizzazione (f) di mercato

market economist economista (mf) di mercato

market forces forze (fpl) di mercato

market forecast previsioni (fpl) di mercato

market leader prodotto-guida (m) del mercato *o* azienda (f) primaria sul mercato

market opportunities possibilità (fpl) di mercato

market penetration penetrazione (f) di mercato

market price prezzo (m) di mercato

market rate prezzo (m) di mercato

market research ricerca (f) di mercato

market share quota (f) di mercato

market trends tendenza (f) di mercato

market value valore (m) di mercato

marketable commerciabile

marketing marketing (m)

marketing agreement accordo (m) di marketing

marketing department servizio (m) di marketing

marketing division reparto (m) marketing

marketing manager direttore di marketing

marketing strategy strategia (f) di marketing

marketing techniques tecniche (fpl) di marketing

marketplace *[in town]* (piazza (f) del) mercato (m)

marketplace *[place where something is sold]* mercato (m)

mass *[of people]* massa (f)

mass *[of things]* massa (f) *o* grande quantità (f)

mass market product prodotto (m) per il mercato di massa

mass marketing marketing (m) di massa

mass media mass-media (mpl) *o* mezzi (mpl) di comunicazione di massa

mass production produzione (f) in serie

mass-produce produrre in serie

mass-produce cars produrre automobili in serie

Master's degree in Business Administration (MBA) master (m) in gestione d'impresa

materials control controllo (m) dei materiali

materials handling movimentazione (f) dei materiali

maternity leave congedo (m) per maternità

matter (n) *[problem]* faccenda (f) *o* problema (f)

matter (n) *[to be discussed]* argomento (m) *o* questione (f)

matter (v) avere importanza

mature (v) scadere

mature economy economia (f) matura

maturity date data (f) di scadenza

maximization massimizzazione (f)

maximize massimizzare

maximum (adj) massimo

maximum (n) massimo (m)

maximum price prezzo (m) massimo

MBA (= Master in Business Administration) master (m) in gestione d'impresa

MBO (= management buyout) acquisto (m) di una società da parte dei suoi stessi dirigenti

MD (= managing director) direttore generale

mean (adj) medio

mean (n) media (f)

mean annual increase aumento (m) medio annuale

means *[money]* mezzi (mpl)

means *[ways]* mezzi (mpl) *o* strumenti (mpl)

means test accertamento (m) patrimoniale

measurement of profitability misura (f) della redditività

measurements misure (fpl)

media coverage diffusione (f) nei mass-media

median valore (m) mediano

mediate mediare

mediation mediazione (f)

mediator mediatore (m)

medium (adj) medio *o* di mezzo

medium (n) mezzo (m)

medium-sized di medie dimensioni

medium-term a medio termine

meet *[be satisfactory]* soddisfare

meet *[expenses]* far fronte *[a una spesa]*

meet *[someone]* incontrare

meet a deadline rispettare una scadenza

meet a demand andare incontro ad una richiesta

meet a target raggiungere un obiettivo

meeting riunione (f)

meeting place luogo (m) d'incontro

member *[of a group]* socio (m)

membership *[all members]* gli iscritti (mpl)

membership *[being a member]* iscrizione (f)

memo memorandum (m)

memorandum memorandum (m)

memory *[computer]* memoria (f)

merchandise (n) merce (f)

merchandize (v) commerciare

merchandize a product esercitare il commercio di un prodotto

merchandizer commerciante (m)

merchandizing attività (f) promozionale

merchant mercante (m)

merchant bank 'merchant bank' (f) *o* banca (f) mercantile

merchant navy marina (f) mercantile

merchant ship *or* **merchant vessel** nave (f) mercantile

merge incorporare

merger fusione (f)

merit merito (n)

merit award *or* **merit bonus** premio (m) di merito

message messaggio (m)

messenger fattorino (m)

micro-economics microeconomia (f)

microcomputer microelaboratore (m)

mid-month accounts contabilità (f) di metà mese

mid-week metà settimana (f)

middle management quadri (mpl) intermedi

middle-sized company società (f) di medie dimensioni

middleman intermediario (m)

million milione (m)

millionaire miliardario (m)

minimum (adj) minimo

minimum (n) minimo (m)

minimum dividend dividendo (m) minimo

minimum payment pagamento (m) minimo

minimum wage salario (m) minimo

minor shareholders azionista (m) di secondaria importanza

minority minoranza (f)

minority shareholder azionista (m) di minoranza

minus meno *o* negativo

minus factor fattore (m) negativo

minute (n) *[time]* minuto (m)

minute (v) verbalizzare *o* mettere a verbale

minutes (n) *[of meeting]* verbale (m) (di assemblea)

misappropriate appropriarsi indebitamente

misappropriation appropriazione (f) indebita

miscalculate fare male i propri calcoli

miscalculation calcolo (m) sbagliato

miscellaneous miscellaneo *o* vario

miscellaneous items articoli (mpl) diversi

mismanage dirigere male

mismanagement cattiva amministrazione (f)

miss *[not to hit]* mancare

miss *[not to meet]* mancare

miss *[train, plane]* perdere

miss a target mancare il bersaglio

miss an instalment non pagare una rata

mistake errore (m)

misunderstanding malinteso (m)

mixed *[different sorts]* misto

mixed *[neither good nor bad]* misto

mixed economy economia (f) di tipo misto

mobility mobilità (f)

mobilize mobilizzare

mobilize capital mobilizzare capitali

mock-up modello (m) in scala

mode modo (m)

mode of payment modalità (fpl) di pagamento

model (n) *[person]* indossatrice (f)

model (n) *[small copy]* modello (m)

model (n) *[style of product]* modello (m)

model (v) *[clothes]* presentare (un modello)

model agreement accordo-tipo (m)

modem modem (m)

moderate (adj) moderato

moderate (v) moderare

monetary monetario

monetary base base (f) monetaria

monetary unit unità (f) monetaria

money denaro (m)

money changer cambiavalute (m)

money markets mercati (mpl) monetari

money order vaglia (m) (mandato di pagamento)

money rates tassi (mpl) monetari

money supply disponibilità (f) di capitali

money up front soldi (mpl) in anticipo

money-making redditizio

money-making plan progetto (m) redditizio

moneylender finanziatore (m) *o* chi fa prestiti

monitor (n) *[screen]* monitor (m)

monitor (v) controllare

monopolization monopolizzazione (f)

monopolize monopolizzare

monopoly monopolio (m)

month mese (m)

month end fine (f) del mese

month-end accounts contabilità (f) di fine mese

monthly (adj) mensile

monthly (adv) mensilmente

monthly payments pagamenti (mpl) mensili

monthly statement resoconto (m) mensile

moonlight (v) lavorare al nero

moonlighter (n) lavoratore (m) al nero

moonlighting (n) lavoro (m) nero

moratorium moratoria (f)

mortgage (n) ipoteca (f)

mortgage (v) ipotecare

mortgage payments pagamenti (mpl) ipotecari

mortgagee creditore (m) ipotecario

mortgager *or* **mortgagor** debitore (m) ipotecario

most-favoured nation nazione (f) più favorita

motivated motivato

motivation motivazione (f)

motor insurance assicurazione (f) auto

mount up aumentare

mounting in aumento

move *[be sold]* vendersi

move *[house, office]* traslocare

move *[propose]* proporre

movement movimento (m)

movements of capital movimenti (m) di capitali

MRP (= manufacturer's recommended price) prezzo (m) consigliato di fabbrica

multicurrency operation operazione (f) a denominazione valutaria multipla

multilateral multilaterale

multilateral agreement accordo (m) multilaterale

multilateral trade commercio (m) multilaterale

multinational (n) multinazionale (f)

multiple (adj) multiplo

multiple entry visa visto (m) consolare multiplo

multiple ownership proprietà (f) multipla

multiple store negozio (m) appartenente ad una catena

multiplication moltiplicazione (f)

multiply moltiplicare

mutual (adj) mutuo *o* reciproco

mutual (insurance) company società (f) mutua (di assicurazioni)

Nn

national nazionale

national advertising pubblicità (f) su tutto il territorio nazionale

nationalization nazionalizzazione (f)

nationalized industry industria (f) statalizzata

nationwide di dimensioni nazionali

natural resources risorse (fpl) naturali

natural wastage numero di lavoratori (mpl) che abbandonano l'attività per pensionamento

near letter-quality (NLQ) ad alta definizione

necessary necessario

negative cash flow reddito (m) societario negativo

neglected business attività (f) trascurata

neglected shares azioni (fpl) trascurate

negligence negligenza (f)

negligent negligente

negligible trascurabile

negotiable trattabile *o* negoziabile

negotiable instrument strumento (m) negoziabile

negotiate negoziare *o* trattare

negotiation negoziato (m) *o* trattativa (f)

negotiator negoziatore (m)

net (adj) netto

net (v) ricavare al netto

net assets *or* **net worth** valore (m) patrimoniale netto

net earnings *or* **net income** utili (mpl) netti

net income *or* **net salary** reddito (m) netto

net loss perdita (f) netta

net margin margine (m) netto

net price prezzo (m) netto

net profit utile (m) netto

net receipts incassi (mpl) netti

net sales ricavi (mpl) netti

net weight peso (m) netto

net yield rendimento (m) netto

network (n) rete (f) *o* sistema (m)

network (v) *[computers]* collegare in rete

news agency agenzia (f) di stampa

newspaper giornale (m)

niche nicchia (f)

night notte (f)

night rate tariffa (f) notturna

night shift turno (m) di notte

nil nulla (m) *o* zero (m)

nil return ricavo (m) nullo

NLQ (= near letter-quality) ad alta definizione

no-claims bonus premio (m) agli assicurati che non hanno denunciato sinistri

no-strike agreement *or* **no-strike clause** accordo (m) *o* clausola (f) che stabilisce il divieto di sciopero

nominal capital capitale (m) nominale

nominal ledger mastro (m) nominale

nominal rent affitto (m) nominale

nominal value valore (m) nominale

nominee candidato (m)

nominee account conto (m) di prestanome

non profit-making senza scopo di lucro

non-delivery mancata consegna (f)

non-executive director direttore (m) senza poteri esecutivi

non-negotiable instrument strumento (m) non negoziabile

non-payment *[of a debt]* omesso pagamento (m) di un debito

non-recurring items articoli (mpl) non ricorrenti

non-refundable deposit deposito (m) non rimborsabile

non-returnable packing imballo (m) a perdere

non-stop senza scalo *o* ininterrotto

non-taxable income reddito (m) non imponibile

nonfeasance reato (m) di omissione

norm norma (f)

notary public notaio (m)

note (n) nota (f)

note (v) *[details]* notare

note of hand pagherò (m) cambiario

notice *[piece of information]* avviso (m)

notice *[that worker is leaving his job]* preavviso (m)

notice *[time allowed]* preavviso (m)

notice *[warning that a contract is going to end]* preavviso (m)

notification notificazione (f)

notify notificare

null nullo

number (n) *[figure]* numero (m)

number (v) numerare

numbered account conto (m) numerato

numeric *or* **numerical** numerico

numeric keypad tastierino (m) numerico

Oo

objective (adj) obiettivo *o* oggettivo

objective (n) obiettivo (m)

obligation *[debt]* debito (m)

obligation *[duty]* dovere (m) *o* impegno (m)

obsolescence invecchiamento (m)

obsolescent obsolescente

obsolete antiquato

obtain ottenere

obtainable conseguibile *o* ottenibile

occupancy occupazione (f)

occupancy rate percentuale (f) di occupazione

occupant occupante (m) *o* chi occupa

occupational occupazionale *o* professionale

occupational accident incidente (m) professionale

odd *[not a pair]* spaiato

odd *[not even]* dispari

odd numbers numeri (mpl) dispari

off *[away from work]* assente

off *[cancelled]* annullato

off *[reduced by]* con sconto di

off the record ufficiosamente

off-peak non di punta

off-season fuori stagione

off-the-job training corsi (mpl) di

addestramento esterni (al posto di lavoro)

offer (n) offerta (f)

offer (v) *[to buy]* offrire *o* proporre

offer (v) *[to sell]* offrire (in vendita)

offer for sale offerta (f) di vendita

offer price prezzo (m) d'offerta

office ufficio (m)

office equipment attrezzatura (f) per ufficio

office furniture arredamento (m) per ufficio

office hours orario (m) d'ufficio

office security sistema (m) di sorveglianza dell'ufficio

office space area (f) uffici

office staff personale (m) d'ufficio

office stationery cancelleria (f) d'ufficio

offices to let affitansi uffici (mpl)

official (adj) ufficiale

official (n) funzionario (m)

official receiver liquidatore (m)

official return reddito (m) ufficiale

officialese linguaggio (m) burocratico

offload scaricare

offshore offshore *o* all'estero

oil *[cooking]* olio (m)

oil *[petroleum]* petrolio (m)

oil price prezzo (m) del petrolio

oil-exporting countries paesi (mpl) esportatori di petrolio

oil-producing countries paesi (mpl) produttori di petrolio

old vecchio

old-established di vecchia istituzione (f)

old-fashioned antiquato

ombudsman difensore (m) civico

omission omissione (f)

omit trascurare *o* omettere

on a short-term basis a breve termine

on account in acconto

on agreed terms secondo i termini convenuti

on an annual basis annualmente

on an average in media

on approval salvo vista e verifica

on behalf of per conto di

on board a bordo

on business per affari

on condition that a condizione che

on credit a credito

on favourable terms a condizioni (fpl) vantaggiose

on line *or* **online** in linea

on order (che è stato) ordinato

on request su richiesta

on sale in vendita

on the increase in aumento

on time puntuale

on-the-job training addestramento (m) sul lavoro

one-off unico

one-off item articolo (m) unico

one-sided parziale

one-sided agreement accordo (m) parziale

one-way fare biglietto (m) di andata

one-way trade commercio (m) a senso unico

OPEC (= Organization of Petroleum Exporting Countries) Organizzazione (f) dei paesi esportatori di petrolio

open (adj) *[not closed]* aperto

open (v) *[begin]* iniziare

open (v) *[start new business]* aprire

open a bank account aprire un conto bancario

open a line of credit aprire una linea di credito

open a meeting aprire una seduta

open account conto (m) aperto

open an account aprire un conto

open cheque assegno (m) non sbarrato

open credit credito (m) aperto

open market mercato (m) libero

open negotiations aprire trattative

open ticket biglietto (m) aperto (senza data di ritorno)

open to offers aperto ad offerte

open-ended agreement accordo (m) aperto

open-plan office ufficio (m) a pianta aperta

opening (adj) iniziale *o* d'apertura

opening (n) apertura (f)

opening balance bilancio (m) d'apertura

opening bid offerta (f) d'apertura

opening hours orario (m) d'apertura

opening price prezzo (m) d'apertura

opening stock rimanenze (fpl) iniziali

opening time orario (m) d'apertura

operate funzionare

operating (n) funzionamento (m)

operating budget budget (m) operativo

operating costs or **operating expenses** costi (mpl) d'esercizio o spese (fpl) d'esercizio

operating manual manuale (m) operativo

operating profit utile (m) d'esercizio

operating system sistema (m) operativo

operation operazione (f)

operational operativo

operational budget budget (m) di gestione

operational costs costi (mpl) di gestione

operative (adj) operativo

operative (n) operatore (m)

operator operatore (m)

opinion poll sondaggio (m) d'opinione

opportunity opportunità (f)

option to purchase opzione (f) per l'acquisto

optional facoltativo

optional extras spese (fpl) supplementari

order (n) *[certain way]* ordine (m)

order (n) *[for goods]* ordinazione (f)

order (n) *[instruction]* ordine (m)

order (n) *[money]* mandato (m) di pagamento o vaglia (m)

order (v) *[goods]* ordinare

order (v) *[put in order]* mettere in ordine

order book registro (m) delle ordinazioni

order fulfilment evasione (f) di un'ordinazione

order number numero (m) d'ordinazione

order picking selezione (f) delle ordinazioni

order processing elaborazione (f) delle ordinazioni

order: on order essere stato ordinato

ordinary ordinario

ordinary shares azioni (fpl) ordinarie

organization *[institution]* organizzazione (f)

organization *[way of arranging]* organizzazione (f)

organization and methods organizzazione (f) e metodo (m)

organization chart organigramma (m)

Organization of Petroleum Exporting Countries (OPEC) Organizzazione (f) dei paesi esportatori di petrolio

organizational organizzativo

organize organizzare

origin origine (f)

original (adj) originario

original (n) originale (m)

OS (= outsize) di taglia forte

out of control fuori controllo

out of date non attuale

out of pocket rimetterci

out of stock esaurito

out of work disoccupato

out-of-pocket expenses piccole spese (fpl)

outbid offrire un prezzo superiore

outgoing in uscita

outgoing mail posta (f) in partenza

outgoings spese (fpl)

outlay esborso (m)

outlet sbocco (m)

output (n) *[computer]* output (m) o dati (mpl) di emissione

output (n) *[goods]* produzione (f)

output (v) *[computer]* emettere

output tax IVA

outright assoluto

outside esteriore

outside director direttore esterno

outside line linea (f) esterna

outside office hours fuori orario d'ufficio

outsize (OS) di taglia forte

outstanding *[exceptional]* straordinario

outstanding *[unpaid]* non pagato

outstanding debts debiti (mpl) insoluti

outstanding orders ordinazioni (fpl) da evadere

overall totale

overall plan piano (m) globale

overbook prenotare più (stanze, posti ecc.) di quanti siano disponibili

overbooking prenotazione (f) di più (stanze, posti, ecc.) di quanti siano disponibili

overcapacity capacità (f) in eccedenza

overcharge (n) prezzo (m) eccessivo

overcharge (v) far pagare troppo

overdraft scoperto (di c/c)

overdraft facility facilitazioni (fpl) di scoperto

overdraw emettere allo scoperto

overdrawn account conto (m) scoperto

overdue scaduto

overestimate (v) sopravvalutare

overhead budget budget (m) generale

overhead costs *or* **expenses** spese (fpl) generali

overheads spese (fpl) generali

overmanning personale (m) in eccedenza

overpayment pagamento (m) in più

overproduce produrre in eccesso

overproduction produzione (f) in eccesso

overseas (adj) all'estero

overseas (n) l'estero (m) *o* i paesi stranieri

overseas markets mercati (mpl) esteri

overseas trade commercio (m) estero

overspend spendere oltre le proprie possibilità

overspend one's budget spendere oltre il proprio budget

overstock (v) saturare di prodotti

overstocks sovraccarico (m) di scorte

overtime lavoro (m) straordinario

overtime ban blocco (m) del lavoro straordinario

overtime pay compenso (m) per lavoro straordinario

overvalue sopravvalutare

overweight: to be overweight di peso eccedente

owe essere debitore

owing dovuto *o* a debito

owing to a causa di

own (v) possedere

own brand goods prodotti (mpl) con marchio proprio

own label goods prodotti (mpl) con etichetta propria

owner proprietario (m)

ownership proprietà (f)

Pp

p & p (= postage and packing) spese (fpl) postali e imballo

PA (= personal assistant) segretaria (f) personale

pack (n) pacco (m)

pack (v) imballare *o* impacchettare

pack goods into cartons imballare le merci

pack of envelopes pacchetto (m) di buste

package *[of goods]* pacco (m)

package *[of services]* contratto (m) globale

package deal pacchetto (m) rivendicativo

packaging *[action]* imballaggio (m)

packaging *[material]* materiale (m) d'imballaggio

packaging material materiale (m) d'imballaggio

packer impacchettatore (m)

packet pacchetto (m)

packet of cigarettes pacchetto (m) di sigarette

packing *[action]* imballaggio (m)

packing *[material]* materiali (mpl) di imballaggio

packing case cassa (f) da imballaggio

packing charges spese (f) d'imballo

packing list or **packing slip** distinta (f) d'imballaggio

paid *[for work]* pagato o remunerato

paid *[invoice]* pagato

pallet paletta (f)

palletize palettizzare o trasportare a mezzo di palette

panel pannello (m)

panic buying incetta (f) in previsione di aumento dei prezzi

paper bag sacchetto (m) di carta

paper feed alimentatore (m) di fogli

paper loss perdita (f) sulla carta

paper profit utili (mpl) ipotetici

paperclip graffetta (f)

papers incartamenti (mpl)

paperwork lavoro (m) d'ufficio

par pari

par value valore (m) nominale

parcel (n) pacco (m)

parcel (v) impacchettare

parcel post servizio (m) pacchi postali

parent company società (f) controllante

parity parità (f)

part (n) parte (f)

part exchange permuta (f) come pagamento parziale

part-owner comproprietario (m)

part-ownership comproprietà (f)

part-time orario (m) ridotto

part-time work or **part-time employment** lavoro (m) a orario ridotto

part-timer lavoratore (m) a orario ridotto

partial loss perdita (f) parziale

partial payment pagamento (m) parziale

particulars dettagli (mpl)

partner socio (m) o compagno/a

partnership società (f) di persone

party parte (f) *[legale]*

patent brevetto (m)

patent agent agente (m) di brevetti

patent an invention brevettare un'invenzione

patent applied for or **patent pending** brevetto (m) richiesto o in attesa di brevetto

patented brevettato

pay (n) *[salary]* paga (f) o retribuzione (f) o stipendio (m)

pay (v) *[bill]* pagare o saldare

pay (v) *[worker]* pagare o remunerare

pay a bill pagare un conto

pay a dividend pagare un dividendo

pay an invoice pagare una fattura

pay back rimborsare

pay by cheque pagare con un assegno

pay by credit card pagare con carta di credito

pay cash pagare in contanti

pay cheque assegno (m) dello stipendio

pay desk banco (m) dei pagamenti

pay in advance pagare anticipatamente

pay in instalments pagare a rate

pay interest pagare gli interessi

pay money down pagare in contanti

pay off *[debt]* estinguere (un debito)

pay off *[worker]* liquidare

pay out sborsare

pay phone telefono (m) a gettoni

pay rise aumento (m) salariale

pay up pagare

payable pagabile

payable at sixty days pagabile a sessanta giorni

payable in advance pagabile anticipatamente

payable on delivery pagabile alla consegna

payable on demand pagabile su richiesta

payback recupero (m) dell'investimento

payback clause clausola (f) di recupero dell'investimento

payback period periodo (m) di recupero

payee beneficiario (m)

payer chi paga

paying (adj) redditizio

paying (n) pagamento (m)

paying-in slip distinta (f) di versamento

payload carico (m) utile

payment pagamento (m)

payment by cheque pagamento (m) tramite assegno

payment by results pagamento (m) in base al lavoro effettuato

payment in cash pagamento (m) in contanti

payment in kind pagamento (m) in natura

payment on account pagamento (m) in acconto

PC (= personal computer) personal computer (m) *o* elaboratore (m) ad uso personale

P/E ratio (= price/earnings ratio) rapporto (m) corso/utili

peak (n) valore (m) massimo

peak (v) raggiungere un punto massimo *o* culminare

peak output livello (m) massimo di produzione

peak period periodo (m) di massima attività

peg prices bloccare i prezzi

penalize penalizzare

penalty penale (f) *o* multa (f)

penalty clause clausola (f) di penalità

pending pendente

penetrate a market realizzare la penetrazione di un mercato

pension pensione (f)

pension fund fondo (m) pensioni

pension scheme piano (m) pensioni

per per *o* per mezzo

per annum all'anno

per capita pro-capite

per cent per cento

per day al giorno

per head per persona

per hour all'ora

per week alla settimana

per year all'anno

percentage percentuale (f)

percentage discount sconto (m) percentuale

percentage increase aumento (m) percentuale

percentage point punto (m) percentuale

performance prestazione (f)

performance rating valutazione (f) della prestazione

period periodo (m)

period of notice periodo (m) di preavviso

period of validity periodo (m) di validità

periodic *or* **periodical (adj)** periodico

periodical (n) pubblicazione (f) periodica

peripherals periferiche (fpl)

perishable deperibile

perishable goods *or* **items** *or* **cargo** merci (fpl) *o* articoli (mpl) *o* derrate (fpl) deperibili

perishables merci (fpl) deperibili

permission autorizzazione (f)

permit (n) permesso (m)

permit (v) autorizzare (qualcuno a fare qualcosa)

personal personale

personal allowances detrazioni (fpl) personali

personal assets attivo (m) mobiliare

personal assistant (PA) segretaria (f) personale

personal computer (PC) personal computer (m) *o* elaboratore (m) ad uso personale

personal income reddito (m) personale

personalized personalizzato

personalized briefcase ventiquattrore (f) personalizzata

personalized cheques assegni (mpl) personalizzati

personnel personale (m)

personnel department ufficio (m) del personale

personnel management direzione (f) del personale

personnel manager capo (m) del personale

peseta *[Spanish currency]* peseta (f)

petty di scarsa importanza

petty cash piccola cassa (f)

petty cash box scatola (f) per la piccola cassa

petty expenses piccole spese (fpl)

phase in introdurre gradualmente

phase out eliminare gradualmente

phoenix syndrome sindrome (f) della fenice

phone (n) telefono (m)

phone (v) telefonare

phone back ritelefonare

phone call chiamata (f) telefonica

phone card carta (f) di credito telefonica

phone number numero (m) di telefono *o* numero telefonico

photocopier fotocopiatrice (f)

photocopy (n) fotocopia (f)

photocopy (v) fotocopiare

photocopying fotocopiatura (f)

photocopying bureau ufficio (m) dove si fanno fotocopie

picking list lista (f) di selezione

pie chart grafico (m) a settori

piece pezzo (m)

piece rate retribuzione (f) a cottimo

piecework lavoro (m) a cottimo

pilferage *or* **pilfering** furto (m) di scarsa entità

pilot (adj) pilota

pilot (n) *[person]* pilota (m)

pilot scheme progetto (m) pilota

pioneer (n) pioniere (m)

pioneer (v) fare da pioniere in

place (n) *[in a competition]* posto (m)

place (n) *[in a text]* segno (m)

place (n) *[job]* posto (m) *o* impiego (m)

place (n) *[situation]* posto (m) *o* luogo (m)

place (v) posare *o* mettere

place an order fare un'ordinazione

place of work posto (m) di lavoro

plaintiff querelante (m)

plan (n) *[drawing]* pianta (f)

plan (n) *[project]* piano (m) *o* progetto (m)

plan (v) progettare *o* organizzare

plan investments pianificare investimenti

plane aereo (m)

planner pianificatore (m)

planning pianificazione (f)

plant (n) *[factory]* fabbrica (f) *o* stabilimento (m)

plant (n) *[machinery]* impianti (mpl)

plant-hire firm ditta (f) di noleggio impianti

platform *[railway station]* binario (m)

PLC *or* **plc (= Public Limited Company)** Società di capitali a sottoscrizione pubblica (SpA)

plug (n) *[electric]* spina (f) elettrica

plug (v) *[block]* tappare

plug (v) *[publicize]* pubblicizzare

plus positivo

plus factor fattore (m) positivo

pocket (n) tasca (f)

pocket (v) incassare

pocket calculator *or* **pocket diary** calcolatrice (f) tascabile *o* agenda (f) tascabile

point punto (m)

point of sale (p.o.s. *or* **POS)** punto (m) di vendita

point of sale material (POS material) materiale (m) per punto di vendita

policy *[plan of action]* politica (f)

policy *[insurance]* polizza (f)

pool resources mettere insieme le risorse

poor quality qualità (f) scadente

poor service servizio (m) scadente

popular popolare

popular prices prezzi (mpl) popolari

port *[computer]* porta (f) *[di computer]*

port *[harbour]* porto (m)

port authority autorità (fpl) portuali

port charges *or* **port dues** diritti (mpl) di porto

port of call porto (m) di scalo

port of embarkation porto (m) d'imbarco

port of registry porto (m) d'armamento

portable portatile

portfolio *[file]* cartella (f) *o* portfolio (m)

portfolio *[of shares]* portafoglio (m)

portfolio management gestione (f) del portafoglio

p.o.s. *or* **POS (= point of sale)** punto (m) di vendita

POS material (point of sale material) materiale (m) per punto di vendita

position *[job]* impiego (m) *o* lavoro (m)

position *[state of affairs]* posizione (f) *o* situazione (f)

positive positivo

positive cash flow flusso (m) di cassa positivo

possess possedere

possibility possibilità (f)

possible possibile

post (n) *[job]* posto (m) di lavoro *o* impiego (m)

post (n) *[letters]* posta (f)

post (n) *[system]* posta (f) *o* servizio (m) postale

post (v) spedire per posta

post an entry registrare una voce (contabile)

post free franco posta

postage spesa (f) postale

postage and packing (p & p) spese postali e imballo

postage paid porto pagato

postal postale

postal charges *or* **postal rates** spese (fpl) postali

postal order vaglia (m) postale

postcode codice (m) d'avviamento postale

postdate postdatare

poste restante fermoposta (m)

postpaid affrancatura (f) pagata

postpone differire *o* rinviare

postponement dilazione (f) *o* rinvio (m)

potential (adj) potenziale

potential (n) potenziale (m)

potential customers clienti (mpl) eventuali

potential market mercato (m) potenziale

pound *[money]* sterlina (f)

pound *[weight: 0.45kg]* libbra (f) *[peso]*

pound sterling lira sterlina

power of attorney procura (f)

PR (= public relations) pubbliche relazioni

pre-empt acquistare con diritto di prelazione

pre-financing prefinanziamento (m)

prefer preferire

preference preferenza (f)

preference shares azioni (fpl) privilegiate

preferential preferenziale

preferential creditor creditore (m) privilegiato

preferential duty *or* **preferential tariff** dazio (m) preferenziale

preferred creditor creditore (m) privilegiato

premises locali (mpl)

premium *[extra charge]* maggiorazione (f)

premium *[insurance]* premio (m) di assicurazione

premium *[on lease]* importo (m) aggiuntivo

premium offer offerta (f) premio

premium quality qualità (f) extra

prepack *or* **prepackage** preconfezionare

prepaid pagato in anticipo

prepay pagare in anticipo

prepayment pagamento (m) anticipato

present (adj) *[being there]* presente

present (adj) *[now]* attuale

present (n) *[gift]* regalo (m)

present (v) *[give]* regalare *o* offrire

present (v) *[show a document]* presentare

present a bill for acceptance presentare un effetto (m) per l'accettazione

present a bill for payment presentare un effetto (m) per il pagamento

present value valore (m) attuale

presentation *[exhibition]* presentazione (f)

presentation *[showing a document]* presentazione (f)

press stampa (f)

press conference conferenza (f) stampa

press release comunicato (m) stampa

prestige prestigio (m)

prestige product prodotto (m) di prestigio

pretax profit utile (m) al lordo delle imposte

prevent prevenire

prevention prevenzione (f)

preventive preventivo

previous precedente

price (n) prezzo (m)

price (v) stabilire il prezzo

price ceiling tetto (m) dei prezzi

price control contollo (m) dei prezzi

price controls controlli (mpl) dei prezzi

price differential disparità (f) dei prezzi

price ex quay prezzi (mpl) franco banchina

price ex warehouse prezzi (mpl) franco magazzino

price ex works prezzo (m) franco stabilimento

price label cartellino (m) del prezzo

price list listino (m) prezzi

price range gamma (f) dei prezzi

price reductions diminuzione (f) dei prezzi

price stability stabilità (f) dei prezzi

price tag cartellino (m) del prezzo

price ticket cartellino (m) del prezzo

price war guerra (f) dei prezzi

price-cutting war guerra (f) della diminuzione dei prezzi

price-sensitive product prodotto (m) sensibile ai cambiamenti di prezzo

price/earnings ratio (P/E ratio) rapporto (m) corso/utili

pricing determinazione (f) del prezzo

pricing policy politica (f) della determinazione dei prezzi

primary primario

primary industry industria (f) primaria

prime primo *o* di prima qualità

prime cost costi (mpl) diretti

prime rate tasso (m) di base

principal (adj) principale

principal (n) *[money]* capitale (m)

principal (n) *[person]* capo (m) *o* direttore (m), direttrice (f)

principle principio (m)

print out stampare

printer *[company]* tipografia (f)

printer *[machine]* stampante (f)

printout stampato (m)

prior precedente

private privato

private enterprise iniziativa (f) privata

private limited company società (f) a responsabilità limitata (Srl)

private ownership proprietà (f) privata

private property proprietà (f) privata

private sector settore (m) privato

privatization privatizzazione (f)

privatize privatizzare

pro forma (invoice) (fattura) proforma

pro rata prorata *o* proporzionale

probation prova (f)

probationary probatorio

problem problema (m)

problem area area (f) problematica

problem solver persona (f) che risolve problemi

problem solving risoluzione (f) di problemi

procedure procedura (f)

proceed procedere

process (n) processo (m)

process (v) *[deal with]* trattare

process (v) *[raw materials]* lavorare *o* trattare

process figures elaborare cifre

processing of information *or* **of statistics** elaborazione (f) delle informazioni *o* delle statistiche

produce (n) *[food]* prodotti (mpl) agricoli

produce (v) *[bring out]* produrre *o* presentare

produce (v) *[interest]* fruttare *o* rendere

produce (v) *[make]* produrre *o* fabbricare

producer produttore (m)

product prodotto (m)

product advertising pubblicità (f) di un prodotto

product cycle vita (f) ciclica di un prodotto

product design progettazione (f) del prodotto

product development sviluppo (m) del prodotto

product engineer responsabile (m) di un prodotto

product line linea (f) di prodotti

product mix gamma (f) di prodotti

production *[making]* produzione (f)

production *[showing]* presentazione (f)

production costs costi (mpl) di produzione

production department ufficio (m) produzioni

production line catena (f) di montaggio

production manager direttore (m) di produzione

production standards standard (m) di produzione

production targets obiettivi (mpl) di produzione

production unit complesso (m) produttivo

productive produttivo

productive discussions discussione (f) produttiva

productivity produttività (f)

productivity agreement accordo (m) sulla produttività

productivity bonus premio (m) di produttività

professional (adj) *[expert]* professionale

professional (n) *[expert]* professionista (m) *o* esperto (m)

professional qualifications qualifiche (fpl) professionali

profit profitto (m) *o* utile (m)

profit after tax utile (m) al netto delle imposte

profit and loss account conto (m) profitti e perdite

profit before tax utile (m) al lordo delle imposte

profit centre centro (m) di profitto

profit margin margine (m) di utile

profit-making a scopo di lucro

profit-oriented company società (f) orientata al profitto

profit-sharing compartecipazione (f) agli utili

profitability *[making a profit]* redditività (f)

profitability *[ratio of profit to cost]* coefficiente (m) di redditività

profitable remunerativo *o* proficuo *o* redditizio

program a computer programmare un computer

programme *or* **program** programma (m)

programming language linguaggio (m) di programmazione

progress (n) progresso (m)

progress (v) avanzare *o* fare progressi

progress chaser addetto (m) al controllo dell'avanzamento

progress payments pagamento (m) progressivo

progress report relazione (f) sull'avanzamento

progressive taxation imposte (fpl) progressive

prohibitive proibitivo

project *[plan]* progetto (m)

project analysis analisi (f) del progetto

project manager direttore (m) del progetto

projected progettato

projected sales vendite (fpl) previste

promise (n) promessa (f)

promise (v) promettere

promissory note pagherò (m)

promote *[advertise]* promuovere

promote *[give better job]* promuovere

promote a corporate image promuovere un'immagine aziendale

promote a new product pubblicizzare un nuovo prodotto

promotion *[publicity]* promozione (f)

promotion *[to better job]* promozione (f)

promotion budget budget (m) per le spese di promozione

promotion of a product promozione (f) di un prodotto

promotional promozionale

promotional budget stanziamento (m) promozionale

prompt sollecito

prompt payment pagamento (m) in contanti

prompt service servizio (m) sollecito

proof prova (f)

proportion proporzione (f)

proportional proporzionale

proposal *[insurance]* proposta (f) (di assicurazione)

proposal *[suggestion]* proposta (f)

propose *[a motion]* proporre

propose to *[do something]* intendere

proprietary company *[US]* società (f) controllante

proprietor proprietario (m)

proprietress proprietaria (f)

prosecute perseguire (legalmente)

prosecution *[legal action]* procedimento (m) giudiziario

prosecution *[party in legal action]* parte (f) querelante

prosecution counsel avvocato (m) della parte querelante

prospective probabile

prospective buyer possibile acquirente (m)

prospects prospettive (fpl)

prospectus prospetto (m)

protective protettivo

protective tariff tariffa (f) protezionistica

protest (n) *[against something]* protesta (f)

protest (n) *[official document]* protesto (m) (per mancato pagamento)

protest (v) *[against something]* protestare contro qualcosa

protest a bill protestare una cambiale

protest strike sciopero (m) di protesta

provide provvedere

provide for provvedere a

provided that *or* **providing** a patto che

provision *[condition]* condizione (f) *o* clausola (f)

provision *[money put aside]* accantonamento (m) *o* riserva (f)

provisional provvisorio

provisional budget budget (m) provvisorio

provisional forecast of sales previsione (f) delle vendite provvisoria

proviso clausola (f) condizionale

proxy *[deed]* procura (f) *o* delega (f)

proxy *[person]* mandatario (m)

proxy vote voto (m) per delega

public (adj) pubblico

public finance finanza (f) pubblica

public funds fondi (mpl) pubblici

public holiday festa (f) nazionale

public image immagine (f) pubblica

Public Limited Company (Plc) società (f) di capitali a sottoscrizione pubblica

public opinion opinione (f) pubblica

public relations (PR) pubbliche relazioni (fpl)

public relations department ufficio (m) delle pubbliche relazioni

public relations man addetto (m) alle pubbliche relazioni

public relations officer dirigente (m) delle pubbliche relazioni

public sector settore (m) pubblico

public transport trasporti (mpl) pubblici

publicity pubblicità (f)

publicity budget budget (m) pubblicitario

publicity campaign campagna (f) pubblicitaria

publicity department ufficio (m) della pubblicità

publicity expenditure spese (f) pubblicitarie

publicity manager direttore (m) della pubblicità

publicize pubblicizzare

purchase (n) acquisto (m)

purchase (v) acquistare *o* comperare

purchase ledger libro (m) mastro degli acquisti

purchase order ordine (m) d'acquisto

purchase price prezzo (m) d'acquisto

purchase tax imposta (f) generale sugli acquisti

purchaser compratore (m)

purchasing acquisto (m)

purchasing department ufficio (m) acquisti

purchasing manager direttore (m) dell'ufficio acquisti

purchasing power potere (m) d'acquisto

put (v) *[place]* mettere

put back *[later]* posticipare

put in writing mettere per iscritto

put money down dare soldi come anticipo

Qq

qty (= **quantity**) quantità (f) (q)

qualified *[skilled]* abile *o* qualificato

qualified *[with reservations]* con riserve *o* condizionato

qualify as qualificarsi

quality qualità (f)

quality control controllo (m) di qualità

quality controller controllore (m) della qualità

quality label marchio (m) di qualità

quantity quantità (f)

quantity discount sconto (m) sul quantitativo

quarter *[25%]* quarto (m)

quarter *[three months]* trimestre

quarter day primo giorno (m) del trimestre

quarterly (**adj**) trimestrale

quarterly (**adv**) trimestralmente

quay molo (m)

quorum numero (m) minimo legale

quota quota (f)

quotation *[estimate of cost]* quotazione (f)

quote (**n**) *[estimate of cost]* quotazione (f)

quote (**v**) *[a reference number]* quotare

quote (**v**) *[estimate costs]* indicare un prezzo *o* quotare

quoted company società (f) quotata in Borsa

quoted shares azioni (fpl) quotate

Rr

R&D (= **research and development**) RS (ricerca e sviluppo)

racketeer organizzatore (m) di attività illegali

racketeering attività (f) illegale

rail ferrovia (f)

rail transport trasporto (m) ferroviario

railroad *[US]* ferrovia (f)

railway *[GB]* ferrovia (f)

railway station stazione (f) ferroviaria

raise (**v**) *[a question]* sollevare

raise (**v**) *[increase]* aumentare

raise (**v**) *[obtain money]* raccogliere fondi

raise an invoice emettere una fattura

rally (**n**) ripresa (f)

rally (**v**) rafforzarsi

random accidentale *o* casuale

random check sondaggio (m)

random error errore (m) casuale

random sample campione (m) casuale

random sampling campionatura (f) casuale

range (**n**) *[series of items]* gamma (f)

range (**n**) *[variation]* variazioni (fpl) *o* scala (f)

range (**v**) variare *o* estendersi

rate (**n**) *[amount]* tasso (m)

rate (**n**) *[price]* quota (f) *o* tariffa (f) *o* tasso (m)

rate of exchange tasso (m) di cambio

rate of inflation tasso (m) d'inflazione

rate of production tasso (m) di produzione

rate of return indice (m) di rendimento

ratification ratifica (f)

ratify ratificare

rating quotazione (f)

ratio rapporto (m)

rationalization razionalizzazione (f)

rationalize razionalizzare

raw materials materie (fpl) prime

re-elect rieleggere

re-election rielezione (f)

re-employ riassumere

re-employment riassunzione (f)

re-export (n) riesportazione (f)

re-export (v) riesportare

reach *[arrive]* raggiungere

reach *[come to]* arrivare a

reach a decision arrivare ad una decisione

reach an agreement giungere ad un accordo

readjust riadattare

readjustment riassestamento (m)

ready pronto

ready cash pronta cassa (f)

real reale

real estate proprietà (f) immobiliare

real income *or* **real wages** reddito (m) effettivo

real-time system sistema (m) in tempo reale

realizable assets attivo (m) esigibile *o* cespiti (mpl) realizzabili

realization of assets realizzazione (f) di cespiti

realize *[sell for money]* realizzare

realize *[understand]* capire *o* rendersi conto di

realize a project *or* **a plan** realizzare un progetto *o* un piano

realize property *or* **assets** realizzare beni *o* cespiti

reapplication nuova domanda (f)

reappoint ricollocare

reappointment ricollocamento (m)

reassess fare una nuova stima

reassessment nuovo accertamento (m)

rebate *[money back]* rimborso (m)

rebate *[price reduction]* riduzione (f) *o* sconto (m)

receipt *[paper]* ricevuta (f)

receipt *[receiving]* ricevimento (m)

receipt book registro (m) delle ricevute

receipts entrate (fpl)

receivable da ricevere

receivables effetti (mpl) attivi

receive ricevere

receiver *[liquidator]* liquidatore (m)

receiving ricevente

reception portineria (f)

reception clerk portiere (f)

reception desk portineria (f) *o* banco (m) d'albergo

receptionist receptionist (m)

recession recessione (f)

reciprocal mutuo *o* reciproco

reciprocal agreement accordo (m) bilaterale

reciprocal trade commercio (m) bilaterale

reciprocity scambio (m)

recognition riconoscimento (m)

recognize a union riconoscere un sindacato

recommend *[say something is good]* raccomandare

recommend *[suggest action]* consigliare

recommendation raccomandazione (f)

reconcile riconciliare

reconciliation riconciliazione (f)

reconciliation of accounts riconciliazione (f) dei conti

record (n) *[better than before]* primato (m)

record (n) *[for personnel]* archivi (mpl)

record (n) *[of what has happened]* rapporto (m)

record (v) registrare

record sales *or* **record losses** *or* **record profits** vendite (fpl) record *o* perdite (fpl) record *o* utili (mpl) record

record-breaking da primato

recorded delivery raccomandata (f) con ricevuta di ritorno

records documentazione (f) *o* archivio (m)

recoup one's losses rifarsi delle perdite

recover *[get better]* riprendersi

recover *[get something back]* ricuperare

recoverable recuperabile

recovery *[getting better]* ripresa (f)

recovery *[getting something back]* ricupero (m)

rectification rettifica (f)

rectify correggere

recurrent ricorrente

recycle riciclare

recycled paper carta (f) riciclata

red tape lungaggine (f) burocratica

redeem estinguere

redeem a bond rimborsare un'obbligazione

redeem a debt estinguere un debito

redeem a pledge riscattare un pegno

redeemable redimibile

redemption *[of a loan]* riscatto (m) (di un prestito)

redemption date data (f) di rimborso

redevelop adibire ad altro uso

redevelopment progetto (m) edilizio di ricostruzione

redistribute ridistribuire

reduce ridurre

reduce a price ridurre un prezzo

reduce expenditure ridurre le spese

reduced rate tasso (m) ridotto

reduction ribasso (m)

redundancy cassa (f) integrazione

redundant in cassa integrazione

refer *[pass to someone]* sottoporre

refer *[to item]* riferirsi *o* fare riferimento a

reference *[dealing with]* riferimento (m)

reference *[person who reports]* persona che è chiamata a dare referenza

reference *[report on person]* referenze (fpl) *o* attestato (m)

reference number numero (m) di riferimento

refinancing of a loan rifinanziamento (m) di un prestito

refresher course corso (m) d'aggiornamento

refund (n) rimborso (m)

refund (v) rimborsare

refundable rimborsabile

refundable deposit caparra (f) rimborsabile

refunding of a loan conversione (f) di un prestito

refusal rifiuto (m)

refuse (v) rifiutare

regarding riguardante

regardless of senza tener conto di

regional regionale

register (n) *[large book]* registro (m) *o* libro (m) contabile

register (n) *[official list]* registro (m)

register (v) *[at hotel]* firmare il registro

register (v) *[in official list]* iscriversi

register (v) *[letter]* fare una lettera raccomandata

register a company iscrivere una società

register a property iscrivere al catasto una proprietà immobiliare

register a trademark depositare un marchio di fabbrica

register of directors registro (m) degli amministratori

register of shareholders registro (m) degli azionisti *o* registro (m) delle azioni

registered (adj) registrato

registered letter raccomandata (f)

registered office sede (f) legale

registered trademark marchio (m) di fabbrica depositato

registrar ufficiale (m) di stato civile

Registrar of Companies Conservatore (m) del Registro delle Società

registration registrazione (f)

registration fee tassa (f) di registrazione

registration form modulo (m) d'iscrizione

registration number numero (m) di matricola

registry registrazione (f)

registry office anagrafe (f)

regular *[always at same time]* consueto *o* fisso

regular *[ordinary]* regolare *o* normale

regular customer cliente (mf) abituale

regular income reddito (m) fisso

regular size formato (m) normale

regular staff personale (m) di ruolo

regulate *[adjust]* regolare

regulate *[by law]* regolarizzare

regulation regolamento (m)

regulations regolamenti (mpl) *o* disposizioni (fpl)

reimbursement rimborso (m)

reimbursement of expenses rimborso (m) delle spese

reimport (n) reimportazione (f)

reimport (v) reimportare

reimportation reimportazione (f)

reinsurance riassicurazione (f)

reinsure riassicurare

reinsurer riassicuratore (m)

reinvest reinvestire

reinvestment reinvestimento (m)

reject (n) scarto (m)

reject (v) rifiutare *o* respingere

rejection rifiuto (m)

relating to relativo a

relations relazioni (fpl)

release (n) rilascio (m)

release (v) *[free]* liberare

release (v) *[make public]* rilasciare

release (v) *[put on the market]* mettere in vendita

release dues liquidare gli ordini arretrati

relevant relativo

reliability attendibilità (f)

reliable attendibile

remain *[be left]* restare

remain *[stay]* restare

remind rammentare

reminder sollecito (m)

remit (n) competenza (f)

remit (v) rimettere

remit by cheque inviare rimessa a mezzo assegno

remittance rimessa (f)

remote control telecomando (m)

removal *[sacking someone]* destituzione (f)

removal *[to new house]* trasloco (m)

remove rimuovere

remunerate retribuire

remuneration retribuzione (f)

render an account presentare un conto

renew rinnovare

renew a bill of exchange *or* **renew a lease** rinnovare una cambiale *o* rinnovare un contratto d'affitto

renew a subscription rinnovare un abbonamento

renewal rinnovo (m)

renewal notice avviso (m) di rinnovo

renewal of a lease *or* **of a subscription** *or* **of a bill** rinnovo (m) di un contratto d'affitto *o* un abbonamento *o* una cambiale

renewal premium premio (m) di rinnovo

rent (n) affitto (m)

rent (v) *[pay money for]* prendere in affitto

rent collector esattore (m) di affitti

rent control blocco (m) degli affitti

rent tribunal sindacato (m) degli inquilini

rent-free esente da canone d'affitto

rental affitto (m)

rental income reddito (m) da affittanze

renunciation rinuncia (f)

reorder (n) nuova ordinazione (f)

reorder (v) riordinare

reorder level livello (m) di riordinazione

reorganization riorganizzazione (f)

reorganize riorganizzare

rep (= representative) rappresentante (m)

repair (n) riparazione (m)

repair (v) aggiustare *o* riparare

repay ripagare

repayable rimborsabile

repayment rimborso (m)

repeat replica (f)

repeat an order ripetere un'ordinazione

repeat order ordinazione (f) rinnovata

replace sostituire

replacement *[item]* sostituzione (f)

replacement *[person]* sostituto (m) *o* rimpiazzo (m)

replacement value valore (m) di sostituzione

reply (n) risposta (f)

reply (v) rispondere

reply coupon coupon (m) con risposta pagata

report (n) rapporto (m)

report (v) riferire

report (v) *[go to a place]* presentarsi

report a loss dichiarare una perdita

report for an interview presentarsi per un colloquio di lavoro

report on the progress of the work *or* **of the negotiations** relazionare sull'andamento di un lavoro *o* dei negoziati

report to someone dover rispondere a qualcuno

repossess recuperare

represent rappresentare

representative (adj) rappresentativo

representative *[company]* ufficio (m) di rappresentanza

representative *[person]* rappresentante (m) di commercio

repudiate ripudiare

repudiate an agreement rifiutare un accordo

request (n) richiesta (f)

request (v) richiedere *o* domandare

request: on request su richiesta

require *[demand]* richiedere

require *[need]* aver bisogno di

requirements richieste (fpl)

resale rivendita (f)

resale price prezzo (m) di rivendita

rescind rescindere

research (n) ricerca (f)

research (v) documentarsi su *o* fare ricerche

research and development (R & D) ricerca (f) e sviluppo (m) (RS)

research programme programma (m) di ricerca

research worker ricercatore (m), ricercatrice (f)

researcher ricercatore (m), ricercatrice (f)

reservation prenotazione (f)

reserve (n) *[money]* fondo (m)

reserve (n) *[supplies]* riserva (f)

reserve (v) riservare

reserve a room *or* **a table** *or* **a seat** riservare una camera *o* un tavolo *o* un posto

reserve currency valuta (f) di riserva

reserve price prezzo (m) minimo

reserves riserve (fpl)

residence residenza (f)

residence permit permesso (m) di soggiorno

resident (adj) residente

resident (n) residente (m) *o* abitante (m)

resign dimettersi

resignation dimissioni (fpl)

resolution risoluzione (f)

resolve decidere

resources risorse (fpl)

respect (v) rispettare

response reazione (f)

responsibilities responsabilità (fpl)

responsibility responsabilità (f)

responsible (for) responsabile di

responsible to someone che deve rispondere a qualcuno

restock rifornire

restocking rifornimento (m)

restraint restrizione (f)

restraint of trade limitazione (f) agli scambi commerciali

restrict limitare

restrict credit limitare il credito

restriction restrizione (f)

restrictive restrittivo

restrictive practices pratiche (fpl) restrittive

restructure ristrutturare

restructuring ristrutturazione (f)

restructuring of a loan rifinanziamento (m) (di un prestito)

restructuring of the company riorganizzazione (f) di una società

result *[general]* risultato (m)

result from derivare

result in avere come risultato

results *[company's profit or loss]* risultati (mpl)

resume riprendere

resume negotiations riprendere le trattative

retail (n) vendita (f) al dettaglio

retail (v) *[goods]* vendere al dettaglio

retail (v) *[sell for a price]* vendersi a

retail dealer dettagliante (m)

retail goods merce per la vendita al dettaglio

retail outlets punto (m) di vendita al dettaglio

retail price prezzo (m) al dettaglio

retail price index Indice (m) dei prezzi al dettaglio

retailer dettagliante (m)

retailing vendita (f) al dettaglio

retire *[from one's job]* andare in pensione

retirement pensionamento (m)

retirement age età (f) della pensione

retiring uscente

retrain riaddestrare

retraining riaddestramento (m)

retrenchment riduzione (f) delle spese

retrieval reperimento (m)

retrieval system sistema (m) di recupero delle informazioni

retrieve reperire

retroactive retroattivo

retroactive pay rise aumento (m) di paga retroattivo

return (n) *[declaration]* dichiarazione (f)

return (n) *[going back]* ritorno (m)

return (n) *[profit]* profitto (m) o guadagno (m)

return (n) *[sending back]* restituzione (f)

return (v) *[declare]* dichiarare

return (v) *[send back]* respingere o mandare indietro

return a letter to sender rimandare una lettera al mittente

return address indirizzo (m) del mittente

return on investment (ROI) reddito (m) sugli investimenti

returnable restituibile

returned empties vuoti (mpl) a rendere

returns *[profits]* incassi (mpl)

returns *[unsold goods]* merce (f) non venduta

revaluation rivalutazione (f)

revalue rivalutare

revenue reddito (m)

revenue accounts conto (m) delle entrate

revenue from advertising ricavo (m) dalla pubblicità

reversal inversione (f)

reverse (adj) inverso

reverse (v) invertire

reverse charge call telefonata (f) a carico del ricevente

reverse takeover acquisizione (f) di controllo inversa

reverse the charges addebitare una telefonata al ricevente

revise riesaminare

revoke revocare

revolving credit credito (m) rinnovabile automaticamente

revolving credit credito (m) rinnovabile automaticamente

rider clausola (f) addizionale

right (adj) *[not left]* destro

right (adj) *[not wrong]* corretto

right (n) *[legal title]* diritto (m)

right of veto diritto (m) di veto

right of way diritto (m) di precedenza

right-hand man uomo (m) di fiducia

rightful giusto

rightful claimant pretendente (m) di diritto

rightful owner proprietario (m) legittimo

rights issue emissione (f) di diritti

rise (n) *[increase]* aumento (m)

rise (n) *[salary]* aumento (m)

rise (v) aumentare

risk (n) rischio (m)

risk (v) *[money]* rischiare

risk capital capitale (m) di rischio

risk premium premio (m) di rischio

risk-free investment investimento (m) privo di rischio

risky rischioso

rival company società (f) rivale

road strada (f)

road haulage trasporto (m) su strada (di merci)

road haulier trasportatore (m) su strada

road tax tassa (f) di circolazione

road transport trasporto (m) su strada

rock-bottom prices prezzo (m) ridottissimo

ROI (= return on investment) reddito (m) sugli investimenti

roll on/roll off ferry roll on/roll off o traghetto (m) per automezzi

rolling plan piano (m) continuo

room *[general]* stanza (f)

room *[hotel]* camera (f)

room *[space]* spazio (m)

room reservations prenotazioni (fpl) di camera

room service servizio (m) in camera

rough approssimativo

rough calculation calcolo (m) approssimativo

rough draft bozza (f)

rough estimate valutazione (f) approssimativa

round down arrotondare diminuendo

round up arrotondare aumentando

routine (adj) abituale

routine (n) routine (f) *o* ordinaria amministrazione (f)

routine call telefonata (f) di routine

routine work lavoro (m) di routine

royalty diritto (m) di concessione

rubber check *[US]* assegno (m) a vuoto

rule (n) norma (f)

rule (v) *[be in force]* essere in vigore

rule (v) *[give decision]* decretare

ruling (adj) corrente

ruling (n) decreto (m)

run (n) *[regular route]* percorso (m)

run (n) *[work routine]* serie (f) *o* sequela (f)

run (v) *[be in force]* essere valido *o* entrare in vigore

run (v) *[buses, trains]* fare servizio

run (v) *[manage]* dirigere

run (v) *[work machine]* far funzionare

run a risk correre un rischio

run into debt contrarre debiti

run out of esaurire

running (n) *[of machine]* marcia (f) *o* funzionamento (m)

running costs *or* **running expenses** spese (fpl) d'esercizio *o* costi (mpl) di gestione di un'azienda

running total totale (m) corrente

rush (n) ressa (f)

rush (v) affrettarsi

rush hour ora (f) di punta

rush job lavoro (m) urgente

rush order ordinazione (f) urgente

Ss

sack someone licenziare qualcuno

safe (adj) sicuro *o* prudente

safe (n) cassaforte (f)

safe deposit deposito (m) in cassetta di sicurezza

safe investment investimento (m) sicuro

safeguard salvaguardia (f)

safety sicurezza (f)

safety measures misure (fpl) di sicurezza

safety precautions misure (fpl) di sicurezza

safety regulations norme (fpl) di sicurezza

salaried stipendiato

salary stipendio (m)

salary cheque assegno (m) dello stipendio

salary review revisione (f) dello stipendio

sale (n) *[at a low price]* saldo (m)

sale (n) *[selling]* vendita (f)

sale by auction vendita (f) all'asta

sale or return venduto con possibilità di resa

saleability vendibilità (f)

saleable vendibile

sales vendite (fpl) *o* fatturato (m)

sales analysis analisi (f) delle vendite

sales book libro (m) vendite

sales budget previsione (f) di vendita

sales campaign campagna (f) di vendite

sales chart grafico (m) delle vendite

sales clerk addetto (m) alle vendite

sales conference raduno (m) dei venditori

sales curve curva (f) delle vendite

sales department ufficio (m) vendite

sales executive dirigente (m) delle vendite

sales figures volume (m) d'affari

sales force forza (f) vendita *o* personale (m) addetto alle vendite

sales forecast previsione (f) di vendita

sales ledger partitario (m) delle vendite

sales ledger clerk impiegato (m) addetto al partitario delle vendite

sales literature materiale (m) illustrativo delle vendite

sales manager direttore (m) commerciale

sales people venditori (mpl)

sales pitch imbonimento (m)

sales promotion promozione (f) delle vendite

sales receipt ricevuta (f) (di vendita)

sales representative rappresentante (m)

sales revenue fatturato (m)

sales target obiettivo (m) di vendita

sales tax imposta (f) sul volume di affari

sales team personale (m) addetto alle vendite

sales volume volume (m) delle vendite

salesman *[in shop]* commesso (m)

salesman *[representative]* rappresentante (m) (di commercio)

salvage (n) *[action]* recupero (m)

salvage (n) *[things saved]* materiale (m) di recupero

salvage (v) salvare *o* recuperare

salvage vessel nave (f) di salvataggio

sample (n) *[group]* campione (m)

sample (n) *[part]* campione (m) *o* saggio (m)

sample (v) *[ask questions]* fare un sondaggio

sample (v) *[test]* campionare

sampling *[statistics]* campionamento (m)

sampling *[testing]* campionamento (m)

satisfaction soddisfazione (f)

satisfy *[customer]* soddisfare

satisfy a demand soddisfare una richiesta

saturate saturare

saturate the market rendere saturo il mercato

saturation saturazione (f)

save (v) *[money]* risparmiare

save (v) *[not waste]* risparmiare *o* economizzare

save (v) *[on computer]* salvare su disco

save on economizzare

save up mettere da parte denaro

savings risparmi (mpl)

savings account conto (m) di risparmio

scale *[system]* scala (f)

scale down ridurre proporzionalmente

scale of charges tariffa (f)

scale up aumentare proporzionalmente

scarcity value valore alto dettato dalla scarsità di fornitura

scheduled flight volo (m) di linea

scheduling elencazione (f)

screen candidates selezionare candidati

scrip documento (m) provvisorio

scrip issue emissione (f) di certificati azionari provvisori

seal (n) sigillo (m)

seal (v) *[attach a seal]* sigillare

seal (v) *[envelope]* chiudere *o* incollare

sealed envelope busta (f) chiusa

sealed tenders offerta (f) in busta chiusa

season *[time for something]* stagione (f) *o* periodo (m)

season *[time of year]* stagione (f)

season ticket tessera (f) (di abbonamento ferroviario)

seasonal stagionale *o* periodico

seasonal adjustments adattamento (m) stagionale

seasonal demand richiesta (f) stagionale

seasonal variations variazioni (fpl) stagionali

seasonally adjusted figures cifre (fpl) destagionalizzate

second (adj) secondo

second (v) *[member of staff]* trasferire *o* distaccare

second quarter secondo trimestre (m)

second-class seconda classe (sui mezzi di trasporto) *o* seconda categoria (di merci)

secondary industry industria (f) secondaria

secondhand usato *o* di seconda mano

seconds prodotti (mpl) di seconda qualità

secret (adj) segreto

secret (n) segreto (m)

secretarial college scuola (f) per segretarie d'azienda

secretary segretaria/o (fm)

secretary *[company official]* segretario (m) del consiglio di amministrazione

secretary *[government minister]* ministro (m)

sector settore (m)

secure funds procurarsi fondi

secure investment investimento (m) garantito

secure job lavoro (m) stabile

secured creditor creditore (m) privilegiato

secured debts debiti (mpl) privilegiati

secured loan mutuo (m) garantito

securities titoli (mpl)

security *[being safe]* sicurezza (f)

security *[guarantee]* garanzia (f)

security guard guardia (f) giurata

security of employment sicurezza (f) dell'impiego

security of tenure sicurezza (f) di possesso

see-safe vendita (f) con possibilità di resa

seize sequestrare

seizure sequestro (m)

selection selezione (f)

selection procedure procedura (f) di selezione

self-employed che lavora in proprio

self-financing (adj) che può autofinanziarsi

self-financing (n) autofinanziamento (m)

self-regulation autoregolazione (f)

self-regulatory autoregolatore

sell vendere

sell forward vendere a termine

sell off svendere

sell out *[all stock]* vendere tutto

sell out *[sell one's business]* vendere (un impresa)

sell-by date data (f) di scadenza

seller venditore (m)

seller's market mercato (m) favorevole ai venditori

selling (n) vendita (f)

selling price prezzo (m) di vendita

semi-finished products prodotti (mpl) semilavorati

semi-skilled workers lavoratori (mpl) parzialmente qualificati

send inviare

send a package by airmail spedire un pacco per via aerea

send a package by surface mail spedire un pacco per posta ordinaria

send a shipment by sea mandare un carico per mare

send an invoice by post spedire una fattura (per posta)

sender mittente (m)

senior anziano *o* piu vecchio

senior manager *or* **senior executive** dirigente (m) in capo *o* direttore (m)

senior partner socio (m) anziano

separate (adj) separato

separate (v) separare

sequester *or* **sequestrate** sequestrare

sequestration sequestro (m)

sequestrator sequestratario (m)

serial number numero (m) di serie

serve servire

serve a customer servire un cliente

service (n) *[business which helps]* società (f) di servizi

service (n) *[dealing with customers]* servizio (m)

service (n) *[of machine]* revisione (f) *o* manutenzione (f)

service (n) *[regular working]* servizio (m)

service (n) *[working for a company]* servizio (m)

service (v) *[a machine]* revisionare

service a debt pagare un debito

service centre centro (m) assistenza

service charge percentuale (f) per il servizio

service department ufficio (m) assistenza

service manual manuale (m) di manutenzione

set (adj) fisso

set (n) serie (f)

set (v) fissare

set against contrapporre

set price prezzo (m) stabilito

set targets fissare obiettivi

set up a company costituire una società (f)

set up in business mettersi in affari

setback battuta (f) d'arresto

settle *[an invoice]* liquidare *o* pagare una fattura

settle *[arrange things]* sistemare

settle a claim definire una domanda d'indennizzo

settle an account saldare un conto

settlement *[agreement]* accordo (m)

settlement *[payment]* pagamento (m)

setup *[company]* organizzazione (f)

setup *[organization]* organizzazione (f)

share (n) *[in a company]* azione (f)

share (v) *[divide among]* spartire *o* dividere

share (v) *[use with someone]* dividere

share an office spartire un ufficio

share capital capitale (m) sociale

share certificate certificato (m) azionario

share issue emissione (f) azionaria

shareholder azionista (m)

shareholding partecipazione (f) azionaria

sharp practice pratica (f) spregiudicata

sheet of paper foglio (m) di carta

shelf scaffale (m)

shelf filler persona addetta al rifornimento degli scaffali

shelf life of a product periodo (m) medio di permanenza di un prodotto

shell company società (f) esistente solo di nome

shelter riparo (m)

shelve accantonare *o* differire

shelving *[postponing]* accantonamento (m)

shelving *[shelves]* scaffalatura (f)

shift (n) *[change]* cambiamento (m)

shift (n) *[team of workers]* turno (m) (di lavoro)

shift key tasto (m) delle maiuscole

shift work lavoro (m) con turni

ship (n) nave (f)

ship (v) trasportare *o* spedire

ship broker agente (m) marittimo

shipment trasporto (m) marittimo

shipper spedizioniere (m) marittimo

shipping spedizione (f) marittima

shipping agent spedizioniere (m) marittimo

shipping charges *or* **shipping costs** costi (mpl) per la spedizione marittima

shipping clerk impiegato (m) di spedizioniere

shipping company società (f) di navigazione

shipping instructions istruzioni (fpl) per la spedizione

shipping line linea (f) di navigazione

shipping note bolla (f) di spedizione

shop negozio (m)

shop around confrontare i prezzi

shop assistant commesso/a (mf) di negozio

shop window vetrina (f)

shop-soiled articolo (m) sciupato per prolungata esposizione

shopkeeper negoziante (m)

shoplifter taccheggiatore (m)

shoplifting taccheggiare

shopper acquirente (mf) *o* cliente (mf)

shopping *[action]* spesa (f)

shopping *[goods bought]* acquisti (mpl)

shopping arcade galleria (f) (con negozi) *o* centro (m) commerciale

shopping centre centro (m) commerciale

shopping mall galleria (f) (con negozi) *o* centro (m) commerciale

shopping precinct zona (f) commerciale

short credit credito (m) a breve termine

short of a meno di

short-dated bills effetti (mpl) a breve termine

short-term (adj) a breve *o* a breve termine

short-term contract contratto (m) a breve termine

short-term credit credito (m) a breve

short-term debts indebitamento (m) a breve

short-term loan mutuo (m) a breve scadenza

shortage scarsità (f)

shortfall ammanco (m)

shortlist (n) lista (f) ristretta (di candidati)

shortlist (v) iscrivere qualcuno in una rosa di candidati

show (n) *[exhibition]* mostra (f)

show (v) mostrare

show a profit indicare un profitto

showcase bacheca (f)

showroom sala (f) di esposizione

shrink-wrapped imballato con metodo termocontrattile

shrink-wrapping imballaggio (m) termocontrattile

shrinkage restringimento (m) *o* deprezzamento (m)

shut (adj) chiuso

shut (v) chiudere

side lato (m)

sideline attività (f) secondaria

sight vista (f)

sight draft tratta (f) a vista

sign (n) insegna (f)

sign (v) firmare

sign a cheque firmare un assegno

sign a contract firmare un contratto

signatory firmatario (m)

signature firma (f)

simple interest interesse (m) semplice

single singolo

Single European Market Mercato Europeo Unico

sister company società (f) sorella

sister ship nave (f) gemella

sit-down protest protesta (f) con occupazione

sit-down strike sciopero (m) con occupazione

site luogo (m)

site engineer ingegnere (m) edile

sitting tenant affittuario (m) occupante

situated situato

situation *[place]* posizione (f) *o* collocazione (f)

situation *[state of affairs]* situazione (f)

situations vacant offerte (fpl) d'impiego

size dimensione (f)

skeleton staff personale (m) ridotto al minimo

skill abilità (f) tecnica

skilled specializzato

skilled labour *or* **skilled workers** manodopera (f) qualificata

slack lento *o* stagnante

slash prices *or* **credit terms** tagliare i prezzi *o* le condizioni di credito

sleeping partner socio (m) accomandante

slip (n) *[mistake]* errore (m)

slip (n) *[piece of paper]* foglietto (m)

slow lento

slow down rallentare

slow payer pagatore (m) tardivo

slowdown rallentamento (m)

slump (n) *[depression]* crollo (m) *o* crisi (f) economica

slump (n) *[rapid fall]* brusca caduta (f)

slump (v) crollare *o* subire una forte flessione

slump in sales discesa (f) delle vendite

small piccolo

small ads piccoli annunci (mpl)

small businesses piccole imprese (fpl)

small businessman piccolo affarista/uomo d'affari

small change moneta (f) spicciola

small-scale in scala (f) ridotta

small-scale enterprise iniziativa (f) su scala ridotta

soar salire alle stelle

social sociale

social costs costi (mpl) sociali

social security previdenza (f) sociale

society *[club]* associazione (f) *o* circolo (m)

society *[general]* società (f)

socio-economic groups gruppi (mpl) socioeconomici

soft currency valuta (f) debole

soft loan prestito (m) agevolato

soft sell tecnica (f) di vendita basata sulla persuasione

software software (m)

sole solo *o* unico

sole agency rappresentanza (f) esclusiva

sole agent rappresentante (m) esclusivo

sole owner unico proprietario (m)

sole trader commerciante (m) in proprio

solicit orders sollecitare un'ordinazione

solicitor procuratore (m) legale

solution soluzione (f)

solve a problem risolvere un problema

solvency solvibilità (f)

solvent (adj) solvente

source of income fonte (f) di reddito

spare part pezzo (m) di ricambio

spare time tempo (m) libero

special speciale

special drawing rights (SDRs) diritti (mpl) speciali di prelievo (DSP)

special offer offerta (f) speciale

specialist specialista (m)

specialization specializzazione (f)

specialize essere specializzato

specification specifica (f)

specify specificare

speech of thanks discorso (m) di ringraziamento

spend *[money]* spendere

spend *[time]* passare il tempo a

spending money denaro (m) per le piccole spese

spending power potere (m) d'acquisto

spinoff sottoprodotto (m)

spoil rovinare *o* viziare

sponsor (n) sponsor (m) *o* garante (m)

sponsor (v) garantire *o* sponsorizzare *o* patrocinare

sponsorship sponsorizzazione (f) *o* avallo (m)

spot *[place]* posto (m) *o* luogo (m)

spot cash pagamento (m) in contanti

spot price prezzo (m) per merce pronta

spot purchase transazione (f) a pronti

spread a risk ripartire un rischio

spreadsheet *[computer]* foglio (m) di calcolo elettronico

stability stabilità (f)

stabilization stabilizzazione (f)

stabilize stabilizzare

stable fermo *o* stabile

stable currency moneta (f) stabile

stable economy economia (f) solida

stable exchange rate tasso (m) di cambio stabile

stable prices prezzi (mpl) stabili

staff (n) personale (m)

staff (v) fornire di personale

staff appointment nomina (f) del personale

staff meeting assemblea (f) del personale

stage (n) stadio (m)

stage (v) *[organize]* organizzare

stage a recovery riprendersi

staged payments pagamenti (mpl) scaglionati

stagger scaglionare

stagnant stagnante

stagnation ristagno (m)

stamp (n) *[device]* timbro (m)

stamp (n) *[post]* francobollo (m)

stamp (v) *[letter]* affrancare *o* mettere francobolli

stamp (v) *[mark]* timbrare

stamp duty imposta (f) di bollo

stand (n) *[at exhibition]* stand (m)

stand down ritirare la propria candidatura

stand security for avallare

stand surety for someone garantire per qualcuno

standard (adj) standard

standard (n) norma (f)

standard letter lettera (f) standard

standard rate (of tax) aliquota (f) d'imposta base

standardization standardizzazione (f)

standardize standardizzare

standby arrangements accordo (m) creditizio di sostegno

standby credit credito (m) di appoggio

standby ticket biglietto (m) aereo privo di prenotazione

standing legittimazione (f)

standing order ordine (m) permanente

staple (n) punto (m) metallico

staple (v) cucire con punti metallici *o* graffare

staple industry industria (f) di base

staple papers together graffare insieme fogli

staple product prodotti (mpl) essenziali

stapler cucitrice (f) *o* graffatrice (f)

start (n) avvio (m)

start (v) iniziare *o* cominciare

start-up avviamento (m)

start-up costs spese (fpl) di avviamento

starting (adj) iniziale

starting date data (f) d'inizio

starting point punto (m) di partenza

starting salary stipendio (m) iniziale

state (n) *[condition]* condizione (f) *o* stato (m)

state (n) *[country]* stato (m) *o* nazione (f)

state (v) dichiarare *o* precisare

state-of-the-art all'avanguardia

statement rendiconto (m)

statement of account estratto (m) conto

statement of expenses rendiconto (m) delle spese

station *[train]* stazione (f)

statistical statistico

statistical analysis analisi (f) statistica

statistician esperto (m) di statistica

statistics statistica (f)

status condizione (f) sociale

status inquiry informazioni (fpl) commerciali

status symbol simbolo (m) di successo

statute of limitations prescrizione (f)

statutory statutario

statutory holiday giorno (m) festivo legale

stay (n) *[time]* permanenza (f)

stay (v) fermarsi

stay of execution sospensiva (f)

steadiness saldezza (f)

sterling lira (f) sterlina

stevedore stivatore (m) *o* scaricatore (m) (di porto)

stiff competition concorrenza (f) dura

stimulate the economy stimolare l'economia

stimulus stimolo (m)

stipulate stipulare

stipulation stipula (f)

stock (adj) *[normal]* standard *o* usuale

stock (n) *[goods]* stock (m) *o* scorte (fpl)

stock (v) *[goods]* rifornire *o* tenere

stock code codice (m) di magazzino

stock control controllo (m) delle scorte

stock controller persona (f) addetta al controllo delle scorte

stock exchange Borsa (f) *o* Borsa Valori

stock level livello (m) delle scorte

stock list inventario (m)

stock market mercato (m) azionario

stock market valuation valutazione (f) del mercato azionario

stock of raw materials riserva (f) di materia prima

stock size misura (f) *o* taglia (f) standard

stock turnover rotazione (f) delle scorte

stock up immagazzinare

stock valuation valutazione (f) delle scorte

stockbroker agente (m) di cambio

stockbroking mediazione (f) di cambio

stockist rivenditore (m)

stocklist inventario (m)

stockpile (n) scorta (f) (di materie prime)

stockpile (v) costruire riserve *o* stoccare

stockroom magazzino (m)

stocktaking inventario (m)

stocktaking sale saldi (mpl) per inventario

stop (n) stop (m) *o* fine (f) *o* arresto (m)

stop (v) *[doing something]* cessare *o* finire

stop a cheque bloccare un assegno

stop an account bloccare un conto

stop payments sospendere i pagamenti

stoppage *[act of stopping]* sospensione (f)

stoppage of payments sospensione (f) dei pagamenti

storage (n) *[computer]* memoria (f)

storage (n) *[cost]* spese (fpl) di immagazzinamento

storage (n) *[in warehouse]* magazzinaggio (m) *o* deposito (m)

storage capacity capienza (f) di magazzino

storage facilities impianti (m) di magazzinaggio

storage unit impianto (m) di magazzinaggio

store (n) *[items kept]* riserva (f)

store (n) *[large shop]* negozio (m) *o* grande magazzino (m)

store (n) *[place where goods are kept]* deposito (m) *o* magazzino (m)

store (v) *[keep for future]* mettere in serbo

store (v) *[keep in warehouse]* immagazzinare

storeroom magazzino (m)

storm damage danni (mpl) causati da un temporale

straight line depreciation ammortamento (m) a quote costanti

strategic strategico

strategic planning pianificazione (f) strategica

strategy strategia (f)

street directory guida (f) stradale

strike (n) sciopero (m)

strike (v) scioperare

striker scioperante (m)

strong forte

strong currency divisa (f) forte

structural strutturale

structural adjustment correzione (f) strutturale

structural unemployment disoccupazione (f) strutturale

structure (n) struttura (f)

structure (v) *[arrange]* strutturare

study (n) studio (m)

study (v) studiare

sub judice in contenzioso

subcontract (n) subappalto (m)

subcontract (v) dare in subappalto

subcontractor subappaltatore (m)

subject to soggetto a

sublease (n) subaffitto (m)

sublease (v) subaffittare

sublessee subaffittuario (m)

sublessor subaffittante (m)

sublet subaffittare

subsidiary (adj) sussidiario

subsidiary (n) filiale (f)

subsidiary company affiliata (f)

subsidize sovvenzionare

subsidy sussidio (m) *o* sovvenzione (f)

subtotal totale (m) parziale

subvention sovvenzione (f)

succeed *[do as planned]* riuscire

succeed *[do well]* riuscire *o* avere successo

succeed *[follow someone]* succedere

success successo (m)

successful di successo

successful bidder miglior offerente (m)

sue citare *o* intentare causa

suffer damage subire un danno

sufficient sufficiente

sum *[of money]* somma (f)

sum *[total]* totale (m)

summons citazione (f) in giudizio

sundries articoli (mpl) vari

sundry items partite (fpl) varie

superior (adj) *[better quality]* superiore

superior (n) *[person]* superiore (m)

supermarket supermercato (m)

superstore grande supermercato (m) *o* ipermercato (m)

supervise sorvegliare

supervision supervisione (f) *o* vigilanza (f)

supervisor supervisore (m)

supervisory ispettivo *o* di supervisione

supplementary supplementare

supplier fornitore (m)

supply (n) *[action]* fornitura (f)

supply (n) *[stock of goods]* provvista (f)

supply (v) fornire *o* approvvigionare

supply and demand offerta (f) e domanda (f)

supply price prezzo (m) d'offerta

supply side economics economia (f) dell'offerta

support price prezzo (m) di sostegno

surcharge sovrapprezzo (m)

surety (n) *[person]* garante (m)

surety (n) *[security]* garanzia (f)

surface mail posta (f) ordinaria

surface transport trasporto (m) di superficie

surplus surplus (m) *o* sovrappiù (m)

surrender (n) *[insurance policy]* riscatto (m)

surrender (v) *[insurance]* riscattare

surrender a policy riscattare una polizza

surrender value valore (m) di riscatto

survey (n) *[examination]* indagine (f) *o* studio (m)

survey (n) *[general report]* quadro (m) generale

survey (v) *[inspect]* esaminare *o* ispezionare

surveyor perito (m)

suspend sospendere

suspension sospensione (f)

suspension of deliveries cessazione (f) delle consegne

suspension of payments sospensione (f) dei pagamenti

swap (n) scambio (m)

swap (v) scambiare

swatch ritaglio (m) (di campioni)

switch (v) *[change]* cambiare

switch over to passare a

switchboard centralino (m)

swop (= swap) scambiare

sympathy strike sciopero (m) di solidarietà

synergy sinergia (f)

system sistema (m)

systems analysis analisi (f) dei sistemi

systems analyst analista (m) dei sistemi

Tt

tabulate tabulare

tabulation tabulazione (f)

tabulator tabulatore (m)

tachograph tachigrafo (m)

tacit agreement tacito accordo (m)

tacit approval tacito consenso (m)

take (n) *[money received]* incasso (m)

take (v) *[need]* volere *o* richiedere

take (v) *[receive money]* guadagnare

take a call prendere una telefonata

take a risk correre un rischio

take action agire

take legal action intentare azione legale

take legal advice ricorrere a consulenza legale

take note prendere nota

take off *[deduct]* dedurre *o* fare uno sconto di

take off *[plane]* decollare

take off *[rise fast]* decollare

take on freight prendere un carico (m) a bordo

take on more staff assumere altro personale

take out a policy sottoscrivere una polizza

take over *[from someone else]* succedere

take place avere luogo

take someone to court portare qualcuno in tribunale

take stock fare l'inventario

take the initiative prendere l'iniziativa

take the soft option scegliere la strada più facile

take time off work prendersi giorni di ferie

take up an option esercitare il diritto d'opzione

takeover acquisizione (f) di controllo

takeover bid offerta (f) pubblica d'acquisto

takeover target obiettivo (m) di rilevamento

takings incassi (mpl)

tangible tangibile

tangible assets beni (mpl) reali

tanker petroliera (f)

tare tara (f)

target (n) obiettivo (m)

target (v) stabilire come obiettivo

target market mercato (m) prescelto

tariff *[price]* tariffa (f)

tariff barriers barriere (fpl) tariffarie

tax (n) tassa (f) *o* imposta (f)

tax (v) tassare *o* gravare d'imposta

tax adjustments adeguamento (m) fiscale

tax allowance riduzione (f) d'imposta

tax assessment accertamento (m) fiscale

tax avoidance evasione (f) fiscale

tax code codice (m) fiscale

tax collection riscossione (f) delle imposte

tax collector esattore (m) delle imposte

tax concession concessione (f) fiscale

tax consultant consulente (m) fiscale

tax credit credito (m) d'imposta

tax deducted at source imposta (f) trattenuta alla fonte

tax deductions *[taken from salary to pay tax]* detrazioni (fpl) d'imposta

tax evasion evasione (f) fiscale

tax exemption esenzione (f) fiscale

tax form modulo (m) delle tasse

tax haven rifugio (m) fiscale

tax inspector ispettore (m) delle tasse

tax loophole sotterfugio (m) fiscale

tax offence infrazione (f) fiscale

tax paid imposta (f) pagata

tax rate aliquota (f) d'imposta

tax reductions riduzioni (fpl) d'imposta

tax relief agevolazione (f) fiscale

tax return *or* **tax declaration** denuncia (f) dei redditi

tax shelter scappatoia (f) fiscale

tax system sistema (m) tributario

tax year anno (m) fiscale

tax-deductible detraibile dal reddito imponibile

tax-exempt esentasse

tax-free esente da tasse

taxable tassabile

taxable income reddito (m) imponibile

taxation tassazione (f)

taxpayer contribuente (m)

telephone (n) telefono (m)

telephone (v) telefonare

telephone book elenco (m) telefonico

telephone call chiamata (f) telefonica

telephone directory elenco (m) telefonico

telephone exchange centralino (m) telefonico

telephone line linea (f) telefonica

telephone number numero (m) telefonico *o* numero di telefono

telephone subscriber abbonato (m) al telefono

telephone switchboard centralino (m) telefonico

telephonist telefonista (mf)

telesales vendite (fpl) per telefono

telex (n) telescrivente (f) *o* telex (m)

teller sportellista (m)

temp (n) segretaria (f) temporanea

temp agency agenzia (f) che fornisce personale temporaneo

temporary employment lavoro (m) *ı* contratto a termine

temporary staff personale (m) avventizio

tenancy *[agreement]* contratto (m) di locazione

tenancy *[period]* locazione (f)

tenant inquilino (m)

tender (n) *[offer to work]* licitazione (f) *o* offerta (f) d'appalto

tender for a contract fare offerta per un contratto d'appalto

tenderer offerente (m)

tendering licitazione (f)

tenure *[right]* diritto (m) di possesso

tenure *[time]* durata (f) in carica

term *[part of academic year]* trimestre (m) scolastico

term *[time of validity]* periodo (m) *o* durata (f)

term insurance assicurazione (f) temporanea

term loan prestito (m) a termine

terminal (adj) *[at the end]* terminale

terminal (n) *[airport]* terminal (m)

terminal bonus premio (m)
(d'assicurazione) finale

terminate terminare

terminate an agreement rescindere un
accordo

termination termine (m)

termination clause clausola (f) di
rescissione

terms condizioni (fpl)

terms of employment condizioni (fpl)
di impiego

terms of payment condizioni (fpl) di
pagamento

terms of reference termini (mpl)
stabiliti

terms of sale condizioni (fpl) di vendita

territory *[of salesman]* territorio (m)

tertiary industry industria (f) terziaria

tertiary sector settore (m) terziario

test (n) prova (f)

test (v) provare

theft furto (m)

third party terza persona (f)

third quarter terzo trimestre (m)

third-party insurance assicurazione
(f) per danni verso terzi

threshold soglia (f)

threshold agreement accordo (m) di
indicizzazione

threshold price prezzo (m) d'entrata

throughput produttività (f)

tie-up *[link]* collegamento (m)

tight money denaro (m) scarso

tighten up on restringere

till (n) cassa (f)

time and motion study studio (m) dei
tempi e dei movimenti

time deposit deposito (m) a termine

time limit termine (m) ultimo

time limitation perenzione (f)

time rate tariffa (f) a tempo

time scale scala (f) temporale

time: on time puntuale *o* in orario

timetable (n) *[appointments]*
programma (m)

timetable (n) *[trains, etc.]* orario (m)

timetable (v) programmare

timing scelta (f) del momento
opportuno

tip (n) *[advice]* informazione (f)
riservata

tip (n) *[money]* mancia (f)

tip (v) *[give money]* dare la mancia a

tip (v) *[say what might happen]*
pronosticare

**TIR (= Transports Internationaux
Routiers)** Trasporto Internazionale su
Strada

token simbolo (m)

token charge costo (m) simbolico

token payment pagamento (m)
simbolico

toll pedaggio (m)

toll free *[US]* esente da pedaggio

toll free number *[US]* servizio (m)
telefonico gratuito

ton tonnellata (f)

tonnage tonnellaggio (m)

tonne tonnellata (f)

tool up attrezzare (una fabbrica)

top (adj) più alto *o* migliore

top (n) *[highest point]* cima (f) *o* vetta
(f)

top (n) *[upper surface]* parte (f)
superiore

top (v) *[go higher than]* superare

top management direzione (f) al
vertice

top quality qualità (f) superiore

top-selling che è in testa alle vendite

total (adj) totale *o* globale

total (n) totale (m)

total (v) ammontare a

total amount importo (m) totale

total assets totale (m) delle attività

total cost costo (m) totale

total expenditure spesa (f) totale

total income reddito (m) totale

total invoice value valore (m) totale
della fattura

total output produzione (f) totale

total revenue reddito (m) complessivo

track record curricolo (m)

trade (n) *[business]* commercio (m)

trade (v) commerciare *o* trafficare

trade agreement trattato (m)
commerciale

trade association associazione (f)
commerciale

trade cycle ciclo (m) economico

trade deficit or **trade gap** deficit (m) della bilancia commerciale

trade description descrizione (f) commerciale

trade directory annuario (m) commerciale

trade discount sconto (m) ai rivenditori

trade fair fiera (f) campionaria

trade in *[buy and sell]* commerciare in o trafficare in

trade in *[give in old item for new]* farsi ritirare l'usato

trade journal giornale (m) di categoria

trade magazine rivista (f) di categoria

trade mission missione (f) commerciale

trade price prezzo (m) al rivenditore

trade terms sconti (mpl) al rivenditore

trade union sindacato (m)

trade unionist sindacalista (m)

trade-in *[old item in exchange]* permuta (f)

trade-in price prezzo (m) di permuta

trademark or **trade name** marchio (m)

trader commerciante (m)

trading commerciale

trading company società (f) commerciale

trading loss perdita (f) d'esercizio

trading partner partner (m) commerciale

trading profit utile (m) d'esercizio

train (n) treno (m)

train (v) *[learn]* fare pratica

train (v) *[teach]* istruire

trainee tirocinante (m)

traineeship apprendistato (m)

training formazione (f)

training levy contributo (m) aziendale per l'addestramento

training officer funzionario (m) addetto all'addestramento

transact business fare affari

transaction transazione (f)

transfer (n) trasferimento (m)

transfer (v) *[move to new place]* trasferire

transfer of funds trasferimento (m) di capitali

transferable trasferibile

transferred charge call telefonata (f) a carico del ricevente

transit transito (m)

transit lounge sala (f) transiti

transit visa visto (m) consolare di transito

translate tradurre

translation traduzione (f)

translation bureau ufficio (m) traduzioni

translator traduttore (m), traduttrice (f)

transport (n) trasporto (m)

transport (v) trasportare

transport facilities servizi (mpl) di trasporto

treasury tesoreria (f)

treble triplo

trend andamento (m)

trial *[court case]* processo (m)

trial *[test of product]* prova (f)

trial and error metodo (m) per tentativi

trial balance bilancio (m) di verifica

trial period periodo (m) di prova

trial sample campione (m) di prova

triple (adj) triplo

triple (v) triplicare

triplicate: in triplicate in triplice copia

troubleshooter mediatore (m)

truck *[lorry]* camion (m)

truck *[railway wagon]* carro (m) merci

trucker camionista (m)

trucking trasporto (m) mediante autocarro

true copy copia (f) autentica

trust company società (f) fiduciaria

turn down rifiutare

turn over (v) *[make sales]* avere un giro d'affari di

turnkey operation operazione (f) chiavi in mano

turnkey operator costruttore (m) chiavi in mano

turnover *[of staff]* ricambio (m)

turnover *[of stock]* movimento (m)

turnover *[sales]* volume (m) d'affari

turnover tax imposta (f) sul volume d'affari

turnround *[goods sold]* rotazione (f)

turnround *[making profitable]* inversione (f) di tendenza

turnround *[of plane]* rotazione (f)

Uu

unaccounted for inspiegato

unaudited non verificato

unaudited accounts contabilità (f) non sottoposta a revisione contabile

unauthorized expenditure spesa (f) non autorizzata

unavailability non disponibilità (f)

unavailable non disponibile

unchanged immutato

unchecked figures cifre (fpl) non verificate

unclaimed baggage bagagli (mpl) non reclamati

unconditional incondizionato

unconfirmed non confermato

undated non datato

undelivered non consegnato

under *[according to]* secondo

under *[less than]* meno di *o* inferiore

under construction in costruzione

under contract sotto contratto

under control sotto controllo

under new management sotto nuova gestione

undercharge far pagare meno

undercut a rival vendere a minor prezzo di un concorrente

underdeveloped countries paesi (mpl) sottosviluppati

underequipped con attrezzatura insufficiente

underpaid malpagato

undersell vendere sotto costo

undersigned sottoscritto

underspend spendere meno

understand capire

understanding intesa (f)

undertake intraprendere

undertaking *[company]* azienda (f) *o* impresa (f)

undertaking *[promise]* compito (m) *o* impegno (m)

underwrite *[guarantee]* garantire

underwrite *[pay costs]* finanziare

underwriting syndicate gruppo (m) di collocamento

undischarged bankrupt fallito (m) non riabilitato

uneconomic rent affitto (m) non redditizio

unemployed disoccupato

unemployment disoccupazione (f)

unemployment pay sussidio (m) di disoccupazione

unfair ingiusto

unfair competition concorrenza (f) sleale

unfair dismissal licenziamento (m) ingiusto

unfavourable sfavorevole

unfavourable exchange rate tasso (m) di cambio sfavorevole

unfulfilled order ordinazione (f) inevasa

unilateral unilaterale

union sindacato (m)

union recognition riconoscimento (m) sindacale

unique selling point *or* **proposition** (USP) proposta (f) unica di vendita

unit *[in unit trust]* azione (f)

unit *[item]* unità (f)

unit cost costo (m) unitario

unit price prezzo (m) unitario

unit trust fondo (m) comune di investimento

unlimited liability responsabilità (f) illimitata

unload *[get rid of]* disfarsi di

unload *[goods]* scaricare

unobtainable non ottenibile

unofficial non ufficiale *o* ufficioso

unpaid non pagato

unpaid invoices fatture (fpl) insolute

unsealed envelope busta (f) aperta

unsecured creditor creditore (m) non garantito

unskilled non specializzato

unsold invenduto

unsubsidized senza sovvenzioni

unsuccessful che non ha successo

up front anticipato

up to fino a *o* conforme a

up to date *[complete]* aggiornato

up to date *[modern]* moderno *o* attuale

up-market rivolto a una fascia alta del mercato

update (n) aggiornamento (m)

update (v) aggiornare *o* mettere al corrente

upset price prezzo (m) d'apertura

upturn miglioramento (m)

upward trend tendenza (f) al rialzo

urgent urgente

use (n) uso (m)

use (v) usare

use up spare capacity impiegare la capacità produttiva inutilizzata

useful utile

user utente (m)

user-friendly facile da usare *o* accessibile

USP (= unique selling point *or* **proposition)** proposta (f) unica di vendita

usual solito *o* abituale

utilization utilizzazione (f)

Vv

vacancy *[for job]* posto (m) vacante

vacant vacante

vacate lasciar vuoto

valid valido

validity validità (f)

valuation valutazione (f)

value (n) valore (m)

value (v) valutare

value added tax (VAT) imposta sul valore aggiunto (IVA)

valuer stimatore (m)

van furgone (m)

variable costs costi (mpl) variabili

variance variazione (f)

variation variazione (f)

VAT (= value added tax) imposta sul valore aggiunto (IVA)

VAT declaration dichiarazione (f) IVA

VAT inspector ispettore (m) IVA

VAT invoice fattura con IVA

vehicle veicolo (m)

vendor venditore (m)

venture (n) *[business]* affare (m) rischioso

venture (v) *[risk]* rischiare

venture capital capitale (m) di rischio

venue luogo (m) di ritrovo

verbal verbale

verbal agreement accordo (m) verbale

verification verifica (f)

verify verificare

vertical communication comunicazione (f) verticale

vertical integration integrazione (f) verticale

vested interest interessi (mpl) costituiti

veto a decision porre il veto a una decisione

via via *o* tramite

viable realizzabile

VIP lounge sala (f) per VIP

visa visto (m) consolare

visible imports importazioni (fpl) visibili

visible trade partite (fpl) visibili

void (adj) *[not valid]* nullo

void (v) invalidare *o* annullare

volume volume (m)

volume discount sconto (m) sul quantitativo

volume of sales volume (m) delle vendite

volume of trade *or* **volume of business** volume (m) degli scambi commerciali

voluntary liquidation liquidazione (f) volontaria

voluntary redundancy cassa (f) integrazione volontaria

vote of thanks ringraziamento (m)

voucher *[document from an auditor]* pezza (f) giustificativa

voucher *[paper given instead of money]* buono (m)

Ww

wage salario (m)

wage claim rivendicazione (f) salariale

wage freeze congelamento (m) salariale

wage levels livelli (mpl) salariali

wage negotiations negoziato (m) salariale

wage scale scala (f) retributiva

waive rinunciare

waive a payment rinunciare ad un pagamento

waiver *[of right]* rinuncia (f)

waiver clause clausola (f) di recessione

warehouse (n) magazzino (m)

warehouse (v) immagazzinare

warehouseman magazziniere (m)

warehousing magazzinaggio (m)

warrant (n) *[document]* autorizzazione (f)

warrant (v) *[guarantee]* garantire

warrant (v) *[justify]* giustificare

warranty (n) garanzia (f)

wastage spreco (m)

waste (n) spreco (m)

waste (v) (use too much) sprecare

waybill lettera (f) di vettura

weak market mercato (m) fiacco

wear and tear deterioramento (m) naturale

week settimana (f)

weekly settimanale

weigh pesare

weighbridge pesa a ponte (f)

weight peso (m)

weight limit limite (m) di peso

weighted average media (f) ponderata

weighted index indice (m) ponderato

weighting ponderazione (f)

well-paid job lavoro (m) ben pagato

wharf molo (m)

white knight 'cavaliere (m) bianco'

whole-life insurance assicurazione (f) sulla vita

wholesale (adv) all'ingrosso

wholesale dealer commerciante (m) all'ingrosso

wholesale discount sconto (m) all'ingrosso

wholesale price index indice (m) dei prezzi all'ingrosso

wholesaler commerciante (m) all'ingrosso

wildcat strike sciopero (m) selvaggio

win a contract vincere un contratto

wind up *[a company]* mettere in liquidazione

wind up *[a meeting]* dichiarare sciolta una riunione

winding up liquidazione (f) *o* scioglimento (m)

window finestra (f)

window display esposizione (f) in vetrina

withdraw *[an offer]* ritirare

withdraw *[money]* prelevare

withdraw a takeover bid ritrattare un'offerta di rilevamento

withdrawal *[of money]* ritiro (m)

withholding tax ritenuta (f) d'acconto

witness (n) testimone (m)

witness (v) *[a document]* firmare come testimone

witness an agreement firmare un accordo come testimone

word-processing videoscrittura (f)

wording dicitura (f)

work (n) lavoro (m)

work (v) lavorare

work in progress lavori in corso

work permit permesso (m) di lavoro

work-to-rule sciopero (m) bianco

worker lavoratore (m), lavoratrice (f)

worker director lavoratore che fa parte del consiglio di amministrazione e che agisce come portavoce del personale

workforce forza (f) lavoro

working (adj) attivo

working capital capitale (m) d'esercizio

working conditions condizioni (fpl) di lavoro

working party commissione (f) di studio

workshop officina (f)

workstation *[at computer]* posto (m) di lavoro

world mondo (m)

world market mercato (m) mondiale

worldwide (adj) mondiale

worldwide (adv) in tutto il mondo

worth (n) *[value]* valore (m)

worth: be worth valere

worthless privo di valore

wrap up *[discussion]* concludere

wrap up *[goods]* impaccare

wrapper confezionatore (m)

wrapping involucro (m) *o* imballaggio (m)

wrapping paper carta (f) da imballaggio

wreck (n) *[company]* impresa (f) fallita

wreck (n) *[ship]* nave (f) naufragata

wreck (v) *[ruin]* distruggere

writ mandato (m)

write scrivere

write down *[assets]* ridurre il valore

write off *[debt]* annullare

write out redigere

write out a cheque compilare un assegno

write-off *[loss]* svalutazione (f)

writedown *[of asset]* svalutazione (f)

writing scrittura (f)

written agreement accordo (m) scritto

wrong sbagliato

wrongful dismissal licenziamento (m) ingiustificato

Xx Yy Zz

year anno (m)

year end fine (f) esercizio

yearly payment pagamento (m) annuale

yellow pages Pagine Gialle (fpl)

yield (n) *[on investment]* rendita (f)

yield (v) *[interest]* rendere

zero zero (m)

zero-rated aliquota (f) nulla

zip code *[US]* codice (m) d'avviamento postale

Italiano-Inglese
Italian-English

Aa

abbandonare *[lasciare]* abandon; leave

abbassare lower (v)

abbassare *[ridurre il prezzo]* knock down *or* knock off *or* reduce price

abbassare i prezzi lower prices

abbassare il prezzo (di articoli) mark down

abbonato (m) al telefono telephone subscriber

abbozzare *[redigere]* draft (v)

abile *[qualificato]* qualified *[skilled]*

abilità (f) *[capacità]* capacity *or* ability

abilità (f) tecnica skill

abitante (m) *[residente]* inhabitant *or* resident (n)

abituale (solito) usual *or* routine

abolire i controlli (mpl) decontrol

abolizione (f) della regolamentazione deregulation

accantonamento (m) shelving *or* postponing

accantonamento (m) *[riserva]* provision *or* money put aside

accantonamento (m) al fondo di ammortamento allowance for depreciation

accantonare (differire) shelve

accantonare *[accumulare]* accumulate

accantonare fondi (mpl) per un progetto earmark funds for a project

accaparramento (m) hoarding *[of goods]*

accaparramento (m) *[monopolio]* corner (n) *or* monopoly

accaparrarsi il mercato (m) corner the market

accertamento (m) dei danni assessment of damages

accertamento (m) fiscale tax assessment

accertamento (m) patrimoniale means test

accertare *[stabilire il valore]* assess

accertare i danni assess damages

accessibile *[facile da usare]* user-friendly

accessori (mpl) fittings

accettabile *[soddisfacente]* acceptable

accettar accept (v)

accettar accept (v) *or* agree

accettare di fare qualcosa agree to do something

accettare una cambiale accept a bill

accettazione (f) acceptance

accettazione (f) di un'offerta acceptance of an offer

accidentale *[casuale]* random

accomodamento (m) composition *[with creditors]*

accomodamento (m) *[accordo]* adjustment

acconsentire a fare qualcosa agree to do something

acconto (m) deposit (n) *[paid in advance]*

accont : in acconto on account

accordare *[cedere]* allow *or* give

accordare *[concedere]* grant (v)

accordo (m) settlement *or* agreement

accord : essere d'accordo con agree with *[be of the same opinion]*

accordo (m) *[accomodamento]* adjustment

accordo (m) *[intesa]* arrangement *or* compromise

accordo (m) aperto open-ended agreement

accordo (m) bilaterale reciprocal agreement

accordo (m) creditizio di sostegno standby arrangements

accordo (m) di indicizzazione threshold agreement

accordo (m) di lunga data long-standing agreement

accordo (m) di marketing marketing agreement

accordo (m) in esclusiva exclusive agreement

accordo (m) multilaterale multilateral agreement

accordo (m) parziale one-sided agreement

accordo (m) scritto written agreement

accordo (m) sulla parola (f) gentleman's agreement

accordo (m) sulla produttività productivity agreement

accordo (m) verbale verbal agreement

accord -tipo (m) model agreement

accreditare (un conto) credit (v)

accumulare accumulate

accumularsi *[maturare]* accrue

accurato *[preciso]* accurate

accusa (f) charge (n) *[in court]*

accusare ricevuta di una lettera acknowledge receipt of a letter

accusato (m) defendant

acquirente (m) *[cliente]* shopper

acquirente (m) genuino genuine purchaser

acquisizione (f) *[acquisto]* acquisition

acquisizione (f) di controllo contestata contested takeover

acquisizione (f) di controllo inversa reverse takeover

acquistare *[comperare]* purchase (v)

acquisti (mpl) shopping *[goods bought]*

acquisto (m) purchase (n); purchasing *or* buying

acquisto (m) a termine forward buying

acquisto (m) centralizzato central purchasing

acquisto (m) di una società da parte dei suoi stessi dirigenti management buyout (MBO)

acquisto (m) fatto per impulso impulse purchase

acquisto (m) in massa bulk buying

acquisto (m) per contanti cash purchase

acquisto (m) rateale hire purchase (HP)

acquisto (m) *[acquisizione]* acquisition *or* purchase

ad alta definizione near letter-quality (NLQ)

ad valorem ad valorem

adattamento (m) stagionale seasonal adjustments

adattare *[adeguare]* adjust

addebitare un acquisto charge a purchase

addebitare un conto debit an account

addebitare una telefonata al ricevente reverse the charges

addebiti (mpl) per interessi interest charges

addebito (m) debit (n)

addebito (m) diretto direct debit

addestramento (m) dei dirigenti management training

addestramento (m) interno (alla ditta) in-house training

addestramento (m) sul lavoro on-the-job training

addetto (m) al controllo dell'avanzamento progress chaser

addetto (m) alle pubbliche relazioni public relations man

addetto (m) alle vendite sales clerk

addetto (m) commerciale commercial attaché

addizionale (supplementare) additional

addizione (f) addition *[calculation]*

adeguamento (m) fiscale tax adjustments

adeguare *[adattare]* adjust

adeguato *[sufficiente]* adequate

adempimento (m) fulfilment

adempimento (m) di un contratto completion of a contract

adibire ad altro uso redevelop

aereo (m) plane

aereo (m) da carico freight plane

aeroplano (m) a noleggio charter plane

aeroporto (m) airport

affare (m) business *[discussion]*

affare (m) *[occasione]* bargain (n) *[cheaper than usual]*

affare (m) *[operazione]* deal (n)

affare (m) poco vantaggioso hard bargain

affare (m) rischioso venture (n) *or* risky deal

affari (mpl) business *[commerce]*

affari: fare affari do business *or* transact business

affermare claim (v) *or* suggest

affermativo affirmative

affidare entrust

affidare fondi ad un progetto commit funds to a project

affiliata (f) subsidiary company

affiliato *[associato]* affiliated

affitansi uffici (mpl) offices to let

affittare *[impianti]* lease equipment

affittar let (v)

affittare *[dare in affitto]* lease out (v) *[of landlord]*

affittare *[tenere in affitto]* lease (v) *[of tenant]*

affittare un negozio let an office

affitto (m) lease (n)

affitto (m) rent

affitto (m) alto high rent

affitto (m) nominale nominal rent

affitto (m) non redditizio uneconomic rent

affittuario (m) lessee

affittuario (m) occupante sitting tenant

affrancar frank (v)

affrancare *[mettere francobolli]* stamp (v) a letter

affrancatura (f) pagata postpaid

affrettarsi hurry up

agenda (f) appointments book

agenda (f) da tavolo desk diary

agenda (f) tascabile pocket diary

agente (m) agent *[working in an agency]*

agente (m) *[rappresentante]* agent *or* representative

agente (m) commissionario commission agent

agente (m) di assicurazione insurance agent

agente (m) di brevetti patent agent

agente (m) di cambio stockbroker

agente (m) di factoring factor (n) *[person]*

agente (m) doganale customs broker

agente (m) in cambi foreign exchange broker

agente (m) marittimo ship broker

agente (m) del credere del credere agent

agenzia (f) agency

agenzia (f) che fornisce personale temporaneo temp agency

agenzia (f) di lavoro employment agency *or* employment bureau

agenzia (f) di stampa news agency

agenzia (f) immobiliare letting agency

agenzia (f) per il recupero dei crediti debt collection agency

agenzia (f) per reperimento di referenze credit agency

agenzia (f) di pubblicità advertising agency

agevolazione (f) concession *[reduction]*

agevolazione (f) fiscale tax relief

agevolazioni (fpl) creditizie credit facilities

aggiornamento (m) update (n)

aggiornamento (m) *[sollecito]* follow up

aggiornare *[mettere al corrente]* update *or* bring up to date

aggiornare *[rimandare]* adjourn

aggiornare una riunione adjourn a meeting

aggiornato up to date *[complete]*

aggirare get round *[a problem]*

aggiudicare un contratto a qualcuno award a contract to someone

aggiudicazione (f) *[giudizio]* adjudication

aggiungere *[sommare]* add

aggiungere il 10% per il servizio add on 10% for service

aggiunta (f) addition *[thing added]*

aggiustare *[riparare]* repair (v)

agire act (v) *or* do something *or* take action

agricolo *o* **agrario** agricultural

aiuto (m) *[assistenza]* assistance

aiuto (m) *[appoggio]* backing

al giorno per day

alla settimana per week

albergo (m) *[hotel]* hotel

albergo (m) selezionato graded hotel

alimentatore (m) di fogli paper feed

alimentazione (f) continua continuous feed

aliquota (f) d'imposta tax rate

aliquota (f) d'imposta base standard rate (of tax)

all'anno per year *or* per annum

all'avanguardia state-of-the-art

all'estero abroad *or* overseas

all'estero *[offshore]* offshore

all'ingrosso wholesale (adv)

all'ora per hour

allargamento (m) expansion

allegare enclose

allegato (m) enclosure

altamente qualificato highly qualified

altamente retribuito highly-paid

alternativa (f) alternative (n)

alternativo alternative (adj)

altezza: essere all'altezza cope *or* be up to

americano American (adj)

Americano, -ana American (n)

ammanco (m) shortfall

ammasso (m) hoard

ammettere admit *or* agree

amministrare *[gestire]* manage

amministrare un patrimonio manage property

amministrativo administrative

amministratore (m) director

amministratore (m) di società company director

amministratore (m) delegato *[direttore generale]* managing director (MD)

amministrazione (f) *[gestione]* administration

ammissione (f) admission

ammontare (m) *[importo]* amount *[of money]*

ammontare a amount to *or* total (v)

ammortamento (m) amortization *or* depreciation

ammortamento (m) a quote costanti straight line depreciation

ammortamento (m) accelerato accelerated depreciation

ammortare *o* **ammortizzare** amortize *or* depreciate

ampliare expand

anagrafe (f) registry office

analisi (f) analysis

analisi (f) dei costi cost analysis

analisi (f) dei sistemi systems analysis

analisi (f) del progetto project analysis

analisi (f) delle mansioni job analysis

analisi (f) delle vendite sales analysis

analisi (f) di mercato market analysis

analisi (f) preventiva della convenienza dei costi cost-benefit analysis

analisi (f) statistica statistical analysis

analista (m) dei costi cost accountant

analista (m) dei sistemi systems analyst

analista (m) di mercato market analyst

analizzare analyse *or* analyze

analizzare il potenziale del mercato analyse the market potential

andamento (m) trend

andare go

andare in pensione retire *[from one's job]*

andare incontro ad una richiesta meet a demand

anno (m) year

anno (m) di base base year

anno (m) fiscale tax year

anno (m) solare calendar year

annotazione (f) entering

annuale *[annuo]* annual

annualmente annually *or* on an annual basis

annuario (m) directory

annuario (m) commerciale commercial directory *or* trade directory

annullamento (m) invalidation

annullare *[cancellare]* cancel

annullare *[invalidare]* void (v)

annullare un assegno cancel a cheque

annullare un contratto cancel a contract

annullato cancelled *or* off

annunci (mpl) economici (su giornale) classified ads *or* classified advertisements

annunciare announce

annuncio (m) announcement

annuncio (m) pubblicitario *[pubblicità]* advertisement

annuo *[annuale]* annual

anticipato advance (adj) *or* up front

anticipazione (f) su un conto advance on account

anticipo (m) advance (n) *[loan]*

anticipo (m) in contanti cash advance

antiquato obsolete *or* old-fashioned

anziano *[piu vecchio]* senior

aperto open (adj)

aperto ad offerte open to offers

apertura (f) opening (n)

apertura: d'apertura *[iniziale]* opening (adj) *or* initial

apertura (f) sul mercato gap in the market

appaltare lavoro farm out work

apparecchiatura (f) equipment

apparecchiatura (f) d'ufficio business equipment

apparecchiatura (f) difettosa faulty equipment

apparecchiatura (f) pesante heavy equipment

appartamento (m) flat (n)

appartenere a belong to

appellare *[ricorrere in appello]* appeal (v) *[against a decision]*

appello (m) *[ricorso]* appeal (n) *[against a decision]*

appendice (f) appendix

applicare enforce

appoggio (m) *[aiuto]* backing

apportare bring in

apporto (m) di capitali contribution of capital

apprendista (m) junior clerk

apprendista (m) in direzione aziendale management trainee

apprendistato (m) traineeship

apprezzamento (m) appreciation *[how good something is]*

apprezzare appreciate *[how good something is]*

appropriarsi indebitamente embezzle *or* misappropriate

appropriazione (f) indebita embezzlement *or* misappropriation

approssimativamente approximately

approssimativo approximate *or* rough

approvare approve *or* agree

approvare: far approvare carry *or* approve in a vote

approvare i termini di un contratto approve the terms of a contract

approvvigionare *[fornire]* supply (v)

appuntamento (m) appointment *[meeting]*

aprire open (v) *[start new business]*

aprire fino a notte tarda late-night opening

aprire trattative open negotiations

aprire un conto open an account

aprire un conto bancario open a bank account

aprire una lettera di credito issue a letter of credit

aprire una linea di credito open a line of credit

aprire una seduta open a meeting

arbitrare una vertenza arbitrate in a dispute

arbitrato (m) arbitration

arbitro (m) arbitrator

archivio (m) (di un computer) computer file

archivio (m) *[documentazione]* records

area (f) *o* regione (f) area *or* region

area (f) *[campo]* field

area (f) del dollaro dollar area

area (f) di carico loading bay

area (f) problematica problem area

area (f) uffici office space

arenarsi (di trattative) break down (v) *[of talks]*

argomento (m) *[questione]* item on agenda *or* matter to be discussed

aria (f) air

armonizzazione (f) harmonization

arredamento (m) per ufficio office furniture

arrestare check (v) *or* stop

arresto (m) check (n) *or* stop

arretrati (mpl) arrears

arrivare arrive

arrivare a reach *or* come to

arrivare ad una decisione reach a decision

arrivi (mpl) arrivals

arrivo (m) arrival

arrotondare aumentando round up

arrotondare diminuendo round down

articoli (mpl) deperibili perishable goods

articoli (mpl) che vendono rapidamente fast-selling items

articoli (mpl) di lusso luxury goods

articoli (mpl) diversi miscellaneous items

articoli (mpl) non ricorrenti non-recurring items

articoli (mpl) vari sundries

articolo (m) *[prodotto]* article *or* item

articolo (m) unico one-off item

ascendere *[salire]* climb

ascensore (m) lift (n)

aspettativa (f) *[congedo autorizzato]* leave of absence

assalire *[attaccare]* attack

assegnare award (v)

assegnatario (m) assignee

assegni (mpl) personalizzati personalized cheques

assegno (m) cheque

assegno (m) a copertura garantita certified cheque

assegno (m) al portatore cheque to bearer

assegno (m) circolare banker's draft *or* bank draft

assegno (m) dello stipendio pay cheque *or* salary cheque

assegno (m) di cassa cashier's check *[US]*

assegno (m) in bianco blank cheque

assegno (m) non sbarrato open cheque

assegno (m) sbarrato crossed cheque

assemblea (f) assembly *or* meeting

assemblea (f) del personale staff meeting

assemblea (f) generale general meeting

Assemblea (f) Generale degli Azionisti annual general meeting (AGM)

assemblaggio (m) *[montaggio]* assembly *[putting together]*

assente absent *or* away from work

assenza (f) *[mancanza]* absence

assicurabile insurable

assicurare insure

assicurare la vita di qualcuno assure someone's life

assicurarsi contro un rischio cover a risk

assicuratore (m) insurer

assicuratore (m) marittimo marine underwriter

assicurazione (f) insurance *or* (life) assurance

assicurazione (f) *[garanzia]* indemnity

assicurazione (f) auto motor insurance

assicurazione (f) contro gli incendi fire insurance

assicurazione (f) globale comprehensive insurance

assicurazione (f) malattie health insurance

assicurazione (f) marittima marine insurance

assicurazione (f) per danni verso terzi third-party insurance

assicurazione (f) sulla casa house insurance

assicurazione (f) sulla vita life assurance *or* life insurance

assicurazione (f) temporanea term insurance

assistente (mf) *[collaboratore]* assistant

assistenza (f) *[aiuto]* assistance

assistenza (f) post-vendita alla clientela after-sales service

assistere assist

assistere a attend (meeting)

associato associate (adj)

associato (m) *[socio]* associate (n)

associato *[affiliato]* affiliated

associazione (f) *[circolo]* association *or* society

associazione (f) commerciale trade association

associazione (f) in compartecipazione copartnership

associazione (f) in partecipazione *['joint venture']* joint venture

assoluto outright

assumere *[impiegare]* employ

assumere del personale hire staff

assumersi la responsabilità di qualcosa accept liability for something

asta (f) auction (n)

attaccare attack

attaccare *[unire]* attach

attendere istruzioni await instructions

attendibile reliable

attendibilità (f) reliability

attenzione (f) attention

attenzione: all'attenzione di FAO (for the attention of)

atterrare land (v) *[of plane]*

atteso due *[expected]*

attestato (m) *[referenze]* reference *[report on person]*

attestazione (f) ufficiale affidavit

attirare appeal to (v) *or* attract

attività (f) activity

attività (fpl) e passività (fpl) assets and liabilities

attività (f) bancaria banking

attività (f) commerciale fiorente flourishing trade

attività (f) esterna di ricerca e di studio field work

attività (f) finanziaria *[finanza]* finance (n)

attività (f) illegale racketeering

attività (fpl) immateriali intangible assets

attività (fpl) liquide current assets

attività (fpl) occulte hidden asset

attività (f) previsionale forecasting

attività (f) promozionale merchandizing

attività (f) secondaria sideline

attività (f) trascurata neglected business

attivo working (adj)

attivo (m) mobiliare personal assets

attivo (m) esigibile *[cespiti realizzabili]* realizable assets

atto (m) deed

atto (m) costitutivo deed of partnership

atto (m) costitutivo di società articles of association

atto (m) di cessione deed of assignment

atto (m) di donazione deed of covenant

atto (m) di trasferimento deed of transfer

atto (m) di vendita *[fattura]* bill of sale

attraccare *[entrare in porto]* dock (v) *[ship]*

attrarre attract

attrezzare (una fabbrica) tool up (a factory)

attrezzatura (f) per ufficio office equipment

attribuire un diritto a qualcuno assign a right to someone

attuale present (adj) *[now]*

attuale *[moderno]* up to date *[modern]*

attuale: non attuale out of date

attuare *[realizzare]* implement (v)

attuario (m) actuary

attuazione (f) implementation

aumentare gain *or* increase *or* rise *[get bigger]*

aumentare raise *or* increase

aumentare di prezzo increase in price

aumentare di valore appreciate *or* increase in value

aumentare il prezzo (di articoli) mark up (an item)

aumentare proporzionalmente scale up

aumento (m) increase *or* rise *[higher salary]*

aumento (m) increase *or* gain *[getting bigger]*

aumento: in aumento on the increase *or* mounting

aumento (m) del costo della vita cost-of-living increase

aumento (m) di paga retroattivo retroactive pay rise

aumento (m) di prezzo mark-up *[action]*

aumento (m) medio annuale mean annual increase

aumento (m) percentuale percentage increase

aumento (m) salariale pay rise

autenticare *[legalizzare]* authenticate

autenticare *[certificare]* certify

autentico *[vero]* genuine

autobus (m) bus

autobus (m) dell'aeroporto airport bus

autocopiante carbonless

autofinanziamento (m) self-financing (n)

autofinanziarsi: che può autofinanziarsi self-financing (adj)

automobile (f) car

automobile (f) di grande successo best-selling car

automobile (f) a noleggio hire car

autoregolatore self-regulatory

autoregolazione (f) self-regulation

autorità (f) authority

autorità (fpl) portuali port authority

autorizzare authorize *or* give permission *or* license

autorizzare (qualcuno a fare qualcosa) allow or permit (someone to do something)

autorizzare un pagamento authorize payment

autorizzato authorized

autorizzazione (f) authorization or permission

autorizzazione (f) warrant (n) *[document]*

avallante (m) guarantor

avallante (m) *[sostenitore]* backer

avallare stand security for

avallo (m) *[sponsorizzazione]* sponsorship

avanzare *[fare progressi]* progress (v)

avaria (f) average (n) *[insurance]*

avaria (f) generale general average

aver bisogno di require *[need]*

avere (v) carry *[have in stock]*

avere (m) *[lato dell'attivo]* credit side

avere come risultato result in

avere indietro get back *[something lost]*

avere lo scopo di aim (v)

avere luogo take place

avere successo *[riuscire]* succeed *[do well]*

avviamento (m) start-up

avviamento (m) commerciale goodwill

avvio (m) start (n)

avvisare *[informare]* advise *[tell what happened]*

avviso (m) notice or piece of information

avviso (m) di ricevimento doganale customs receipt

avviso (m) di rinnovo renewal notice

avvocato (mf) lawyer; counsel

avvocato (mf) della parte querelante prosecution counsel

avvocato (mf) difensore defence counsel

azienda (f) *[impresa]* business or firm or company

azienda (f) autonoma independent company

azienda (f) commerciale business establishment

azienda (f) con forte indebitamento highly-geared company

aziende (f) in concorrenza competing firms

azione (f) share (n) *[in a company]*

azione (f) action *[thing done]*

azione (f) *[causa]* action or lawsuit

azioni (fpl) ordinarie ordinary shares or equities

azioni (fpl) privilegiate preference shares

azioni (fpl) privilegiate cumulative cumulative preference shares

azioni (fpl) quotate quoted shares

azioni (fpl) trascurate neglected shares

azionista (m) shareholder

azionista (m) di maggioranza majority shareholder

azionista (m) di minoranza minority shareholder

azionista (m) principale major shareholder

Bb

bacheca (f) showcase

bacino (m) dock (n)

bagagli (mpl) non reclamati unclaimed baggage

bagaglio (m) luggage

bagaglio (m) a mano hand luggage

bagaglio (m) in eccesso excess baggage

banca (f) bank (n)

banca (f) centrale central bank

banca (f) d'emissione issuing bank

banca (f) di compensazione clearing bank

banca (f) di sconto discount house *[bank]*

Banca (f) Europea per gli Investimenti (BEI) European Investment Bank (EIB)

banca (f) mercantile merchant bank

banchiere (m) banker

banco (m) counter

banco (m) dei pagamenti pay desk

banco (m) di esposizione display stand

banconota (f) banknote; bill (n) *[US]*

barattare barter (v)

baratto (m) *[scambio]* barter (n)

barriera (f) barrier

barriera (f) *[protezione]* hedge (n)

barriera (f) doganale customs barrier

barriere (fpl) tariffarie tariff barriers

base (f) base (n) *[place]*

base: di base basic (adj)

base (f) *[fondamento]* basis

base (f) di dati database

base (f) monetaria monetary base

basilare *[di base]* basic (adj) *[simple]*

basso *[scadente]* low (adj)

basso: a basso prezzo cheap

basso livello (m) low (n)

battuta (f) d'arresto setback

bene (m) *[cespite]* asset

bene (m) *[merce]* commodity

beneficiario (m) beneficiary

beneficio (m) *[utilità]* benefit (n)

benestare (m) approval

beni (mpl) di consumo consumer goods

beni (mpl) di consumo durevoli consumer durables

beni (mpl) durevoli durable goods

beni (mpl) invisibili invisible assets

beni (mpl) reali tangible assets

beni (mpl) strumentali capital goods

benzina (f) a prezzo ridotto cut-price petrol

biasimare blame (v)

biasimo (m) *[colpa]* blame (n)

biglietto (m) business card; ticket

biglietto (m) aereo privo di prenotazione standby ticket

biglietto (m) aperto (senza data di ritorno) open ticket

biglietto (m) da visita business card

biglietto (m) di andata one-way fare

biglietto (m) di banca note (n)

biglietto (m) omaggio complimentary ticket

bilancia (f) balance (n)

bilancia (f) commerciale attiva favourable balance of trade

bilancia (f) commerciale in dollari dollar balance

bilancia (f) dei pagamenti balance of payments

bilancia (f) commerciale balance of trade

bilanciare balance (v)

bilancio (m) balance (n)

bilancio (m) d'apertura opening balance

bilancio (m) dello Stato budget (n) *[government]*

bilancio (m) di chiusura closing balance

bilancio (m) di verifica trial balance

bilancio (m) preventivo budget (n) *[personal, company]*

bilancio (m) d'esercizio balance sheet

bilaterale bilateral

bilione (m) billion (UK)

binario (m) platform *[in railway station]*

bloccare block (v)

bloccare i salari e i prezzi freeze *or* peg wages and prices

bloccare un assegno stop a cheque

bloccare un conto stop an account

bloccato *[congelato]* frozen

blocco (m) *[commerciale]* freeze (n)

blocco (m) degli affitti rent control

blocco (m) del credito credit freeze

blocco (m) del lavoro straordinario overtime ban

blocco (m) di fogli per lavagna flip chart

boicottaggio (m) boycott (n)

boicottare boycott (v)

bolla (f) di spedizione dispatch note *or* shipping note *or* delivery note

bolletta (f) bill *[list of charges]*

bolletta (f) d'avviso advice note

bollettino (m) bulletin

bonifico (m) bank transfer

boom (m) boom (n)

bordo: a bordo on board

borsa (f) bag

borsa (f) *[cartella]* briefcase

borsa (f) **di studio** grant (n)

Borsa (f) **Merci** commodity exchange

Borsa (f) **Valori** stock exchange

bozza (f) rough draft

bozza (f) **di un piano** draft plan

bozza (f) **di un progetto** draft project

breve: a breve *o* **a breve termine** short-term (adj) *or* on a short-term basis

breve: nel più breve termine as soon as possible (asap)

brevettare un'invenzione patent an invention

brevettato patented

brevetto (m) patent

brevetto (m) **richiesto** *o* **in attesa di brevetto** patent applied for *or* patent pending

britannico *[inglese]* British

broker (m) broker

budget (m) *[bilancio preventivo]* budget (n) *[personal, company]*

budget (m) **di gestione** operational budget

budget (m) **generale** overhead budget

budget (m) **operativo** operating budget

budget (m) **per le spese di promozione** promotion budget

budget (m) **provvisorio** provisional budget

budget (m) **pubblicitario** publicity budget *or* advertising budget

budgetario *[relativo al budget]* budgetary

budgettare budget (v)

buon affare (m) good buy

buon guadagno (m) healthy profit

buona gestione (f) good management

buona qualità (f) good quality

buono good

buono (m) coupon *or* voucher

buono (m) **premio** gift coupon *or* gift voucher

busta (f) **aperta** unsealed envelope

busta (f) **chiusa** sealed envelope

bustarella (f) *[tangente]* bribe (n)

Cc

cadere fall (v) *or* go lower

cadere *[calare]* drop (v)

cadere *[crollare]* collapse (v)

caduta (f) *[crollo]* fall (n) *or* collapse

caduta (f) *[ribasso]* drop (n)

calare *[cadere]* drop (v)

calcolare calculate

calcolare 10% per il trasporto allow 10% for carriage

calcolare una media average (v)

calcolatore (m) calculator

calcolatrice (f) **tascabile** pocket calculator

calcolo (m) calculation

calcolo (m) **approssimativo** rough calculation

calcolo (m) **sbagliato** miscalculation

calligrafia (f) handwriting

calo (m) lowering

cambiale (f) bill of exchange

cambiale (f) *[effetto]* bill (n) *[written promise to pay]*

cambiale (f) **di favore** *[effetto di comodo]* accommodation bill

cambiali (fpl) **da incassare** *[effetti attivi]* bills receivable

cambiali (fpl) **da pagare** *[effetti passivi]* bills payable

cambiamento (m) change *or* difference *or* shift

cambiamento (m) *[modifica]* alteration

cambiare change *or* exchange *[money]*

cambiare switch *or* change

cambiare *[modificare]* alter

cambiavalute (m) money changer

cambio (m) exchange (n) *[currency]*

cambio (m) incrociato cross rate

camera (f) room

Camera (f) di Commercio Chamber of Commerce

camion (m) lorry *or* truck

camion (m) articolato articulated lorry

camionista (m) lorry driver *or* trucker

campagna (f) campaign *or* drive

campagna (f) country *[not town]*

campagna (f) aggressiva hard selling

campagna (f) di vendite sales campaign

campagna (f) promozionale a mezzo posta mail shot

campagna (f) pubblicitaria publicity campaign *or* advertising campaign

campionamento (m) sampling

campionare sample (v) *or* test

campionatura (f) casuale random sampling

campionatura (f) per accettazione acceptance sampling

campione (m) sample (n)

campione (m) casuale random sample

campione (m) di prova trial sample

campione (m) gratuito free sample

campione (m) per dimostrazione demonstration model

campione (m) (statistico) di controllo check sample

campo (m) (area) area *or* field

canale (m) channel (n)

canali (mpl) di distribuzione distribution channels *or* channels of distribution

canalizzare channel (v)

cancellare cross out

cancellare *[annullare]* cancel

cancellazione (f) *[disdetta]* cancellation

cancelleria (f) d'ufficio office stationery

candidato (m) candidate

candidato (m) a un posto di lavoro applicant for a job

capace di capable of

capacità (f) capacity *[space]*

capacità (f) *[abilità]* capacity *[ability]*

capacità (f) di guadagno earning capacity

capacità (f) di produzione manufacturing capacity

capacità (f) in eccedenza overcapacity

capacità (f) industriale industrial capacity

capacità (f) produttiva capacity *[production]*

capacità (f) produttiva in eccesso excess capacity

capacità (f) produttiva inutilizzata spare capacity

caparra (f) rimborsabile refundable deposit

capi (mpl) d'intesa heads of agreement

capienza (f) di magazzino storage capacity

capire (rendersi conto di) realize *or* understand

capitale (m) *o* **capitali (mpl)** capital

capitale (m) d'apporto initial capital

capitale (m) d'esercizio working capital

capitale (m) di rischio risk capital

capitale (m) di rischio venture capital

capitale (m) disponibile available capital

capitale (m) effettivo equity capital

capitale (m) in fuga flight of capital

capitale (m) mutuato loan capital

capitale (m) nominale nominal capital

capitale (m) obbligazionario loan stock

capitale (m) sociale share capital

capitali (mpl) capital

capitalizzare capitalize

capitalizzazione (f) capitalization

capitalizzazione (f) di mercato market capitalization

capitalizzazione (f) delle riserve capitalization of reserves

capo (m) boss (informal)

capo (m) (direttore) principal (n) *[person]*

capo (m) del personale personnel manager

capo (m) reparto head of department; floor manager

capo (m) servizio departmental manager

capo (m) ufficio chief clerk

carenza (f) di manodopera manpower shortage

caricabile chargeable

caricare *[un camion o una nave]* load a lorry *or* a ship

caricare *[programma]* load (v) *[a computer program]*

carico (m) load (n) *or* cargo

carico (m) di camion lorry-load

carico (m) di coperta deck cargo

carico (m) di ritorno homeward freight

carico (m) lordo deadweight cargo

carico (m) utile payload

carnet (m) carnet *[document]*

caro dear

carovita (m) *[costo della vita]* cost of living

carrello (m) elevatore (a forche) fork-lift truck

carro (m) merci railway goods wagon

carta (f) assegni cheque (guarantee) card

carta (f) carbone carbon paper

carta (f) d'imbarco boarding card *or* boarding pass

carta (f) d'imbarco embarkation card

carta (f) da imballaggio wrapping paper

carta (f) da pacco brown paper

carta (f) di credito credit card; charge card

carta (f) di credito d'oro gold card

carta (f) di credito telefonica phone card

carta (f) di sbarco landing card

carta (f) riciclata recycled paper

cartella (f) *[borsa]* briefcase

cartella (f) *[portfolio]* portfolio

cartellino (m) del prezzo price ticket *or* price tag *or* price label

cartello (m) cartel

cartolina (f) postale card *or* postcard

cartoncino (m) card *[material]*

cartoncino (m) della società compliments slip

cartone (m) cardboard

cartone (m) carton *[material]*

cartone (m) *[imballo di cartone]* carton *[box]*

casa (f) house *[for family]*

casa: di casa in casa house-to-house

casella (f) postale P.O. box number

cassa (f) case *or* crate *or* box

cassa (f) checkout *or* till *[in supermarket]*

cassa (f) automatica prelievi cash dispenser

cassa (f) da imballaggio packing case

cassa (f) integrazione volontaria voluntary redundancy

cassa: in cassa integrazione redundant

cassaforte (f) safe (n)

cassiere (m), cassiera (f) cashier

casuale (accidentale) random

catalogo (m) catalogue *or* list

catalogo (m) di vendita per corrispondenza mail-order catalogue

categoria (f) category *or* class

catena (f) chain *[of stores]*

catena (f) di montaggio assembly line *or* production line

cattiva amministrazione (f) mismanagement *or* maladministration

cattivo acquisto (m) bad buy

causa: a causa di owing to

causa (f) *[azione]* action *[lawsuit]*

causa (f) di forza maggiore act of God; force majeure

causa (f) legale court case

causa (f) per risarcimento action for damages

cavaliere (m) bianco white knight

cavarsela get along

cedente (m) *[parte venditrice]* assignor

cedere *[accordare]* allow *or* give

cedola (f) di dividendo dividend warrant

centrale central

centralino (m) telefonico telephone exchange *or* switchboard

centralizzare centralize

centralizzazione (f) centralization

centro (m) centre

centro (m) (di città) downtown (n)

centro: in centro downtown (adv)

centro (m) assistenza service centre

centro (m) commerciale shopping centre; shopping mall *or* arcade

centro (m) d'affari business centre

centro (m) di costi cost centre

centro (m) **di profitto** profit centre

centro (m) **industriale** industrial centre

certificare *[autenticare]* certify

certificato certificated

certificato (m) certificate

certificato (m) **azionario** share certificate

certificato (m) **d'iscrizione** certificate of registration

certificato (m) **d'origine** certificate of origin

certificato (m) **di accettazione** certificate of approval

certificato (m) **di deposito** certificate of deposit

certificato (m) **di garanzia** certificate of guarantee

certificato (m) **di sdoganamento** clearance certificate

certificato (m) **medico** doctor's certificate

certificazione (f) *[revisione contabile]* auditing

cespite (m) **(bene)** asset

cespiti (mpl) **congelati** frozen assets

cespiti (mpl) **realizzabili** *[attivo esigibile]* realizable assets

cessare (finire) stop (v) *[doing something]*

cessare di lavorare stop work *or* knock off

cessazione (f) **delle consegne** suspension of deliveries

cessione (f) *[trasferimento]* cession *or* assignment

cessione (f) **di una cambiale** delivery *[of bill of exchange]*

check in (m) check-in counter

chiamare call (v) *or* telephone (v)

chiamata (f) **telefonica** phone call *or* telephone call

chiaro clear (adj) *[easy to understand]*

chiave key (adj) *[important]*

chiave (f) key *[to door]*

chiedere apply for *[ask for]*

chiedere (a qualcuno di fare qualcosa) ask *[someone to do something]*

chiedere *[domandare]* ask for *[something]*

chiedere informazioni enquire *or* inquire

chiedere ulteriori dettagli *o* **particolari** ask for further details *or* particulars

chiedere un rimborso ask for a refund

chilo (m) *o* **chilogrammo** (m) kilo *or* kilogram

chiudere shut (v)

chiudere *[finire]* close (v) *[after work]*

chiudere *[incollare]* seal (v) *[envelope]*

chiudere *[sospendere un'attività]* close down

chiudere a chiave lock (v)

chiudere a chiave un negozio *o* **un ufficio** lock up a shop *or* an office

chiudere un conto close an account

chiudere un conto bancario close a bank account

chiuso closed *or* shut

chiusura (f) closing *or* close *or* end

chiusura (f) *[termine]* closure

ciclico cyclical

ciclo (m) cycle

ciclo (m) **economico** economic cycle *or* trade cycle

cifra (f) figure *or* digit

cifra (f) **preventivata** estimated figure

cifre (fpl) *[numeri]* figures

cifre (fpl) **destagionalizzate** seasonally adjusted figures

cifre (fpl) **effettive** historical figures

cifre (fpl) **non verificate** unchecked figures

cima (f) *[vetta]* top (n) *[highest point]*

circolazione (f) circulation *[of money]*

circolo (m) *[associazione]* society *or* club

citare *[intentare causa]* sue

citazione (f) **in giudizio** summons

classe (f) class

classe (f) **business** business class

classe (f) **turistica** economy class *or* tourist class

classificare classify

classificazione (f) classification

clausola (f) clause; article

clausola (f) **addizionale** rider

clausola (f) **condizionale** proviso

clausola (f) **di esclusione** exclusion clause

clausola (f) **di penalità** penalty clause

clausola (f) **di recessione** waiver clause

clausola (f) di recupero dell'investimento payback clause

clausola (f) di rescissione cancellation clause or termination clause

clausola (f) di salvaguardia escape clause

cliente (mf) client or customer

cliente (mf) abituale regular customer

clientela (f) clientele

clienti (mpl) eventuali potential customers

coassicurazione (f) co-insurance

codice (m) code

codice (m) a barre bar code

codice (m) d'avviamento postale postcode or zip code [US]

codice (m) di etica professionale code of practice

codice (m) di magazzino stock code

codice (m) di zona area code

codice (m) fiscale tax code

codici (mpl) leggibili dal computer computer-readable codes

codifica (f) o **codificazione (f)** coding

coefficiente (m) di redditività profitability [ratio of profit to cost]

coefficiente (m) di carico load factor

cogliere [raccogliere] collect or fetch

coincidenza (f) connection

collaborare collaborate

collaboratore (m) [assistente] assistant

collaborazione (f) collaboration

collaterale collateral (adj)

collegamento (m) tie-up or link

collegare connect

collegare in rete network (v) [computers]

collettivo collective

collocazione (f) [posizione] situation [place]

colloquio (m) [intervista] interview (n)

colmare una lacuna (f) fill a gap

colonna (f) del dare debit column

colonna (f) dell'avere credit column

colpa (f) fault or blame

colpevole (mf) di appropriazione indebita embezzler

come consigliato as per advice

come da campione as per sample

come da fattura as per invoice

cominciare [iniziare] begin or start

comitato (m) commission or committee

commerciabile marketable

commerciale commercial (adj)

commercializzare [vendere] commercialize or market (v)

commercializzazione (f) commercialization

commerciante (m) dealer or trader

commerciante (m) all'ingrosso wholesaler or wholesale dealer

commerciante (m) in proprio sole trader

commerciare handle or deal in or sell

commerciare in o **trafficare in** trade in [buy and sell]

commercio (m) commerce or trade or business

commercio (m) a senso unico one-way trade

commercio (m) bilaterale reciprocal trade

commercio (m) d'esportazione export trade

commercio (m) estero foreign trade or overseas trade

commercio (m) internazionale international trade

commercio (m) interno domestic trade

commercio (m) invisibile invisible trade

commercio (m) legittimo lawful trade

commercio (m) libero fair trading

commercio (m) marittimo maritime trade

commercio (m) multilaterale multilateral trade

commesso (m) o **commessa (f) (di negozio)** salesman or saleswoman or shop assistant

commesso (m) viaggiatore commercial traveller

commettere commit [crime]

commissione (f) [percentuale] commission [money]

commissione (f) di mediazione brokerage or broker's commission

commissione (f) di studio working party

comodo convenient

compagnia (f) [società di capitali] company

compagnia (f) aerea airline

compagnia (f) di assicurazione insurance company

compagno (m) o compagna (f) [socio] partner

comparabilità (f) comparability

compartecipazione (f) agli utili profit-sharing

compensare compensate; make up for

compensare un assegno clear a cheque

compensazione (f) di un assegno clearance of a cheque

compenso (m) [ricompensa] compensation

compenso (m) [emolumento] fee [for services]

compenso (m) per lavoro straordinario overtime pay

comperare buy or purchase

comperare a termine buy forward

comperare in contanti buy for cash

competenza (f) remit (n)

competere con qualcuno o con un'azienda compete with someone or with a company

competitività (f) competitiveness

competitivo competitive

competizione (f) [concorrenza] competition

compilare make out [invoice]

compilare un assegno write out a cheque

compito (m) [impegno] undertaking or promise

complementare complementary

complesso (m) produttivo production unit

completamento (m) completion

completare complete (v) or finalize

completo complete (adj)

comporre (formare) form (v)

comporre un numero dial a number

compratore (m) purchaser or buyer

compravendita (f) di azioni da parte degli stessi amministratori della Società insider dealing

comprensivo comprehensive

comprese tasse (fpl) inclusive of tax

compromesso (m) compromise (n)

comproprietà (f) co-ownership or joint ownership or part-ownership

comproprietario (m) co-owner or joint owner or part-owner

computer (m) computer

computerizzare computerize

comune common

comune: in comune jointly

comunicare communicate

comunicato (m) stampa press release

comunicazione (f) communication

comunicazione (f) orizzontale horizontal communication

comunicazione (f) verticale vertical communication

comunicazioni (fpl) communications

comunità (f) community

con cum

con coupon (m) cum coupon

con dividendo (m) cum dividend

concedente (m) franchiser

concedere [accordare] grant (v)

concedere il diritto di esclusiva franchise (v)

concessionario (m) franchisee; licensee; concessionaire

concessione (f) concession or right; franchise

concessione (f) di licenze licensing

concessione (f) di vendita distributorship; franchising

concessione (f) fiscale tax concession

conciliazione (f) conciliation

concludere conclude [agreement]

concludere [finire] end (v)

concludere definitivamente clinch

concordare [corrispondere a] agree with or be the same as

concordato [convenuto] agreed

concorrente (m) competitor

concorrenza (f) [competizione] competition

concorrenza: in concorrenza competing (adj)

concorrenza (f) accanita keen competition

concorrenza (f) dura stiff competition

concorrenza (f) sleale unfair competition

concorrenza (f) spietata cut-throat competition

condirettore (m) joint managing director

condirezione (f) joint management

condizionato *[con riserve]* qualified *[with reservations]*

condizione (f) condition *[terms]*

condizione: a condizione che on condition that

condizione (f) *[stato]* condition *[state]*

condizione (f) sociale status

condizioni (fpl) terms

condizioni: a condizioni vantaggiose on favourable terms

condizioni (fpl) di assunzione conditions of employment

condizioni (fpl) di impiego terms of employment

condizioni (fpl) di lavoro working conditions

condizioni (fpl) di pagamento terms of payment

condizioni (fpl) di vendita terms of sale

condizioni (fpl) moderate easy terms

condizioni (fpl) per pagamento in contanti cash terms; cash price

conducente (m) driver

condurre (guidare) drive (v) *[a car]*

condurre una trattativa conduct negotiations

conferenza (f) *[congresso]* conference

conferenza (f) stampa press conference

conferire il diritto entitle

conferma (f) confirmation *or* acknowledgement

confermare confirm

confermare l'assunzione di una persona confirm someone in a job

confermare una prenotazione confirm a booking

confermato: non confermato unconfirmed

confezionatore (m) wrapper

confezione (f) a bolla di plastica trasparente bubble pack

confezione (f) finta dummy pack

confezione (f) per esposizione display pack

conflitto (m) di interessi conflict of interest

conformarsi a (osservare) comply with

confrontare (paragonare) compare

confronto (m) comparison

congedo (m) leave (n)

congedo (m) autorizzato *[aspettativa]* leave of absence

congedo (m) per maternità maternity leave

congegno (m) device

congelamento (m) salariale wage freeze

congelare freeze (v) *[prices]*

congelare un credito freeze credits

congelato *[bloccato]* frozen

congiunto (unito) joint

congiuntura (f) economic trends

conglomerato (m) conglomerate

congresso (m) *[conferenza]* conference

consegna (f) di merci delivery of goods

consegna (f) gratuita free delivery

consegnare deliver; consign

consegnare: non consegnato undelivered

consegnatario (m) consignee

conseguibile *[ottenibile]* obtainable

Conservatore (m) del Registro delle Società Registrar of Companies

conservazione (f) in ambiente frigorifero cold storage

considerare consider

consigliare *[raccomandare]* advise *or* recommend *[what should be done]*

Consiglio (m) di Amministrazione board of directors

consistere in consist of

consocio (m) copartner

consolidamento (m) consolidation

consolidare consolidate

consolidare spedizioni consolidate *[shipments]*

consolidato consolidated

consorzio (m) consortium

consueto *[fisso]* regular *[always at same time]*

consulente (m) consultant *or* adviser

consulente (m) di direzione aziendale management consultant

consulente (m) fiscale tax consultant

consulente (m) legale legal adviser

consulente (m) tecnico consulting engineer

consulenza (f) consultancy

consulenza (f) legale   legal advice

consultarsi   consult

consumatore (m)   consumer

consumo (m)   consumption

consumo (m) interno *o* nazionale   home consumption

contabile (mf) *[ragioniere]*   bookkeeper

contabilità (f)   accounting; bookkeeping

contabilità (f) a costi correnti   current cost accounting

contabilità (f) basata sui conti   cost accounting

contabilità (f) di bilancio   budget account *[in bank]*

contabilità (f) di fine mese   month-end accounts

contabilità (f) di metà mese   mid-month accounts

contabilità (f) non sottoposta a revisione contabile   unaudited accounts

contabilità (f) semestrale   half-yearly accounts

container (m)   container *[for shipping]*

containerizzare   containerize *[put into containers]*

containerizzazione (f)   containerization *[putting into containers]*

contanti: in contanti   in cash

contare   count (v) *[add]*

contare su   depend on

contatto (m)   contact (n)

contenere   contain *or* hold

contenitore (m)   container; holder

contenitore (m) di contanti   cash till

contenuto (m)   contents

contenzioso: in contenzioso   sub judice

conti (mpl) attivi   accounts receivable

conti (mpl) gestione   management accounts

conti (mpl) passivi   accounts payable

contingente (m) di importazione   import quota

contingenza (f)   contingency; cost-of-living bonus

continuamente   continually

continuare   continue

continuazione (f)   continuation

continuo   continual *or* continuous

conto (m)   account; bill *[in restuarant]*

conto: per conto di   on behalf of

conto (m) *[dell'albergo]*   hotel bill

conto (m) a garanzia   escrow account

conto (m) aperto   open account

conto (m) assegni   cheque account

conto (m) bancario   bank account

conto (m) bloccato   account on stop

conto (m) capitale   capital account

conto (m) chiuso   dead account

conto (m) congelato   frozen account

conto (m) congiunto   joint account

conto (m) corrente   current account

conto (m) creditori   credit account

conto (m) delle entrate   revenue accounts

conto (m) dettagliato   itemized account

conto (m) di cassa   cash account

conto (m) di contropartita   contra account

conto (m) di deposito   deposit account

conto (m) di prestanome   nominee account

conto (m) di risparmio   savings account

conto (m) in credito   account in credit

conto (m) numerato   numbered account

conto (m) personale   charge account

conto (m) profitti e perdite   profit and loss account

conto (m) scoperto   overdrawn account

conto (m) spese   expense account

contraffare   counterfeit (v)

contraffatto *[falso]*   counterfeit (adj)

contraffazione (f)   forgery *[action]*

contrapporre   set against

contrario   contrary

contrarre   contract (v)

contrarre debiti   incur debts *or* run into debt

contrassegno (m)   countersign

contrasto (m)   contrast (n)

contrattare *[tirare sul prezzo]*   bargain (v)

contrattazione (f)   bargaining

contratti (mpl) a termine su materie prime   commodity futures

contratto (m)   contract (n)

contratto (m) a breve termine   short-term contract

contratto (m) a prezzo fisso fixed-price agreement

contratto (m) a termine forward contract

contratto (m) salariale collettivo collective wage agreement

contratto (m) di assicurazione insurance contract

contratto (m) di lavoro contract of employment

contratto (m) di locazione tenancy *[agreement]*

contratto (m) globale package *[of services]*

contrattuale contractual

contrattualmente contractually

contribuente (m) taxpayer

contribuire contribute

contributo (m) contribution

controfferta (f) counter-offer *or* counterbid

controllabile *[trattabile]* manageable

controllante controlling (adj)

controllare control (v)

controllare *[esaminare]* check (v) *or* examine

controlli (mpl) dei prezzi price controls

controlli (mpl) valutari exchange controls

controllo (m) examination *or* check

controllo: a controllo statale government-controlled *or* government-regulated

controllo (m) *[verifica]* control (n) *or* check

controllo (m) budgetario budgetary control

controllo (m) dei materiali materials control

controllo (m) dei prezzi price control

controllo (m) del credito credit control

controllo (m) delle scorte stock control

controllo (m) di magazzino inventory control

controllo (m) di qualità quality control

controllo (m) doganale customs examination

controllo (m) passeggeri check-in *[at airport]*

controllore (m) controller *[who checks]*

controllore (m) della qualità quality controller

controreazione (f) feedback

controrichiesta (f) counter-claim (n)

contumace: essere contumace default (v)

conveniente good value (for money)

convenire covenant (v)

convenuto *[concordato]* agreed

convenzione (f) covenant (n)

conversione (f) conversion

conversione (f) della valuta currency conversion

conversione (f) di fondi conversion of funds

conversione (f) di un prestito refunding of a loan

convertibilità (f) convertibility

convertire convert

convocare call (v) *or* convene *[meeting]*

cooperare co-operate

cooperativa (f) co-operative (n)

cooperativo *[cooperativa]* co-operative (adj)

cooperazione (m) *[collaborazione]* co-operation

cooptare qualcuno co-opt someone

copertura (f) cover (n) *[top]*

copertura (f) assicurativa insurance cover

copia (f) copy (n)

copia (f) *[esemplare]* copy (n) *[book, newspaper]*

copia (f) autentica certified copy *or* true copy

copia (f) carbone carbon copy

copia (f) di riserva backup copy

copia (f) in chiaro hard copy

copiare *[riprodurre]* copy (v)

copiatrice (f) copier *or* copying machine

coprire cover (v)

coprire i costi cover costs

corona (f) (danese, norvegese) krone *[currency used in Denmark and Norway]*

corona (f) (svedese) krona *[currency used in Sweden]*

corporazione (f) corporation

corporazione (f) *[gilda]* guild

correggere correct (v) *or* amend *or* rectify

corrente current *or* ruling

correre un rischio run a risk *or* take a risk

corretto correct (adj) *or* right

correzione (f) correction

correzione (f) strutturale structural adjustment

corriere (m) *[messaggero]* courier *[messenger]*

corrispondente (mf) correspondent *[who writes letters]*

corrispondenza (f) correspondence

corrispondenza: essere in corrispondenza con qualcuno correspond with someone

corrispondere a *[concordare]* agree with *or* be the same as

corrompere (con denaro *o* **doni)** bribe (v)

corso (m) a indirizzo commerciale commercial course

corso (m) d'aggiornamento refresher course

corso (m) in amministrazione management course

corso (m) introduttivo induction course *or* induction training

corso (m) per operazioni a termine forward rate

corte (f) di Giustizia court

costante constant

costare cost (v)

costi (mpl) d'esercizio operating costs *or* operating expenses

costi (mpl) di distribuzione distribution costs

costi (mpl) di factoring factoring charges

costi (mpl) di gestione operational costs *or* running costs *or* running expenses

costi (mpl) di lancio launching costs

costi (mpl) di produzione production costs *or* manufacturing costs

costi (mpl) diretti prime cost

costi (mpl) eccessivi excessive costs

costi (mpl) fissi fixed costs

costi (mpl) fondiari landed costs

costi (mpl) indiretti del lavoro indirect labour costs

costi (mpl) per la spedizione marittima shipping charges *or* shipping costs

costi (mpl) sociali social costs

costi (mpl) variabili variable costs

costituire incorporate *[a company]*

costituire una società (f) set up a company

costituzione (f) incorporation

costo (m) cost (n)

costo (m) della manodopera labour costs

costo (m) della vita *[carovita]* cost of living

costo (m) delle vendite cost of sales

costo (m) diretto direct cost

costo (m) effettivo historic(al) cost

costo (m) marginale marginal cost *or* incremental cost

costo (m) più una percentuale cost plus

costo (m) simbolico token charge

costo (m) totale total cost

costo (m) unitario unit cost

costo (m), assicurazione (f) e nolo (m) cost, insurance and freight (c.i.f.)

costoso costly *or* expensive

costruire *[sviluppare]* develop *[build]*

costruire riserve *[stoccare]* stockpile (v)

costruttore (m) chiavi in mano turnkey operator

costruzione: in costruzione under construction

coupon (m) con risposta pagata reply coupon

crediti (mpl) congelati frozen credits

credito (m) credit (n) *or* credit balance

credito: a credito on credit

credito (m) a breve short-term credit

credito (m) a breve termine short credit

credito (m) a lungo termine long credit

credito (m) al consumatore consumer credit

credito (m) aperto open credit

credito (m) bancario bank credit

credito (m) d'imposta tax credit

credito (m) di appoggio standby credit

credito (m) esente da interessi interest-free credit

credito (m) esigibile debts due

credito (m) immediato instant credit

credito (m) inesigibile bad debt

credito (m) prorogato extended credit

credito (m) rinnovabile automaticamente revolving credit

creditore (m) creditor

creditore (m) differito deferred creditor

creditore (m) in solido co-creditor

creditore (m) ipotecario mortgagee

creditore (m) non garantito unsecured creditor

creditore (m) privilegiato preferential creditor *or* secured creditor

crescente increasing

crescita (f) growth

crescita (f) economica economic growth

crisi (f) del dollaro dollar crisis

crisi (f) di mancanza di liquidità liquidity crisis

crisi (f) economica *[crollo]* slump (n) *or* depression

crisi (f) finanziaria financial crisis

crollare *[cadere]* collapse (v) *or* crash *or* fail

crollo (m) *[crisi economica]* slump (n) *[depression]*

crollo (m) *[caduta]* fall (n) *or* collapse (n) *or* crash (n)

cronico chronic

cubico cubic

cucire con punti metallici *[graffare]* staple (v)

cucitrice (f) *[graffatrice]* stapler

culminare *[raggiungere un punto massimo]* peak (v)

cumulativo cumulative

curricolo (m) track record

curriculum (m) vitae curriculum vitae (CV)

curva (f) curve

curva (f) delle vendite sales curve

Dd

da non restituire *o* **da gettare** disposable

da primato record-breaking

da ricevere receivable

danneggiare damage (v)

danneggiato damaged

danni (mpl) *[rotture]* damage; breakages

danni (mpl) causati da un temporale storm damage

danno (m) alla proprietà damage to property

danno (m) causato da un incendio fire damage

dare give

dare corso ad un'ordinazione deal with an order

dare e avere debits and credits

dare in affitto *[affittare]* lease out (v)

dare in prestito *[prestare]* loan (v)

dare in subappalto subcontract (v)

dare istruzioni brief (v)

dare la caccia a chase *[an order]*

dare soldi come anticipo put money down

data (f) date (n)

data (f) d'inizio starting date

data (f) del lancio launching date

data (f) di chiusura *[termine ultimo]* closing date

data (f) di consegna delivery date

data (f) di entrata in vigore effective date

data (f) di ricevimento date of receipt

data (f) di rimborso redemption date

data (f) di scadenza sell-by date; expiry date *or* maturity date

data (f) di scadenza *[termine ultimo]* deadline

data (f) di ultimazione completion date

datare date (v)

datario (m) date stamp

datato dated

datato: non datato undated

dati (mpl) data

dati (mpl) **di emissione** computer output

datore (m) **di lavoro** employer

daziere (m) Excise officer

dazio (m) duty *[tax]*

dazio (m) **d'esportazione** export duty

dazio (m) **doganale** customs duty *or* import duty

dazio (m) **preferenziale** preferential duty *or* preferential tariff

debiti (mpl) **a lungo termine** long-term debts

debiti (mpl) **insoluti** outstanding debts

debiti (mpl) **privilegiati** secured debts

debito (m) debt

debito: a debito *[dovuto]* owing

debito (m) *[registrazione]* debit entry

debito (m) **inesigibile** irrecoverable debt

debitore (m) debtor

debitore: essere debitore owe

debitore (m) **autorizzato al concordato preventivo** certificated bankrupt

debitore (m) **ipotecario** mortgager *or* mortgagor

debitore (m) **riconosciuto da tribunale** judgment debtor

decentramento (m) decentralization

decentrare decentralize

decidere decide *or* resolve

decidere una linea di condotta decide on a course of action

decimale (m) decimal (n)

decisione (f) decision

decisione (f) *[verdetto]* judgement *or* judgment

decisivo deciding

declino (m) decline (n)

decollare take off

decrescente decreasing (adj)

decretare rule (v) *[give decision]*

decreto (m) ruling (n)

decurtare dock (v) *or* deduct money

dedurre *[fare uno sconto di]* take off *or* deduct

deficit (m) *[disavanzo]* deficit

deficit (m) **della bilancia commerciale** trade deficit *or* trade gap

definire una domanda d'indennizzo settle a claim

deflazione (f) deflation

deflazionistico deflationary

degrado (m) *[normale usura]* fair wear and tear

delega (f) delegation *[action]*

delega (f) *[procura]* proxy *[deed]*

delegare delegate (v)

delegato (m) delegate (n)

delegato (m) *[sostituto]* deputy

delegazione (f) delegation

denaro (m) money

denaro (m) **a buon mercato** cheap money

denaro (m) **contante** cash (n) *[money]*

denaro (m) **per le piccole spese** spending money

denaro (m) **scarso** tight money

denominazione (f) **della mansione** job title

denuncia (f) **dei redditi** tax return *or* tax declaration

depennare cross off

deperibile perishable

deporto (m) backwardation

depositante (m) depositor

depositare documenti file documents

depositare in banca bank (v)

depositare un marchio di fabbrica register a trademark

depositi (mpl) **bancari** bank deposits

depositi (mpl) **fruttiferi** interest-bearing deposits

deposito (m) deposit (n) *[in bank]*

deposito (m) *[magazzino]* store (n) *[place where goods are kept]*

deposito (m) *[magazzinaggio]* storage (n) *[in warehouse]*

deposito (m) **a termine** time deposit

deposito (m) **a vista** demand deposit

deposito (m) **in cassetta di sicurezza** safe deposit

deposito (m) **in contanti** cash deposit

deposito (m) **merci** goods depot

deposito (m) **non rimborsabile** non-refundable deposit

deposito (m) vincolato fixed deposit

depressione (f) depression

deregolamentazione (f) deregulation

derivare result from

descrivere describe

descrizione (f) description

descrizione (f) commerciale trade description

descrizione (f) dei compiti job description

design (m) *[progettazione]* design (n)

desktop publishing (m) desk-top publishing (DTP)

destinare appropriate (v) *[funds]*

destinatario (m) addressee

destinazione (f) destination

destituzione (f) removal *or* sacking *[of someone]*

destro right (adj) *[not left]*

deterioramento (m) naturale wear and tear

determinare determine

determinazione (f) del prezzo pricing

determinazione (f) del prezzo di concorrenza competitive pricing

determinazione (f) marginale del prezzo marginal pricing

detraibile deductible

detraibile dal reddito imponibile tax-deductible

detrazione (f) deduction

detrazioni (fpl) d'imposta tax deductions *[from salary to pay tax]*

detrazioni (fpl) personali personal allowances

dettagli (mpl) particulars

dettagliante (m) retailer *or* retail dealer

dettagliare detail (v) *or* break down (v) *or* itemize

dettagliato detailed

dettaglio (m) detail (n)

dettare dictate

dettatura (f) dictation

di mezzo *[medio]* medium (adj)

diagramma (m) diagram

diagramma (m) a barre bar chart

diagramma (m) del ciclo di lavorazione flow diagram

diario diary

dichiarare declare *or* state

dichiarare le merci alla dogana declare goods to customs

dichiarare qualcuno fallito declare someone bankrupt

dichiarare sciolta una riunione wind up a meeting

dichiarare una perdita report a loss

dichiarato declared

dichiarazione (f) declaration

dichiarazione (f) doganale customs declaration

dichiarazione dei redditi declaration of income

dichiarazione di fallimento declaration of bankruptcy

dichiarazione IVA VAT declaration

dicitura (f) wording

difendere defend

difendere una causa defend a lawsuit

difensore (m) civico ombudsman

difesa (f) defence *[legal]*

difetto (m) defect *or* mechanical fault

difettoso defective *[faulty]*

differenza (f) difference

differenza (f) a credito credit balance

differenze (fpl) di prezzo differences in price

differenziale differential (adj)

differire (rinviare) defer *or* postpone *or* shelve

differire un pagamento defer payment

differito deferred

diffusione (f) nei mass-media media coverage

digitare keyboard (v)

dilazione (f) *[rinvio]* postponement

diluizione (f) della partecipazione azionaria dilution of equity

dimensione (f) size

dimensioni: di medie dimensioni medium-sized

dimettersi resign

diminuire decrease (v) *or* fall off

diminuzione (f) decrease (n)

diminuzione (f) dei prezzi price reduction *or* reduction in price; mark-down

diminuzione (f) del valore decrease in value

dimissioni (fpl) resignation

dimostrare demonstrate

dimostratore (m) demonstrator

dimostrazione (f) demonstration

dinamismo (m) *[energia]* human energy

dipartimentale departmental

dipartimento (m) department

dipartimento (m) design design department

dipendente (m) employee

dipendenti (m) pagati a ore hourly-paid workers

diramare istruzioni issue instructions

direttamente direct (adv)

direttiva (f) directive *or* guideline

direttivo *[gestionale]* managerial

diretto direct (adj)

direttore (m), direttrice (f) manager; senior executive

direttore (m) commerciale sales manager

direttore (m) d'albergo hotel manager

direttore (m) del progetto project manager

direttore (m) del reparto esportazioni export manager

direttore (m) del servizio marketing sales executive

direttore (m) dell'ufficio acquisti purchasing manager

direttore (m) della pubblicità advertising manager *or* publicity manager

direttore (m) delle distribuzioni distribution manager

direttore (m) delle finanze finance director

direttore (m) delle vendite sales executive

direttore (m) di banca bank manager

direttore (m) di filiale branch manager

direttore (m) di marketing marketing manager

direttore (m) di produzione production manager

direttore (m) di zona area manager

direttore (m) esecutivo executive director

direttore (m) esterno outside director

direttore (m) facente funzione acting manager

direttore (m) generale *[amministratore delegato]* managing director (MD); chief executive

direttore (m) generale general manager

direttore (m) senza poteri esecutivi non-executive director

direttore (m) vendite esterne field sales manager

direzione (f) management *[managers]*

direzione (f) *[istruzione]* directions *or* instructions

direzione (f) al vertice top management

direzione (f) centrale *[sede centrale]* main office

direzione (f) del personale personnel management

dirigente (m) executive (n)

dirigente (m) delle pubbliche relazioni public relations officer

dirigente (m) delle vendite sales executive

dirigente (m) di grado inferiore junior executive *or* junior manager

dirigente (m) in capo senior manager *or* senior executive

dirigere direct (v) *or* run (v) *or* manage

dirigere male mismanage

diritti (mpl) di porto port charges *or* port dues

diritti (mpl) portuali harbour dues

diritti (mpl) speciali di prelievo (DSP) special drawing rights (SDRs)

diritto (m) right *or* entitlement; legal title

diritto (m) law *[study]*

diritto (m) civile civil law

diritto (m) commerciale commercial law

diritto (m) contrattuale contract law

diritto (m) della navigazione maritime law

diritto (m) di concessione royalty

diritto (m) di possesso tenure *[right]*

diritto (m) di precedenza right of way

diritto (m) di veto right of veto

diritto (m) internazionale international law

diritto (m) societario company law

disavanzo (m) *[deficit]* deficit

discendente *[giù]* down *or* downward

discesa (f) delle vendite slump in sales

dischetto (m) diskette

disco (m) disk

discorso (m) di ringraziamento speech of thanks

discrepanza (f) discrepancy

discussione (f) discussion

discussione (f) *[disputa]* argument

discussione (f) collettiva joint discussions

discussione (f) produttiva productive discussions

discutere discuss

disdetta (f) *[cancellazione]* cancellation

disdire un affare call off a deal

disegno (m) industriale industrial design

disfarsi di get rid of

disoccupato out of work *or* unemployed

disoccupazione (f) unemployment

disoccupazione (f) strutturale structural unemployment

disonestamente fraudulently

disonesto *[fraudolento]* fraudulent

dispari odd *[not even]*

disparità (f) dei prezzi price differential

dispersione (f) leakage

disponibile available

disponibile: non disponibile unavailable

disponibilità (f) availability

disponibilità: non disponibilità (f) unavailability

disponibilità (f) di capitali money supply

disponibilità (fpl) finanziarie financial assets

disporre *[sistemare]* arrange *or* set out

disposizione (m) *[sistemazione]* arrangement *or* system

disposizioni (fpl) *[regolamenti]* regulations

disputa (f) argument

dissentire differ

dissolvere *[risolvere]* dissolve

distinta (f) d'imballaggio packing list *or* packing slip

distinta (f) di versamento paying-in slip *or* deposit slip

distretto (m) commerciale commercial district

distribuire distribute

distributore (m) distributor

distribuzione (f) distribution

distruggere wreck (v) *or* ruin

ditta (f) (impresa) firm (n) *or* business *or* company

ditta (f) a conduzione familiare family company

ditta (f) di consulenza consultancy firm

ditta (f) di vendita a rate hire-purchase company

ditta (f) di noleggio impianti plant-hire firm

dittafono (m) dictating machine

divario (m) gap

diversificare diversify

diversificazione (f) diversification

diverso different

dividendo (m) dividend

dividendo (m) finale final dividend

dividendo (m) in acconto interim dividend

dividendo (m) minimo minimum dividend

dividere share (v)

divieto (m) di importazione import ban

divisa (f) forte strong currency

divise (fpl) *[moneta straniera]* foreign currency

divisione (f) division *[part of a group]*

divulgare *[rivelare]* disclose

divulgare un'informazione disclose a piece of information

divulgazione (f) *[rivelazione]* disclosure

divulgazione (f) di un'informazione riservata disclosure of confidential information

documentario (m) documentary

documentarsi su *[fare ricerche]* research (v)

documentazione (f) documentation; records

documenti (mpl) documents

documenti (mpl) falsi faked documents

documento (m) document

documento (m) provvisorio scrip

dogana (f) customs

doganiere (m) customs officer

dollaro (m) dollar

domanda (f) demand (n)

domanda: fare domanda scritta apply in writing

domanda (f) *[istanza]* application

domanda (f) d'impiego application for a job

domanda d'impiego: fare domanda d'impiego apply for a job

domanda (f) d'indennizzo claim (n)

domanda (f) di lavoro job application

domanda (f) effettiva effective demand

domanda (f) finale final demand

domandare demand (v)

domandare *[chiedere]* ask for *[something]*

domandare *[richiedere]* request (v)

domestico domestic

domicilio (m) domicile

domicilio: a domicilio door-to-door

donna (f) d'affari businesswoman

dono (m) *[omaggio]* free gift

doppia tassazione (f) double taxation

doppio double (adj)

dorso (m) *[retro]* back (n)

dossier (m) *[pratica]* dossier

dover rispondere a qualcuno report to someone

dovere (m) *[impegno]* obligation *or* duty

dovutamente *[regolarmente]* duly *or* legally

dovuto *[a debito]* due *or* owing

dovuto: essere dovuto fall due *or* be due

dozzina (f) dozen

dracma (f) drachma *[Greek currency]*

DSP (diritti speciali di prelievo) special drawing rights (SDRs)

duplicare duplicate (v)

duplicato (m) duplicate (n)

duplicato: fare il duplicato di una fattura duplicate an invoice

duplicazione (f) duplication

durata (f) *[periodo]* term *[of validity]*

durata (f) in carica tenure *[time]*

duty free shop *[negozio esente da tasse]* duty-free shop

Ee

eccellente excellent

eccessivo excessive

eccesso excess

eccetto *[tranne]* except

eccezionale *[straordinario]* exceptional

economia (f) economy

economia (f) *[scienze economiche]* economics

economia (f) controllata controlled economy

economia (f) dell'offerta supply side economics

economia (f) di massa economies of scale

economia (f) di mercato libero free market economy

economia (f) di tipo misto mixed economy

economia (f) matura mature economy

economia (f) nera black economy

economia (f) solida stable economy

economico *[a basso prezzo]* economical *or* cheap

economico *[finanziario]* economic *or* financial

economista (mf) economist

economista (mf) di mercato market economist

economizzare economize *or* save

ecu (m) (Unità di Conto Europea) ecu *or* ECU (= European currency unit)

edificio (m) facility *[building]*

edificio (m) principale main building

effetti (mpl) a breve termine short-dated bills

effetti (mpl) all'incasso bills for collection

effetti (mpl) attivi receivables *or* bills receivable

effetti (mpl) bancabili *[strumenti scontabili]* bankable paper

effetti (mpl) passivi *[cambiali da pagare]* bills payable

effettivo effective

effettivo (reale) actual

effetto (m) effect (n)

effetto (m) *[cambiale]* bill (n) *or* promise to pay

effetto (m) a catena knock-on effect

effetto (m) a lunga scadenza long-dated bill

effetto (m) accettato irrevocabilmente irrevocable acceptance

effetto (m) bancario bank bill *[GB]*

effetto (m) di comodo *[cambiale di favore]* accommodation bill

effettuare effect (v)

efficacia (f) effectiveness

efficiente efficient

efficienza (f) efficiency

elaborare cifre process figures

elaborato a mezzo computer computerized

elaboratore (m) ad uso personale *[personal computer]* personal computer (PC)

elaborazione (f) delle ordinazioni order processing

elaborazione (f) dei dati data processing

elaborazione (f) delle informazioni processing of information

elaborazione (f) di massa batch processing

elasticità (f) elasticity

eleggere elect

elementi (m) ciclici cyclical factors

elemento (m) decisivo deciding factor

elencare list (v) *or* index (v)

elencazione (f) scheduling

elenco (m) classificato classified directory

elenco (m) delle cause docket

elenco (m) di indirizzi mailing list

elenco (m) telefonico telephone book *or* telephone directory

elezione (f) election

eliminare delete

eliminare gradualmente phase out

eliminare le scorte in eccesso dispose of excess stock

embargo (m) embargo (n)

emendamento (m) *[rettifica]* amendment

emergenza (f) emergency

emettere issue (v) *[shares]*

emettere allo scoperto overdraw

emettere un assegno draw *[a cheque]*

emettere una fattura raise an invoice

emissione (f) azionaria share issue

emissione (f) di certificati azionari provvisori scrip issue

emissione (f) di diritti rights issue

emissione (f) gratuita di azioni bonus issue

emolumento (m) *[compenso]* fee *[for services]*

energia (f) elettrica energy *[electricity]*

energia (f) *[dinamismo]* human energy

ente (m) locale local government

entrare enter *or* go in

entrare: far entrare admit *or* let in

entrare in porto *[attraccare]* dock (v) *[ship]*

entrare in possesso di una società acquire a company

entrare in vigore run (v) *or* be in force

entrata (f) entry *[going in]*

entrate (fpl) receipts

equalizzazione (f) equalization

equipaggiare equip

equivalere a qualcosa correspond with something

equo (giusto) fair (adj)

erodere erode

errore (m) error *or* mistake

errore (m) casuale random error

errore (m) di computer computer error

errore (m) di trascrizione clerical error

esame (f) examination

esame: in esame on approval

esaminare examine *or* inspect

esaminare *[controllare]* check (v) *or* examine

esatto exact (adj)

esattamente exactly

esattore (m) dei crediti debt collector

esattore (m) delle imposte tax collector

esattore (m) di affitti rent collector

esaurire *[vendere tutto]* sell out *[all stock]*

esaurire run out of

esaurito out of stock

esborso (m) outlay *or* disbursement

escludere exclude

esclusione (f) exclusion

esclusività (f) exclusivity

escluso excluding; exclusive of

escudo (m) escudo (Portuguese currency)

esecutivo executive (adj)

esecuzione (f) execution

eseguire execute

esemplare (m) *[copia]* copy (n) *[of book, newspaper]*

esentare exempt (v)

esentasse tax-exempt

esente exempt (adj)

esente da canone d'affitto rent-free

esente da dazio duty-free

esente da pedaggio toll free *[US]*

esente da tassa exempt from tax

esente da tasse tax-free *or* free of tax

esenzione (f) exemption

esenzione (f) fiscale tax exemption *or* exemption from tax

esercitare exercise (v)

esercitare il commercio di un prodotto merchandize a product

esercitare un'opzione exercise an option *or* take up an option

esercizio (m) exercise (n)

esercizio (m) di un'opzione exercise of an option

esercizio (m) finanziario financial year

esibire exhibit (v)

esigenza (f) di manodopera manpower requirements

esigere exact (v)

espansione (f) industriale industrial expansion

esperto experienced

esperto (m) *[professionista]* expert (n) *or* professional (n)

esperto (m) di statistica statistician

esplorare explore

esporre display (v)

esportare export (v)

esportatore exporting (adj)

esportatore (m) exporter

esportazione (f) export (n)

esportazioni (fpl) exports

espositore (m) *[standista]* exhibitor

esposizione (f) *[mostra]* exhibition *or* display

esposizione (f) in vetrina window display

espresso express (adj)

esprimere express (v) *[state]*

espropriazione (f) per pubblica utilità compulsory purchase

essere in ritardo (nel fare una cosa) fall behind *or* be late

essere valido run (v) *or* be in force

estendersi *[variare]* range (v)

esteriore outside

esterno external *[outside a company]*

estero *[straniero]* external *or* foreign

estero (m) *[i paesi stranieri]* overseas (n)

estero: all'estero abroad *or* overseas

estinguere *[un debito]* redeem *or* pay off *or* clear *[a debt]*

estratto (m) conto statement of account

estratto (m) conto bancario bank statement

età (f) della pensione retirement age

etichetta (f) label (n)

etichetta (f) di posta aerea airmail sticker

etichetta (f) indirizzata address label

etichettare label (v)

etichettatura (f) labelling

ettaro (m) hectare

euroassegno (m) Eurocheque

eurodollaro (m) Eurodollar

euromercato (m) Euromarket

euromoneta (f) Eurocurrency

evadere evade

evadere un'ordinazione fulfil an order

evasione (f) d'imposta evasion

evasione (f) di un'ordinazione order fulfilment

evasione (f) fiscale tax avoidance *or* tax evasion

evidenziatore (m) marker pen

ex cedola (f) ex coupon

ex dividendo (m) ex dividend

expertise (f) *[perizia]* expertise

extra extra

Ff

fabbrica (f) factory *or* plant

fabbricante (m) *[produttore]* manufacturer

fabbricare *[produrre]* manufacture (v) *or* produce *or* make

fabbricazione (f) *[lavorazione]* manufacture (n)

faccenda (f) *[problema]* matter (n) *or* problem

facente funzione di *[sostituto]* acting

facile easy

facile da usare *[accessibile]* user-friendly

facilitazioni (fpl) di scoperto overdraft facility

facoltativo optional

factoring (m) factoring

factoring: fare del factoring factor (v)

fallimento (m) bankruptcy

fallire fail

fallire: fare fallire ruin (v) *or* bankrupt (v)

fallire *[non arrivare a compimento]* fall through

fallito bankrupt (adj)

fallito (m) bankrupt (n)

fallito (m) non riabilitato undischarged bankrupt

falsificare falsify *or* fake (v) *or* forge

falsificazione (f) falsification

falso (m) forgery *[copy]*

falso *[contraffatto]* false *or* counterfeit (adj)

falso *[fittizio]* dummy

far entrare admit *[let in]*

far pagare charge (v) *[money]*

far pagare meno undercharge

far pagare troppo overcharge (v)

fare pratica train (v) *[learn]*

fare progressi *[avanzare]* progress (v)

fare riferimento a refer *[to item]*

fare soldi make money

fare un'ordinazione place an order

farsi ritirare l'usato trade in *[give in old item for new]*

fascia (f) tax bracket

fascicolo (m) file (n) *[documents]*

fascicolo (m) dello schedario card-index file

fascicolo (m) supplementare (in una rivista) magazine insert

fattibilità (f) feasibility

fatto appositamente custom-built *or* custom-made

fattore (m) factor (n) *[influence]*

fattore (m) costo cost factor

fattore (m) negativo minus factor *or* downside factor

fattore (m) positivo plus factor

fattori (mpl) di produzione factors of production

fattorino (m) deliveryman *or* messenger

fattura (f) invoice (n) *or* bill

fattura (f) *[atto di vendita]* bill of sale

fattura (f) con IVA VAT invoice

fattura (f) dettagliata itemized invoice

fattura (f) proforma pro forma (invoice)

fatturare invoice (v) *or* bill (v)

fatturato (m) *[vendite]* sales (revenue)

fatturazione (f) invoicing *or* billing

fatture (fpl) insolute unpaid invoices

favorevole favourable

fax (m) fax (n)

fedeltà (f) alla marca brand loyalty

fede: in buona fede bona fide; in good faith

fedeltà (f) dei clienti customer loyalty

fermare countermand

fermarsi stay (v)

fermo (stabile) stable

fermoposta (m) poste restante

ferrovia (f) railway *or* rail *or* railroad *[US]*

festa (f) nazionale public holiday; bank holiday

fiasco: fare fiasco fail (v) *or* flop (v)

fiducia (f) confidence

fiera (f) campionaria trade fair

file (m) *[archivio]* computer file

filiale (f) branch office; subsidiary

finale final

finanza (f) *[attività finanziaria]* finance (n)

finanza (f) pubblica public finance

finanze (fpl) finances

finanziamento (m) financing

finanziamento (m) del disavanzo (m) deficit financing

finanziare finance (v) *or* fund (v) *or* pay costs

finanziare un'operazione finance an operation

finanziariamente financially

finanziario *[economico]* financial

finanziatore (m) moneylender

fine fine (adv) *[very small]*

fine (f) *[scadenza]* expiry

fine (f) *[termine]* end (n)

fine (f) del mese month end

fine (f) esercizio year end

finestra (f) window

finire *[concludere]* end (v)

finire *[portare a termine]* complete (v)

finire *[cessare]* stop (v) *[doing something]*

finito finished

fino a *[conforme a]* up to

fiorente booming *or* flourishing

fiorino (m) (olandese) guilder *[Dutch currency]*

firma (f) signature

firmare sign (v)

firmare come testimone witness (v) *[a document]*

firmare il registro check in *or* register *[at hotel]*

firmare un accordo come testimone witness an agreement

firmare un assegno sign a cheque

firmare un contratto sign a contract

firmatario (m) signatory

firmatario (m) congiunto joint signatory

fiscale fiscal

fissaggio (m) fixing

fissare fix *or* arrange

fissare obiettivi set targets

fissare una riunione per le 3 del pomeriggio fix a meeting for 3 p.m.

fissato fixed

fissato (m) bollato contract note

fisso fixed *or* flat

fisso (consueto) regular *[always at same time]*

fittizio (falso) dummy

flessibile flexible

flessibilità (f) flexibility

fluire flow (v)

flusso (m) flow (n)

flusso (m) di cassa cash flow

flusso (m) di cassa positivo positive cash flow

fluttuante fluctuating

fluttuante *[galleggiante]* floating

fluttuare *[oscillare]* fluctuate

fluttuare: far fluttuare float (v) *[a currency]*

fluttuazione (f) fluctuation

foglietto (m) slip (n) *[piece of paper]*

foglio (m) di calcolo elettronico spreadsheet *[computer]*

foglio (m) di carta sheet of paper

fondamentale *[di base]* basic *or* most important

fondamento (m) *[base]* basis

fondi (mpl) insufficienti insufficient funds *[US]*

fondi (mpl) pubblici public funds

fondo (m) fund *or* reserve (n)

fondo (m) comune di investimento unit trust

fondo (m) di cassa cash float; cash in hand

fondo (m) di previdenza contingency fund

fondo (m) pensioni pension fund

Fondo Monetario Internazionale (FMI) International Monetary Fund (IMF)

fonte (f) di reddito source of income

formale formal

formalità (f) formality

formalità (fpl) doganali customs formalities

formare (comporre) form (v)

formare un numero telefonico dial (v) a number

formato (m) normale regular size

formazione (f) training

formulazione (f) form of words

fornire (approvvigionare) supply (v)

fornire di personale staff (v)

fornitore (m) supplier

fornitore (m) allo stato *o* statale government contractor

fornitura (f) supply (n) *[action]*

forte strong

forte richiesta (f) keen demand

forti costi (mpl) heavy costs

forza (f) lavoro labour force *or* workforce

forza (f) vendita *[personale addetto alle vendite]* sales force

forzato forced

forze (fpl) di mercato market forces

fotocopia (f) photocopy (n)

fotocopiare photocopy (v)

fotocopiatrice (f) photocopier

fotocopiatura (f) photocopying

fragile fragile

franco (m) franc

franco *[senza spese]* franco

franco a bordo free on board (f.o.b.)

franco di porto carriage free

franco di spese *[gratuito]* free of charge

franco dogana free of duty

franco posta post free

franco su rotaia free on rail

francobollo (m) postage stamp

fraudolento fraudulent

frequente frequent

frode (f) fraud

fronte: far fronte a una spesa meet an expense

frontiera (f) border

fruttare *[rendere]* earn *or* bear *or* produce (v) *[interest]*

fuga (f) *[di denaro]* flight *[of money]*

fungere da interfaccia interface (v)

funzionamento (m) *[marcia]* running (n) *[of machine]*

funzionare *[operare]* act *or* operate *or* work

funzionare: far funzionare operate (v) *or* run a machine

funzionario (m) official (n)

funzionario (m) addetto all'addestramento training officer

funzionario (m) di banca banker

fuoco (m) *[incendio]* fire (n)

fuori controllo out of control

fuori orario d'ufficio outside office hours

fuori stagione off-season

furgone (m) van

furgone (m) per le consegne delivery van

furto (m) theft

furto (m) di scarsa entità pilferage *or* pilfering

fusione (f) merger

futura consegna (f) future delivery

Gg

galleria (f) *[con negozi]* shopping mall *or* shopping arcade

gamma (f) range (n) *or* series of items

gamma (f) dei prezzi price range

gamma (f) di prodotti product mix

garante (m) surety; sponsor (n)

garantire guarantee (v)

garantire *[sponsorizzare]* sponsor (v)

garantire per qualcuno stand surety for someone

garantire un debito guarantee a debt

garanzia (f) guarantee (n) *or* security

garanzia (f) collaterale collateral (n)

generale general

generi (mpl) di consumo consumables

gestionale *[direttivo]* managerial

gestione (f) *[amministrazione]* administration *or* management

gestione (f) del portafoglio portfolio management

gestire *[amministrare]* manage

gettare throw away

gettare: da gettare disposable

giacenze (fpl) finali alla chiusura dell'esercizio closing stock

gilda (f) *[corporazione]* guild

giornale (m) newspaper

giornale (m) di categoria trade journal

giorno (m) day

giorno (m) festivo legale statutory holiday

giorno (m) per giorno day-to-day

giovane *[junior]* junior (adj)

girante (m) endorser

girare un assegno endorse a cheque

girata (f) endorsement *[action]*

giratario (m) endorsee

giroconto (m) giro system

giù *[discendente]* down

giudicare judge (v)

giudice (m) adjudicator

giudice (m) *[magistrato]* judge (n)

giudizio (m) *[aggiudicazione]* adjudication

giudizio (m) arbitrale award (n)

giungere ad un accordo reach an agreement

giungere al punto di pareggio break even (v)

giuridico legal *[referring to law]*

giurisdizione (f) jurisdiction

giustificare justify *or* warrant (v)

giusto rightful

giusto *[equo]* fair (adj)

globale *[totale]* all-in *or* total (adj)

governativo *[del governo]* government (adj)

governo (m) government (n)

grado (m) di solvibilità credit rating

graduale gradual

graduato graduated

graffare *[cucire con punti metallici]* staple (v)

graffare insieme fogli staple papers together

graffatrice (f) *[cucitrice]* stapler

graffetta (f) paperclip

grafico (m) a settori pie chart

grafico (m) delle vendite sales chart

grammo (m) gram *or* gramme

grande magazzino (m) department store

grande quantità (f) *[massa]* mass *[of things]*

grande quantità (f) *[volume]* bulk

grande supermercato (m) superstore

gratifica (f) (premio) bonus

gratifica (f) di bilancio incentive bonus

gratifica (f) natalizia *[tredicesima]* Christmas bonus

gratis gratis *or* free

gratuitamente free (adv) *[no payment]*

gratuito *[franco di spese]* free of charge

gravare d'imposta *[tassare]* tax (v)

grave heavy *[important]*

griglia (f) *[reticolo]* grid

grinta (f) drive (n) *[energy]*

grossa (f) *[dodici dozzine]* gross (n) (= 144)

gru (f) crane

gruppi (mpl) socioeconomici socio-economic groups

gruppo (m) batch (n) *[of orders]*; group *[of people]*

gruppo (m) di collocamento underwriting syndicate

gruppo (m) industriale group *[of businesses]*

gruppo (m) selezionato di consumatori consumer panel

guadagnare earn *[money]*

guadagni (mpl) earnings *[salary]*

guadagno (m) gain (n) *[increase in value]*

guadagno (m) *[profitto]* return (n) *[profit]*

guadagno (m) lordo gross earnings

guardia (f) giurata security guard

guasto (m) breakdown (n) *[machine]*

guerra (f) dei prezzi price war

guerra (f) della diminuzione dei prezzi price-cutting war

guida (f) (turistica) courier *[guide]*

guida (f) stradale street directory

guidare *[condurre]* drive (v) *[a car]*

Hh

hard disk (m) hard disk

holding (f) *[società controllante]* holding company

hotel (m) *[albergo]* hotel

Ii

illecito illicit

illegale illegal

illegalità (f) illegality

illegalmente illegally

imballaggio (m) packing *or* packaging; wrapping

imballaggio (m) ermetico airtight packaging

imballaggio (m) termocontrattile shrink-wrapping

imballare *[impacchettare]* pack (v)

imballare (merce) in casse crate (v) *or* pack goods into cartons

imballato con metodo termocontrattile shrink-wrapped

imballo (m) a perdere non-returnable packing

imballo (m) di cartone carton *or* box

imbarcare *o* **imbarcarsi** embark *or* board

imbarcarsi in embark on

imbarco (m) embarkation

imbonimento (m) sales pitch

imbrogliare fiddle (v)

imbroglio (m) *[truffa]* fiddle (n)

imitazione (f) imitation *or* fake (n)

immagazzinare store *or* stock up *or* keep in warehouse

immagine (f) aziendale corporate image

immagine (f) del prodotto brand image

immagine (f) pubblica public image

immediatamente immediately

immediato *[istantaneo]* immediate *or* instant

immettere *[informazioni nel computer]* input information *[on computer]*

immissione (f) mediante tastiera keyboarding

immobile (m) con chiusura di sicurezza lock-up premises

immobilizzazioni (fpl) capital assets

immobilizzi (mpl) fixed assets

immobilizzi (mpl) tecnici capital equipment

immutato unchanged

impaccare wrap up *[goods]*

impacchettare *[imballare]* pack (v) *or* parcel (v)

impacchettatore (m) packer

impadronirsi capture

impegni (mpl) commitments

impegno (m) *[compito]* undertaking *or* promise

impegno (m) *[dovere]* obligation *or* duty

imperfetto imperfect

imperfezione (f) imperfection

impianti (mpl) plant (n) *or* machinery

impianti (mpl) di magazzinaggio storage facilities

impianti (mpl) portuali harbour facilities

impianto (m) di magazzinaggio storage unit

impiegare *[assumere]* employ

impiegatizio *[d'ufficio]* clerical

impiegato employed

impiegato (m) clerk

impiegato (m) addetto al partitario delle vendite sales ledger clerk

impiegato (m) addetto alle informazioni information officer

impiegato (m) alla biglietteria booking clerk

impiegato (m) di spedizioniere shipping clerk

impieghi (mpl) disponibili appointments vacant

impiego (m) *[lavoro]* job *or* employment

impiego (m) *[posto]* position *or* post *or* job

impiego (m) a tempo pieno full-time employment

imporre impose

imporre *[una tassa]* levy (v) *[a duty]*

importante important

importanza (f) importance

importanza: avere importanza be important *or* matter (v)

importanza: di scarsa importanza petty *or* minor

importare *[merci]* import (v)

importatore (m) importer

importatore, -trice importing (adj)

importazione (f) importation

importazioni (fpl) imports

importazioni (fpl) visibili visible imports

importazioni-esportazioni import-export (adj)

importo (m) *[ammontare]* amount *[of money]*

importo (m) aggiuntivo premium *[on lease]*

importo (m) dovuto amount owing

importo (m) fisso flat rate

importo (m) forfettario lump sum

importo (m) maturato accrual

importo (m) pagato amount paid

importo (m) totale total amount

imposizione (f) enforcement

imposta (f) *[tassa]* tax (n) *or* duty

imposta (f) arretrata back tax

imposta (f) di bollo stamp duty

imposta (f) diretta direct tax

imposta (f) generale sugli acquisti purchase tax

imposta (f) indiretta excise duty

imposta (f) pagata tax paid

imposta (f) progressiva graded tax

imposta (f) progressiva sul reddito graduated income tax

imposta (f) sul reddito income tax

imposta (f) sul valore aggiunto (IVA) value added tax (VAT)

imposta (f) sul volume di affari sales tax *or* turnover tax

imposta (f) sulla società corporation tax

imposta (f) sulle plusvalenze capital gains tax

imposta (f) trattenuta alla fonte tax deducted at source

imposte (f) indirette indirect tax

imposte (f) progressive progressive taxation

imprenditore (m) contractor; entrepreneur

imprenditoriale entrepreneurial

impresa (f) business *or* company

impresa (f) di trasporti *[trasportatore]* carrier *or* haulage contractor

impronta (f) mark (n)

impulso (m) impulse

in acconto on account

in aumento on the increase *or* mounting

in buona fede bona fide

in comune jointly

in concorrenza competing (adj)

in contanti cash (adv)

in media on an average

in orario *[puntuale]* on time

in ritardo *[tardi]* late (adv)

in scala naturale full-scale (adj)

in scala ridotta small-scale (adj)

in vendita for sale

inabile *[privo di validità]* invalid

inabilità (f) *[invalidità]* invalidity

inadempiente (m) defaulter

inadempienza (f) default (n)

inadempienza (f) nel pagamento default on payments

inadempimento (m) del contratto breach of contract

incapace incompetent

incarico (m) assignment *[work]*

incartamenti (mpl) papers

incassabile cashable

incassare cash (v) *or* encash

incassare un assegno cash a cheque

incassi (mpl) takings *or* returns

incassi (mpl) netti net receipts

incasso (m) take (n) *[money received]*

incendio (m) *[fuoco]* fire (n)

incentivo (m) incentive

incidente (m) accident *or* crash (n)

incidente (m) professionale occupational accident

includere count (v) *or* include

incluso inclusive

incollare *[chiudere]* seal (v) *[an envelope]*

incondizionato unconditional

incontrare meet *[someone]*

incorporare merge

incorporato *[inserito]* built-in

incorrere (in) incur

incrementativo incremental

incremento (m) increment

indagare inquire

indagine (f) *[analisi]* investigation *or* examination

indebitamento (m) indebtedness

indebitamento (m) a breve short-term debts

indebitarsi get into debt

indebitato indebted

indennità (f) *[indennizzo]* indemnification

indennità (f) di contingenza cost-of-living allowance

indennizzare *[risarcire]* indemnify; make good *[a defect or loss]*

indennizzo (m) *[indennità]* indemnification

indicare un prezzo *[quotare]* quote (v) *or* estimate costs

indicare un profitto show a profit

indicatore (m) indicator

indicatori (mpl) economici economic indicators

indice (m) index (n)

indice (m) dei prezzi al consumo consumer price index

Indice (m) dei prezzi al dettaglio retail price index

indice (m) dei prezzi all'ingrosso wholesale price index

indice (m) del costo della vita cost-of-living index

indice (m) di crescita growth index

indice (m) di rendimento rate of return

indice (m) economico index number

indice (m) ponderato weighted index

indicizzato index-linked

indicizzazione (f) indexation *or* index-linking

indipendente independent

indiretto indirect

indirizzare una lettera *o* **un pacco** address a letter *or* a parcel

indirizzo (m) *[recapito]* address (n)

indirizzo (m) cablografico cable address

indirizzo (m) d'inoltro forwarding address

indirizzo (m) d'ufficio business address

indirizzo (m) del mittente return address

indirizzo (m) di comodo accommodation address

indirizzo (m) personale home address

indiscriminato *[uniforme]* across-the-board

indispensabile essential

indossatrice (f) model (n) *[person]*

industria (f) industry

industria (f) a forte assorbimento di capitali capital-intensive industry

industria (f) che si è sviluppata rapidamente boom industry

industria (f) chiave key industry

industria (f) di base staple industry

industria (f) pesante heavy industry

industria (f) primaria primary industry

industria (f) secondaria secondary industry

industria (f) statalizzata nationalized industry

industria (f) terziaria tertiary industry

industriale industrial

industriale (m) industrialist

industrializzare industrialize

industrializzazione (f) industrialization

inefficiente inefficient

inefficienza (f) inefficiency

inferiore *[più basso]* lower (adj)

inferiore *[meno di]* under *or* less than

inflazione (f) inflation

inflazione (f) da costi cost-push inflation

inflazionistico inflationary

influenza (f) influence (n)

influenzare influence (v)

informare *[avvisare]* inform *or* advise

informazione (f) riservata tip (n) *[advice]*

informazioni (fpl) commerciali status inquiry

informazioni (fpl) di volo flight information

infortunio (m) sul lavoro industrial accident

infrangere infringe

infrangere un accordo break an agreement

infrastruttura (f) infrastructure

infrazione (f) fiscale tax offence

ingegnere (m) edile site engineer

ingiusto unfair

inglese *[britannico]* English *or* British

ingranaggio (m) gear

ingrosso: all'ingrosso wholesale (adv)

ininterrotto *[senza scalo]* non-stop

iniziale initial (adj) *or* starting *or* opening

iniziare *[cominciare]* begin *or* start (v) *or* initiate

iniziare un dibattito (m) initiate discussions

iniziativa (f) initiative

iniziativa (f) commerciale commercial undertaking

iniziativa (f) privata private enterprise

iniziativa (f) su scala ridotta small-scale enterprise

inizio (m) beginning

innovare innovate

innovativo innovative

innovatore (m) innovator

innovazione (f) innovation

inoltrare file (v) *[a request]*

inoltrare una domanda di brevetto file a patent application

inoltro (m) forwarding

inondare flood (v)

inondazione (f) flood (n)

inquilino (m) tenant

insegna (f) sign (n)

inseguire chase *or* follow up

inserimento (m) in un nuovo lavoro induction

inserire insert *or* put in

inserire in una lista di proscrizione blacklist (v)

inserito *[incorporato]* built-in

inserzione (m) advertisement

inserzione: pubblicare un'inserzione per un impiego disponibile advertise a vacancy

inserzioni (fpl) *[annunci economici su giornale]* classified ads

inserzionista (m) advertiser

insolvente insolvent

insolvenza (f) insolvency

inspiegato unaccounted for

insuccesso (m) failure *or* flop

insuccesso (m) commerciale commercial failure

intangibile intangible

integrazione (f) orizzontale horizontal integration

integrazione (f) verticale vertical integration

intendere propose to *[do something]*

intensificare escalate

intentare azione legale take legal action

intentare causa *[citare]* sue

intentare causa civile bring a civil action

interdire *[vietare]* ban (v)

interdizione (f) ban (n)

interessare interest (v)

interessarsi di concern (v) *or* deal with

interesse (m) interest (n)

interesse (m) alto high interest

interesse (m) composto cumulative interest

interesse (m) composto compound interest

interesse (m) fisso fixed interest

interesse (m) maturato accrued interest

interesse (m) semplice simple interest

interessi (mpl) costituiti vested interest

interfaccia (f) interface (n)

intermediario (m) intermediary *or* intermediary

internazionale international

interno internal *or* in-house

interno (m) telephone extension

interno (del territorio nazionale) inland

intero (pieno) full

interpretare interpret

interprete (mf) interpreter

interrompere discontinue

intervallo (m) *[fra ordinazione e consegna]* lead time

intervista (f) *[colloquio]* interview (n)

intervistare interview (v)

intervistato (m) interviewee

intervistatore (m) interviewer

intesa (f) understanding

intesa (f) *[accordo]* arrangement *or* understanding *or* compromise

intraprendente go-ahead (adj)

intraprendere undertake

introdurre introduce

introdurre gradualmente phase in

introduzione (m) introduction *or* bringing into use

invalidare *[annullare]* invalidate *or* void (v)

invalidità (f) *[inabilità]* invalidity

invecchiamento (m) obsolescence

invenduto unsold

inventariare *[fare l'inventario]* take stock *or* inventory (v)

inventario (m) stocklist; inventory

inventario (m) *[stock]* stock *or [US]* inventory

inventario (m) stocktaking

inventario: fare l'inventario inventory (v) *or* take stock

inversione (f) reversal

inversione (f) di tendenza turnround *[making profitable]*

inverso reverse (adj)

invertire reverse (v)

investigare investigate

investimenti (mpl) ad interessi fissi fixed-interest investments

investimenti (mpl) esteri foreign investments

investimenti (mpl) in titoli di prim'ordine blue-chip investments

investimento (m) investment

investimento (m) garantito secure investment

investimento (m) privo di rischio risk-free investment

investimento (m) sicuro safe investment

investire invest

investire capitali invest in *or* lock up capital

investito invested *or* employed *[money]*

investitore (m) investor

investitori (mpl) istituzionali institutional investors

inviare send

inviare per fax fax (v)

inviare rimessa a mezzo assegno remit by cheque

inviato (m) correspondent *[journalist]*

invio (m) consignment *[things sent, received]*

invio (m) *[per posta]* mailing

invio (m) di riviste per posta magazine mailing

invitare invite *or* call *[on someone to do something]*

invito (m) invitation

involucro (m) *[imballaggio]* wrapping

ipermercato (m) hypermarket

ipoteca (f) mortgage (n)

ipotecare mortgage (v)

irregolare irregular

irregolarità (fpl) irregularities

irrevocabile irrevocable

iscrivere una società register a company

iscriversi register (v) *[in official list]*

iscrizione (f) membership *[being a member]*

ispettivo *[di supervisione]* supervisory

ispettore (m) aziendale factory inspector

ispettore (m) delle tasse tax inspector

ispettore (m) IVA VAT inspector

ispezionare *[esaminare]* survey (v) *or* inspect

ispezione (f) inspection

istantaneo *[immediato]* instant (adj) *or* immediate

istanza (f) *[domanda]* application

istituire institute (v) *or* establish

istituto (m) institute (n)

istituto (m) di credito credit bank

istituto (m) di credito fondiario building society

istituto (m) finanziario financial institution

istituzionale institutional

istituzione (f) institution

istruire train (v) *or* teach

istruzione (f) instruction

istruzioni (fpl) per l'uso directions for use

istruzioni (fpl) per la spedizione shipping instructions *or* forwarding instructions

itinerario (m) itinerary

IVA (imposta sul valore aggiunto) VAT (= value added tax)

Jj

joint venture (f) *[associazione in partecipazione]* joint venture

junior *[giovane]* junior (adj)

Ll

lanciare launch (v) *or* bring out

lanciare una società float a company

lancio (m) launch (n) *or* launching

lancio (m) di una società flotation *or* floating of a company

lasciar vuoto vacate

lasciare *[abbandonare]* leave (v) *[resign]*

lasciare *[partire]* leave (v) *or* go away

lasciare libera la camera dell'albergo check out of hotel

lato (m) side

lato (m) dell'attivo *[avere]* credit side

laureato (m) **che fa tirocinio come dirigente** graduate trainee

lavorare work (v)

lavorare al nero moonlight (v)

lavorare: che lavora in proprio self-employed

lavorare *[trattare]* process (v) *[raw materials]*

lavoratore (m), **lavoratrice** (f) worker

lavoratore (m) **a domicilio** homeworker

lavoratore (m) **al nero** moonlighter

lavoratore (m) **a orario ridotto** part-timer

lavoratore (m) **saltuario** casual worker

lavoratore che fa parte del consiglio di amministrazione e che agisce come portavoce del personale worker director

lavoratori (mpl) **parzialmente qualificati** semi-skilled workers

lavorazione (f) *[fabbricazione]* manufacture (n)

lavoro (m) labour; job *or* piece of work

lavoro (m) *[impiego]* position *or* job

lavoro (m) **a contratto** contract work

lavoro (m) **a contratto a termine** temporary employment

lavoro (m) **a cottimo** piecework

lavoro (m) **a orario ridotto** part-time work *or* part-time employment

lavoro (m) **arretrato** backlog

lavoro (m) **ben pagato** well-paid job

lavoro (m) **con turni** shift work

lavoro (m) **d'ufficio** clerical work

lavoro (m) **di routine** routine work

lavoro (m) **in corso** work in progress

lavoro (m) **manuale** manual work

lavoro (m) **nero** moonlighting

lavoro (m) **saltuario** casual work

lavoro (m) **stabile** secure job

lavoro (m) **straordinario** overtime

lavoro (m) **urgente** rush job

leasing (m) leasing

leasing (m) **immobiliare** lease-back

legale legal *or* according to the law

legalizzare *[autenticare]* authenticate

legge (f) law *[rule]*

legge (f) **del rendimento decrescente** law of diminishing returns

legge (f) **dell'offerta e della domanda** law of supply and demand

leggibile dal computer computer-readable

legislazione (f) legislation

legittimazione (f) standing

legittimo lawful

lento slow

lento *[stagnante]* slack

lettera (f) letter

lettera: fare una lettera raccomandata register (v) *[letter]*

lettera (f) **aerea** air letter

lettera (f) **circolare** circular letter

lettera (f) **circolare** circular (n)

lettera (f) **d'affari** business letter

lettera (f) **di accompagnamento** covering letter

lettera (f) **di assunzione** letter of appointment

lettera (f) **di credito** letter of credit (L/C)

lettera (f) **di credito circolare** circular letter of credit

lettera (f) **di credito irrevocabile** irrevocable letter of credit

lettera (f) **di intenti** letter of intent

lettera (f) **di presentazione** letter of introduction

lettera (f) **di reclamo** letter of complaint

lettera (f) **di referenze** letter of reference

lettera (f) **di sollecito** follow-up letter

lettera (f) **di vettura** consignment note; waybill

lettera (f) **espresso** express letter

lettera (f) **standard** standard letter

leva (f) **finanziaria** leverage

levata (f) postal collection

libbra (f) *[peso]* pound *[weight: 0.45kg]*

liberare free (v) *or* release

liberarsi di qualcosa get rid of something

libero free (adj)

libero professionista (m) freelancer

libero scambio (m) free trade

libretto (m) **assegni** cheque book

libretto (m) di versamento bank book

libro (m) book (n)

libro (m) cassa cash book

libro (m) contabile *[registro]* register (n) *or* journal

libro (m) giornale journal *or* accounts book

libro (m) mastro ledger

libro (m) mastro degli acquisti purchase ledger

libro (m) vendite sales book

licenza (f) licence

licenza (f) d'esportazione export licence *or* export permit

licenza (f) di importazione import licence *or* import permit

licenziamento (m) dismissal

licenziamento (m) ingiustificato wrongful dismissal

licenziamento (m) ingiusto unfair dismissal

licenziare discharge *or* sack *or* dismiss *[employees]*

licenziare: essere licenziato get the sack

licitazione (f) tendering

licitazione (f) *[offerta d'appalto]* tender (n) *[offer to work]*

limitare limit (v) *or* restrict

limitare il credito restrict credit

limitato limited

limitazione (f) agli scambi commerciali restraint of trade

limite (m) limit (n)

limite (m) del prestito lending limit

limite (m) di credito credit limit

limite (m) di peso weight limit

limite (m) massimo ceiling

linea (f) line (n)

linea: in linea on line *or* online

linea (f) aerea *[compagnia aerea]* airline

linea (f) di carico load line

linea (f) di navigazione shipping line

linea (f) di prodotti product line

linea (f) esterna outside line

linea (f) gerarchica line management

linea (f) telefonica telephone line

linguaggio (m) burocratico officialese

linguaggio (m) di computer computer language

linguaggio (m) di programmazione programming language

liquidare clear (v) *[stock]*

liquidare (pagare) una fattura settle *[an invoice]*

liquidare le ordinazioni inevase release dues

liquidatore (m) liquidator *or* official receiver

liquidazione (f) liquidation *or* winding up

liquidazione (f) coatta compulsory liquidation

liquidazione (f) volontaria voluntary liquidation

liquidità (f) liquid assets *or* liquidity

lira (f) (italiana) lira *[currency used in Italy]*

lira (f) sterlina pound sterling

lista (f) list (n)

lista (f) di indirizzi address list

lista (f) di selezione picking list

lista (f) nera black list (n)

lista (f) ristretta (di candidati) shortlist (n)

listino (m) *[catalogo]* list (n) *or* catalogue

listino (m) prezzi price list

litro (m) litre

livelli (mpl) salariali wage levels

livello (m) level (n)

livello: di livello inferiore low-level

livello (m) delle scorte stock level

livello (m) di organico manning levels

livello (m) di riordinazione reorder level

livello (m) massimo di produzione peak output

locale *[del luogo]* local

locali (mpl) premises

locali (mpl) d'azienda *o* **locali commerciali** business premises

locatore (m) landlord

locazione (f) tenancy *[period]*

logogramma (m) logo

lordo gross (adj)

lungaggine (f) burocratica red tape

lungo *[per molto tempo]* long

lungo: a lungo termine long-term

luogo (m) site *or* place

luogo: avere luogo take place

luogo (m) **d'incontro** meeting place

luogo (m) **di ritrovo** venue

Mm

macchina (f) machine; car

macchina (f) **affrancatrice** franking machine

macchina (f) **che cambia denaro in spiccioli** change machine

macchinario (m) **pesante** heavy machinery

macroeconomia (f) macro-economics

magazzinaggio (m) *[deposito]* warehousing *or* storage (n) *[in warehouse]*

magazziniere (m) warehouseman

magazzino (m) warehouse (n); stockroom *or* storeroom; store

magazzino (m) **a prezzi scontati** discount store

magazzino (m) **doganale** bonded warehouse

magazzino (m) **frigorifero** cold store

maggioranza (f) majority

maggiorazione (f) premium *or* extra charge

maggiore major

magistrato (m) *[giudice]* magistrate *or* judge (n)

malinteso (m) misunderstanding

malpagato underpaid

mancanza (f) *[assenza]* absence

mancanza (f) **di fondi** lack of funds

mancare miss

mancare il bersaglio miss a target

mancata consegna (f) non-delivery

mancia (f) tip (n) *[money]*

mandare indietro *[respingere]* return (v) *or* send back

mandare un carico per mare send a shipment by sea

mandatario (m) proxy *[person]*

mandato (m) mandate; writ

mandato (m) **di pagamento** *[vaglia]* money order

maneggevole *[pratico]* handy

maneggio (m) *[gestione]* handling

manifatturiero manufacturing

manifesto (m) manifest

manodopera (f) manpower

manodopera (f) **qualificata** skilled labour

manodopera (m) **a basso prezzo** cheap labour

manodopera (m) **locale** local labour

manovale (m) manual worker

mantenere maintain *[keep at same level]*

mantenere una promessa keep a promise

mantenimento (m) maintenance

mantenimento (m) **delle provvigioni** maintenance of supplies

mantenimento (m) **di contatti** maintenance of contacts

manuale manual (adj)

manuale (m) manual (n)

manuale (m) **di manutenzione** service manual

manuale (m) **operativo** operating manual

manufatti (mpl) manufactured goods

manutenzione (f) *[revisione]* maintenance *or* service (n) *[of machine]*

marca (f) *[nome del prodotto]* brand name

marca (f) *[marchio]* brand

marchio (m) trademark *or* trade name *or* brand

marchio (m) **di fabbrica depositato** registered trademark

marchio (m) **di qualità** quality label

marcia (f) *[funzionamento]* running (n) *[of machine]*

marco (m) tedesco Deutschmark *or* mark

marginale marginal

margine (m) margin *[profit]*

margine (m) di errore margin of error

margine (m) di utile profit margin

margine (m) lordo gross margin

margine (m) netto net margin

marina (f) mercantile merchant navy

marittimo marine *or* maritime

marketing (m) marketing

marketing (m) di massa mass marketing

mass-media (m) *[mezzi di comunicazione di massa]* mass media

massa (f) mass

massimale (m) di credito credit ceiling

massimizzare maximize

massimizzazione (f) maximization

massimo maximum (adj)

massimo (m) maximum (n)

master (m) in gestione d'impresa Master's degree in Business Administration (MBA)

mastro (m) dei conti dei creditori bought ledger

mastro (m) nominale nominal ledger

materiale (m) d'imballaggio packaging material

materiale (m) da esposizione display material

materiale (m) di recupero salvage (n) *or* things saved

materiale (m) illustrativo delle vendite sales literature

materiale (m) per punto di vendita point of sale material (POS material)

materiale (m) pubblicitario con buono coupon ad

materie (fpl) prime raw materials

matrice (f) counterfoil

matrice (f) dell'assegno cheque stub

maturare *[accumularsi]* accrue

maturazione (f) degli interessi accrual of interest

media (f) average (n) *or* mean (n)

media: in media on an average

media (f) ponderata weighted average

mediare mediate

mediatore (m) mediator *or* troubleshooter

mediatore (m) assicurativo insurance broker

mediazione (f) mediation

mediazione (f) di cambio stockbroking

medio average (adj) *or* medium

medio: a medio termine medium-term

meglio: il meglio best (n)

memorandum (m) memorandum *or* memo

memoria (f) del computer computer memory

meno *[negativo]* minus

meno di *[inferiore]* under *or* less than

meno: a meno di short of

mensile monthly (adj)

mensilmente monthly (adv)

mercanteggiare haggle

mercante (m) merchant

mercati (mpl) esteri overseas markets

mercati (mpl) monetari money markets

mercato (m) market (n)

mercato (m) a termine forward market

mercato (m) al rialzo bull market

mercato (m) al ribasso buyer's market

mercato (m) azionario stock market

mercato (m) chiuso closed market

mercato (m) controllato da un solo fornitore captive market

mercato (m) dei cambi foreign exchange market

mercato (m) delle materie prime commodity market

mercato (m) favorevole ai venditori seller's market

mercato (m) fiacco weak market

mercato (m) interno domestic market

mercato (m) libero open market

mercato (m) limitato limited market

mercato (m) mondiale world market

mercato (m) nazionale home market

mercato (m) nero black market

mercato (m) potenziale potential market

mercato (m) prescelto target market

Mercat (m) Europeo Unico Single European Market

merce (f) merchandise (n) *or* goods

merce (f) **a prezzo ridotto** cut-price goods

merce (f) **con dazio pagato** duty-paid goods

merce (f) **danneggiata da incendio** fire-damaged goods

merce (f) **in transito** goods in transit

merce (f) **non venduta** returns *or* unsold goods

merce (f) **per la vendita al dettaglio** retail goods

merchant bank (f) *[banca mercantile]* merchant bank

merci (fpl) **deperibili** perishable goods

merci (fpl) **vendute sottocosto** distress merchandise

merito (n) merit

mese (m) month

mese (m) **solare** calendar month

messaggero (m) *[corriere]* courier *or* messenger

messaggio (m) message

metà (f) half (n)

metà settimana (f) mid-week

metodo (m) **LIFO (ultimo a entrare, primo a uscire)** LIFO (= last in first out)

metodo (m) **per tentativi** trial and error

mettere put (v) *or* place

mettere *[posare]* place (v)

mettere a verbale *[verbalizzare]* minute (v)

mettere al corrente *[aggiornare]* update (v)

mettere da parte denaro save up

mettere francobolli *[affrancare]* stamp (v) *[a letter]*

mettere in liquidazione scorte di magazzino liquidate stock

mettere in liquidazione una società liquidate *or* wind up *[a company]*

mettere in ordine put in a certain order

mettere in serbo store (v) *[keep for future]*

mettere in vendita release (v) *or* put on the market

mettere insieme batch (v)

mettere insieme le risorse pool resources

mettere l'embargo su embargo (v)

mettere per iscritto put in writing

mettersi in affari go into business *or* set up in business

mettersi in contatto con contact (v)

mezza dozzina (f) half a dozen *or* a half-dozen

mezzi (mpl) means *[money]*

mezzi (mpl) *[strumenti]* means *[ways]*

mezzi (mpl) **di comunicazione di massa** mass media

mezzo half (adj)

mezzo (m) medium (n)

microeconomia (f) micro-economics

microelaboratore (m) microcomputer

miglior offerente (m) successful bidder

miglioramento (m) upturn

migliore best (adj)

migliore *[piu alto]* top (adj)

migliore offerente (m) highest bidder

miliardario (m) millionaire

miliardo billion *[US]*

milione (m) million

millantato credito (m) false pretences

minimo minimum (adj)

minimo (m) minimum (n)

ministero (m) ministry *or* government department

Ministero del Tesoro Treasury

ministro (m) government minister *or* secretary

minoranza (f) minority

minuto (m) minute (n) *[time]*

miscellaneo *[vario]* miscellaneous

missione (f) **commerciale** trade mission

misto mixed

misura (f) **della redditività** measurement of profitability

misura (f) **standard** stock size

misure (fpl) measurements

misure (fpl) **cubiche** cubic measure

misure (fpl) **di sicurezza** safety measures *or* safety precautions

mittente (m) sender *or* consignor

mobilità (f) mobility

mobilizzare mobilize

mobilizzare capitali mobilize capital

modalità (fpl) **di pagamento** mode of payment

modello (m) model (n)

e (f) omission

honour (v)

rare dishonour

rare un effetto dishonour a bill

una cambiale honour a bill

una firma honour a signature

o (m) honorarium

o operational or operative (adj)

re (m) operator or operative (n)

re (m) in cambi foreign
nge dealer

re (m) su tastiera keyboarder

one (f) operation

one (f) *[affare]* deal (n)

**one (f) a denominazione
la multipla** multicurrency
ation

one (f) chiavi in mano turnkey
ation

one (f) disonesta fraudulent
action

oni (fpl) *[transazioni]* dealing

e (f) pubblica public opinion

unità (f) opportunity

li (mpl) pubblicitari junk mail

e (f) d'acquisto call (n) *[stock
ange]*

e (f) per l'acquisto option to
hase

hour

di accettazione check-in time

di chiusura closing time

di punta rush hour

lavorativa man-hour

hourly

(m) timetable (n) *[trains, etc.]*

in orario *[puntuale]* on time

(m) d'apertura opening hours

(m) d'ufficio office hours

(m) di banca banking hours

(m) pieno full-time

(m) ridotto part-time

re order (v) *[goods]*

ria amministrazione (f)
ine (n)

rio ordinary

to on order

azione (f) order (n) *[for goods]*

---

ordinazioni (fpl) inevase back orders
or dues or unfulfilled orders

ordinazione (f) rinnovata repeat order

ordinazione (f) urgente rush order

ordinazioni (fpl) da evadere
outstanding orders

ordinazioni (fpl) per corrispondenza
mail-order

ordine (m) order (n)

ordine (m) alfabetico alphabetical order

ordine (m) bancario banker's order

ordine (m) cronologico chronological
order

ordine (m) d'acquisto purchase order

ordine (m) del giorno agenda

ordine (m) di consegna delivery order

**ordine (m) di pagamento di valuta
estera** foreign money order

ordine (m) permanente standing order

ore (fpl) d'ufficio business hours

organico (m) manning

organigramma (m) organization chart

organizzare organize or arrange or plan

organizzativo organizational

organizzazione (f) organization

**Organizzazione (f) dei paesi
esportatori di petrolio** Organization of
Petroleum Exporting Countries (OPEC)

organizzazione (f) e metodo (m)
organization and methods

organizzazione (f) gerarchica line
organization

**Organizzazione (f) Internazionale del
Lavoro (OIL)** International Labour
Organization (ILO)

originale (m) original (n)

originario original (adj)

origine (f) origin

ormeggiare berth (v)

ormeggio (m) berth (n)

oro (m) in verghe gold bullion

oscillare *[fluttuare]* fluctuate

osservare *[conformarsi]* comply with

ottenere obtain or gain or get

**ottenere la liberazione (su cauzione) di
qualcuno** bail someone out

ottenibile *[conseguibile]* obtainable

ottenibile: non ottenibile unobtainable

output (m) *[dati di emissione]*
computer output

---

modello (m) economico economic
model

modello (m) in scala scale model or
mock-up

modem (m) modem

moderare moderate (v)

moderato moderate (adj)

moderno *[attuale]* modern or up to date

modifica (f) *[cambiamento]* alteration

modificare *[cambiare]* alter

modo (m) mode

moduli (mpl) a striscia continua
continuous stationery

modulo (m) form (n)

modulo (m) d'iscrizione registration
form

modulo (m) delle tasse tax form

modulo (m) di dichiarazione doganale
customs declaration form

**modulo (m) per domanda di
assunzione** application form

molo (m) quay or wharf

moltiplicare multiply

moltiplicazione (f) multiplication

molto bene fine (adv) or very good

mondiale worldwide (adj)

mondo (m) world

mondo: in tutto il mondo worldwide
(adv)

moneta (f) (metallica) coin

moneta (f) a corso legale legal tender

moneta (f) inflazionata inflated
currency

moneta (f) legale legal currency

moneta (f) spicciola small change

moneta (f) stabile stable currency

moneta (f) straniera foreign currency

monetario monetary

monitor (m) monitor (n) or screen

---

monopolio (m) monopoly

monopolio perfetto (m) absolute
monopoly

monopolizzare monopolize

monopolizzazione (f) monopolization

montacarichi (m) goods elevator

montaggio (m) *[assemblaggio]*
assembly *[putting together]*

montatura (f) giornalistica hype (n)

moratoria (f) moratorium

morto dead (adj) *[person]*

mostra (f) *[esposizione]* exhibition or
display

mostrare show (v)

motivato motivated

motivazione (f) motivation

movimentazione (f) dei materiali
materials handling

movimenti (m) di capitali movements
of capital

movimento (m) movement or turnover
[of stock]

multa (f) (penale) fine or penalty

multare fine (v)

multilaterale multilateral

multinazionale (f) multinational (n)

multiplo multiple (adj)

mutuare borrow; lend

mutuatario (m) borrower

mutuo (m) borrowing

mutuo (m) *[prestito]* loan (n)

mutuo (m) a breve scadenza
short-term loan

mutuo (m) a lunga scadenza
long-term loan

mutuo (m) garantito secured loan

mutuo (reciproco) mutual (adj) or
reciprocal

Nn

nastro (m) magnetico magnetic tape or
mag tape

navale (marittimo) maritime

nave (f) ship (n)

nave (f) da carico cargo ship or
freighter

nave (f) di salvataggio salvage vessel

nave (f) gemella sister ship

nave (f) mercantile merchant ship or merchant vessel

nave (f) per trasporto di container container ship

nazionale national

nazionale: di dimensioni nazionali nationwide

nazionalizzazione (f) nationalization

nazione (f) [paese] country [state]

nazione (f) più favorita most-favoured nation

necessario necessary

negativo (meno) minus

negligente negligent

negligenza (f) negligence

negoziabile negotiable

negoziante (m) shopkeeper

negoziare negotiate

negoziare [commerciare] deal in (v)

negoziato (m) [negoziazione] negotiation

negoziato (m) salariale wage negotiations

negoziatore (m) negotiator

negoziazione (f) [negoziato] negotiation

negozio (m) shop or store

negozio (m) appartenente a una catena multiple store

negozio (m) che fa parte di una catena chain store

negozio (m) con merce a prezzi ridotti cut-price store

negozio (m) d'angolo corner shop

negozio (m) di vendita a prezzi ridotti discount store

negozio (m) esente da tasse duty-free shop

negozio (m) per articoli da regalo gift shop

netto net (adj)

nicchia (f) niche

nodo (m) della questione bottom line

noleggiare charter (v)

noleggiare un aeroplano charter an aircraft

noleggiare un'automobile hire a car

noleggiatore (m) (di navi, aerei) charterer

noleggio (m) chartering or charter (n)

noleggio (m) in blocco block booking

nome (m) name

nome: a nome di on behalf of

nome (m) del prodotto [marca] brand name

nomina (f) appointment [to a job]

nomina (f) del personale staff appointment

nomina (f) di amministratore giudiziario letters of administration

nominare appoint

non datato undated

non disponibile unavailable

non disponibilità (f) unavailability

non pagato outstanding or unpaid

non specializzato unskilled

non ufficiale [ufficioso] unofficial

non verificato unaudited

norma (f) standard (n) or rule (n) or norm

normale [regolare] regular or ordinary

normale usura e degrado fair wear and tear

norme (fpl) antincendio fire regulations

norme (fpl) di sicurezza safety regulations

nota (f) note (n)

nota (f) di accredito credit note

nota (f) di addebito debit note

notaio (m) notary public

notare note (v) or mark (v) [details]

notificare notify

notificazione (f) notification

notte (f) night

nulla (m) [zero] nil

nullo null or void or not valid

numerare number (v)

numeri (mpl) [cifre] figures

numeri (m) dispari odd numbers

numerico numeric or numerical

numero (m) number (n) or figure

numero (m) dell'assegno cheque number

numero (m) di conto corrente di corrispondenza giro account number

numero (m) di fattura invoice number

numero (m) di matricola registration number

numero (m) di partita batch number

numero (m) di riferimento reference number

numero (m) di serie serial number

numero (m) di telefono phone number

numero (m) minimo legale quorum

numero (m) telefonico number or phone num...

nuova domanda (f) re...

nuova ordinazione (f)

nuovo accertamento (...

nuovo di zecca brand...

nuovo orientamento (...
[new venture]

Oo

obbligatorio compulsory

obbligazione (f) bond [borrowing by government]

obbligazione (f) [di società private] debenture

obbligazione (f) al portatore bearer bond

obbligazione (f) irredimibile irredeemable bond

obbligazione (f) redimibile callable bond

obbligazioni (fpl) 'cartastraccia' junk bonds

obbligazioni (fpl) convertibii convertible loan stock

obbligazionista (m) debenture holder

obbligo (m) liability

obiettivi (mpl) di produzione production targets

obiettivo (m) objective (n) or target (n)

obiettivo (m) di rilevamento takeover target

obiettivo (m) di vendita sales target

obiettivo [oggettivo] objective (adj)

obsolescente obsolescent

occasione (f) [affare] bargain (n) [cheaper than usual]

occultamento (m) di beni concealment of assets

occupante (m) occupant

occupare occupy

occuparsi: chi occupa occupant

occuparsi di attend to or handle (v) or deal with

occupato busy; engaged [telephone]

occupazionale [profes... occupational

occupazione (f) occup...

offerente (m) tendere...

offerta (f) offer (n); b...

offerta (f) d'apertur...

offerta (f) d'appalto...
to work]

offerta (f) d'occasion...

offerta (f) di propag...
offer

offerta (f) di vendita...

offerta (f) e domand...
demand

offerta (f) in busta c...
tenders

offerta (f) per conta...

offerta (f) premio p...

offerta (f) pubblica...
takeover bid

offerta (f) reale cas...

offerta (f) speciale s...

offerte (fpl) d'impie...
vacant

officina (f) worksho...

offrire [proporre] o...

offrire [presentare]...

offshore [all'estero...

olio (m) edible oil o...

omaggio (m) [dono...

omaggio: in omagg...

omesso pagamento...
non-payment [of...

omettere [trascura...

Pp

pacchetto (m) packet

pacchetto (m) *[azionistico]* block (n) *[of shares]*

pacchetto (m) di buste pack of envelopes

pacchetto (m) di sigarette packet of cigarettes

pacchetto (m) rivendicativo package deal

pacco (m) package *or* pack *or* parcel

paese (m) *[nazione]* country *[state]*

paese (m) d'origine country of origin

paese (m) in via di sviluppo developing country

paesi (mpl) esportatori di petrolio oil-exporting countries

paesi (mpl) industrializzati industrialized societies

paesi (mpl) produttori di petrolio oil-producing countries

paesi (mpl) sottosviluppati underdeveloped countries

paesi (mpl) stranieri *[l'estero]* overseas (n)

paga (f) *[salario]* pay (n) *[salary]*

pagabile payable

pagabile a sessanta giorni payable at sixty days

pagabile alla consegna payable on delivery

pagabile anticipatamente payable in advance

pagabile su richiesta payable on demand

pagamenti (mpl) ipotecari mortgage payments

pagamenti (mpl) mensili monthly payments

pagamenti (mpl) scaglionati staged payments

pagamento (m) payment *or* settlement

pagamento (m) *[esborso]* disbursement

pagamento (m) a carico del destinatario charges forward

pagamento (m) a saldo *o* totale full payment

pagamento (m) alla consegna cash on delivery (c.o.d.)

pagamento (m) annuale yearly payment

pagamento (m) anticipato advance payment *or* prepayment

pagamento (m) degli arretrati back payment

pagamento (m) di un debito discharge (n) *[of debt]*

pagamento (m) differito deferred payment

pagamento (m) in acconto payment on account

pagamento (m) in base al lavoro effettuato payment by results

pagamento (m) in contanti payment in cash *or* cash payment; prompt payment

pagamento (m) in natura payment in kind

pagamento (m) in più overpayment

pagamento (m) minimo minimum payment

pagamento (m) parziale partial payment

pagamento (m) progressivo progress payments

pagamento (m) provvisiorio interim payment

pagamento (m) semestrale half-yearly payment

pagamento (m) simbolico token payment

pagamento (m) tramite assegno payment by cheque

pagare *[remunerare]* pay (v) *[worker]*

pagare *[saldare]* pay (v) *[bill]*

pagare: far pagare charge someone

pagare: far pagare meno undercharge (v)

pagare: far pagare troppo overcharge (v)

pagare a rate pay in instalments

pagare anticipatamente pay in advance

pagare con carta di credito pay by credit card

pagare con un assegno pay by cheque

pagare gli interessi pay interest

pagare in anticipo prepay

pagare in contanti pay cash

pagare un conto pay a bill

pagare un debito service a debt

pagare un dividendo pay a dividend

pagare una fattura pay *or* settle an invoice

pagato paid *[invoice]*

pagato *[remunerato]* paid *[for work]*

pagato: non pagato outstanding *or* unpaid

pagato in anticipo prepaid

pagatore (m) tardivo slow payer

pagherò (m) promissory note *or* IOU

pagherò (m) cambiario note of hand

Pagine Gialle (fpl) yellow pages

palazzo (m) block (n) *or* large building

paletta (f) pallet

palettizzare *[trasportare a mezzo di palette]* palletize

pannello (m) panel

paragonabile comparable

paragonabile: essere paragonabile compare with

paragonare *[confrontare]* compare

pareggiare un budget balance (v) *[a budget]*

pari par

parità (f) parity

parte (f) part (n)

parte (f) *[leg]* party

parte (f) contraente contracting party

parte (f) querelante prosecution *[party in legal action]*

parte (f) superiore top (n) *or* upper surface

parte (f) venditrice *[cedente]* assignor

partecipazione (f) investment *or* interest (n)

partecipazione (f) azionaria shareholding

partenza (f) departure *or* going away

partenze (fpl) departures

partire (lasciare) leave (v) *or* go away

partita (f) (di merci) batch *or* lot *[of items]*

partitario (m) delle vendite sales ledger

partite (fpl) varie sundry items

partite (fpl) visibili visible trade

partner (m) commerciale trading partner

parziale one-sided

passare a switch over to

passare il tempo a spend *[time]*

passibile di liable to

passività (fpl) liabilities

passività (fpl) a lungo termine long-term liabilities

passività (fpl) correnti current liabilities

passivo (m) patrimoniale equity

patto: a patto che provided that *or* providing

pausa (f) break (n)

pavimento (m) floor *[surface]*

pedaggio (m) toll

penale (f) penalty

penalità (f) *[multa]* forfeit (n)

penalizzare penalize

pendente pending

pendolare (m) commuter

pendolare: fare il pendolare commute *[travel]*

penetrazione (f) di mercato market penetration

pensionamento (m) retirement

pensione (f) pension

per affari on business

per cento per cent

per conto di on behalf of

per persona per head

percentuale (f) percentage

percentuale (f) d'errore error rate

percentuale (f) di crescita growth rate

percentuale (f) di occupazione occupancy rate

percentuale (f) per il servizio service charge

percorso (m) run (n) *or* regular route

perdere miss *[train, plane]*

perdere *[un diritto]* forfeit (v) *[a right]*

perdere denaro lose money

perdere un deposito forfeit a deposit

perdere un'ordinazione lose an order

perdita (f) loss

perdita (f) *[di un diritto]* forfeiture *[of a right]*

perdita (f) d'esercizio trading loss

perdita (f) di capitale capital loss

perdita (f) di clientela loss of customers

perdita (f) di un'ordinazione loss of an order

perdita (f) netta net loss

perdita (f) parziale partial loss

perdita (f) secca dead loss

perdita (f) sulla carta paper loss

perdite (fpl) record record losses

perenzione (f) time limitation

perfetta sintonia (f) fine tuning

periferiche (fpl) peripherals

periodico periodic or periodical (adj)

periodico (m) *[rivista]* journal or magazine

periodico *[stagionale]* seasonal

periodo (m) period or term

periodo (m) *[stagione]* season *[time for something]*

periodo (m) di avviamento make-ready time

periodo (m) di massima attività peak period

periodo (m) di preavviso period of notice

periodo (m) di prova trial period

periodo (m) di recupero payback period

periodo (m) di validità period of validity

periodo (m) medio di permanenza di un prodotto shelf life of a product

perito (m) surveyor

perizia (f) d'avaria damage survey

permanenza (f) stay (n) *[time]*

permesso (m) permit (n)

permesso (m) di lavoro work permit

permesso (m) di soggiorno residence permit

permettere allow or permit

permuta (f) come pagamento parziale part exchange; trade-in

perseguire *[legalmente]* prosecute

persona (f) addetta al controllo delle scorte stock controller

persona (f) che prende decisioni decision maker

persona (f) che risolve problemi problem solver

personal computer (m) *[elaboratore]* personal computer (PC)

personale personal

personale (m) staff (n) or personnel

personale (m) addetto alle vendite *[forza vendita]* sales force or sales team

personale (m) al banco counter staff

personale (m) alberghiero hotel staff

personale (m) avventizio temporary staff

personale (m) d'ufficio office staff

personale (m) di ruolo regular staff

personale (m) dirigente managerial staff

personale (m) impiegatizio clerical staff

personale-chiave key personnel or key staff

personalizzato personalized

pesa a ponte (f) weighbridge

pesante heavy *[weight]*

pesare weigh

peseta (f) peseta *[Spanish currency]*

peso (m) weight

peso (m) lordo gross weight

peso (m) morto deadweight

peso (m) netto net weight

petroliera (f) tanker

petrolio (m) oil or petroleum

pezza (f) giustificativa di cassa cash voucher

pezzo (m) piece

pezzo (m) di ricambio spare part

pianificare investimenti plan investments

pianificatore (m) planner

pianificazione (f) planning

pianificazione (f) a lunga scadenza long-term planning

pianificazione (f) strategica strategic planning

piano (m) *[di edificio]* floor

piano (m) *[progetto]* plan (n) or project

piano (m) continuo rolling plan

piano (m) di contingenza contingency plan

piano (m) globale overall plan

piano (m) pensioni pension scheme

piano *[livello]* level

pianta (f) plan (n) or drawing

piatto flat *or* dull

piazza (f) del mercato marketplace *[in town]*

piccola cassa (f) petty cash

piccole imprese (fpl) small businesses

piccole spese (fpl) petty expenses

piccoli annunci (mpl) small ads

piccolo small

piccolo affarista *o* uomo d'affari small businessman

pieno *[intero]* full

pieno scarico (m) di un debito full discharge of a debt

PIL (prodotto interno lordo) gross domestic product (GDP)

pilota pilot (adj)

pilota (m) pilot (n) *[person]*

pioniere (m) pioneer (n)

pioniere: fare da pioniere in pioneer (v)

più alto *[migliore]* top (adj)

più basso *[inferiore]* lower (adj)

planimetria (f) floor plan

plusvalenza (f) capital gains

PNL (prodotto nazionale lordo) gross national product (GNP)

politica (f) policy *[way of working]*

politica (f) creditizia credit policy

politica (f) dei prezzi flessibile flexible pricing policy

politica (f) della determinazione dei prezzi pricing policy

politica (f) di budget budgetary policy

polizza (f) policy *[insurance]*

polizza (f) contro tutti i rischi all-risks policy

polizza (f) di assicurazione insurance policy

polizza (f) di carico bill of lading

polizza (f) provvisoria covering note

ponderazione (f) weighting

popolare popular

porta (f) door

porta (f) di computer computer port

portafoglio (m) portfolio *or* shareholding

portare bring *or* bear *or* carry

portare *[trasportare]* carry *or* transport

portare qualcuno in tribunale take someone to court

portata (f) lorda deadweight tonnage

portatile portable

portatore (m), portatrice (f) bearer

portfolio (m) *[cartella]* portfolio

portiere (m) reception clerk

portineria (f) reception (desk)

porto (m) port *or* harbour

porto (m) assegnato carriage forward *or* freight forward

porto (m) d'armamento port of registry

porto (m) d'imbarco port of embarkation

porto (m) di scalo port of call

porto (m) di transito entrepot port

porto (m) franco free port

porto (m) pagato carriage paid *or* postage paid

posare (mettere) place (v) *or* put

positivo positive

posizione (f) *[collocazione]* situation *or* place

posizione (f) *[situazione]* position *[state of affairs]*

posizione (f) finanziaria financial position

posporre hold over

possedere possess *or* own (v)

possibile acquirente (m) prospective buyer

possibilità (f) possibility

possibilità (fpl) di mercato market opportunities

possibile possible

possibile: se non è possibile failing that

posta (f) post (n) *or* mail (n)

posta (f) aerea airmail (n)

posta (f) elettronica electronic mail *or* e-mail

posta (f) in arrivo incoming mail

posta (f) in partenza outgoing mail

posta (f) ordinaria surface mail

postale postal

postdatare postdate

posticipare put back *[till later]*

posto (m) *[impiego]* place (n) *or* position *or* job

posto (m) *[luogo]* spot *or* place

posto (m) chiave key post

posto (m) di lavoro place of work; computer workstation

posto (m) vacante job vacancy

potenziale potential (adj)

potenziale (m) potential (n)

potere (m) *[controllo]* power *or* control (n)

potere (m) contrattuale bargaining power

potere (m) d'acquisto purchasing power; spending power

potere (m) per ricorrere al prestito borrowing power

pranzo (m) d'affari business lunch

pratica (f) *[dossier]* dossier

pratica (f) spregiudicata sharp practice

pratiche (fpl) restrittive restrictive practices

pratica: fare pratica train (v) *[learn]*

pratico *[maneggevole]* practical *or* handy

preavviso (m) notice *[time allowed]*

precedente previous *or* prior

precisare *[dichiarare]* state (v)

preciso *[accurato]* precise *or* accurate

preconfezionare prepack *or* prepackage

predere parte in enter into *[discussion]*

preferenza (f) preference

preferenziale preferential

preferire prefer

prefinanziamento (m) pre-financing

prefisso (m) telefonico dialling code

prelevare withdraw *[money]*

prelievo (m) sulle importazioni import levy

premio (m) *[gratifica]* bonus

premio (m) addizionale additional premium

premio (m) agli assicurati che non hanno denunciato sinistri no-claims bonus

premio (m) d'operosità incentive payments

premio (m) di assicurazione insurance premium

premio (m) di merito merit award *or* merit bonus

premio (m) di produttività productivity bonus

premio (m) di rinnovo renewal premium

premio (m) di rischio risk premium

premio (m) finale terminal bonus

prendere a prestito *[mutuare]* borrow

prendere in affitto rent (v) *[pay money for]*

prendere in consegna un carico di merce accept delivery of a shipment

prendere l'iniziativa take the initiative

prendere nota take note

prendere un carico (m) a bordo take on freight

prendere una telefonata take a call

prendersi giorni di ferie take time off work

prenotare book (v)

prenotare una camera *o* **un tavolo** *o* **un posto** reserve a room *or* a table *or* a seat

prenotazione (f) *[registrazione]* booking *or* reservation

prenotazione anticipata (f) advance booking

prenotazioni (fpl) di camera room reservations

preoccupazione (f) concern (n) *or* worry

preparare lo schema di un contratto draft a contract

preparazione (f) del budget budgeting

prescrizione (f) statute of limitations

presentare present (v) *[show a document]*

presentare *[un modello]* model (v) *[clothes]*

presentare *[introdurre]* introduce

presentare *[offrire]* present (v) *or* give *[a gift]*

presentare (produrre) produce (v) *or* bring out

presentare un conto render an account

presentare un effetto (m) per il pagamento present a bill for payment

presentare un effetto (m) per l'accettazione present a bill for acceptance

presentare una controrichiesta counter-claim (v)

presentarsi report (v) *[go to a place]*

presentarsi al check in check in *[at airport]*

presentarsi per un colloquio di lavoro report for an interview

presentazione (f) production *or* presentation

presentazione (f) in cofanetto boxed set

presente present (adj) *[being there]*

presidente (m) chairman

presidente e amministratore delegato chairman and managing director

presso care of (c/o)

prestanome (m) nominee

prestare lend *or* advance *[money]*

prestatore (m) lender

prestazione (f) performance

prestigio (m) prestige

prestiti (mpl) bancari bank borrowings

prestito (m) *[mutuo]* loan (n)

prestito (m) a termine term loan

prestito (m) agevolato soft loan

prestito (m) bancario bank loan

presto: al più presto possibile as soon as possible (asap)

pretendente (m) di diritto rightful claimant

prevedere forecast (v)

prevenire prevent

preventivo preventive

preventivo (m) estimate (n) *or* quote (n)

prevenzione (f) prevention

previdenza (f) sociale social security

previsione (f) forecast (n)

previsione (f) a lungo termine long-term forecast

previsione (f) della necessità di manodopera manpower forecasting

previsione (f) provvisoria delle vendite provisional forecast of sales

previsione (f) di vendita sales budget

previsione (f) di vendita sales forecast

previsioni (fpl) del flusso di cassa cash flow forecast

previsioni (fpl) di mercato market forecast

prezzi (mpl) concorrenziali keen prices

prezzi (mpl) correnti common pricing

prezzi (mpl) effettivi di vendita actuals

prezzi (mpl) equi fair price

prezzi (mpl) flessibili flexible prices

prezzi (mpl) franco banchina price ex quay

prezzi (mpl) franco magazzino price ex warehouse

prezzi (mpl) franco stabilimento price ex works

prezzi (mpl) inflazionati inflated prices

prezzi (mpl) popolari popular prices

prezzi (mpl) stabili stable prices

prezzo (m) price (n)

prezzo: ad alto prezzo highly-priced

prezzo (m) al dettaglio retail price

prezzo (m) al rivenditore trade price

prezzo (m) allineato competitive price

prezzo (m) concordato agreed price

prezzo (m) consigliato di fabbrica manufacturer's recommended price

prezzo (m) corrente current price

prezzo (m) d'acquisto purchase price

prezzo (m) d'apertura opening price

prezzo (m) d'entrata threshold price

prezzo (m) d'intervento intervention price

prezzo (m) d'occasione bargain price

prezzo (m) d'offerta supply price

prezzo (m) del coperto cover charge

prezzo (m) del petrolio oil price

prezzo (m) del trasporto haulage costs *or* haulage rates

prezzo (m) di catalogo catalogue price

prezzo (m) di chiusura closing price

prezzo (m) di fabbrica factory price

prezzo (m) di fattura invoice value

prezzo (m) di listino list price

prezzo (m) di mercato market price *or* market rate

prezzo (m) di permuta trade-in price

prezzo (m) di rivendita resale price

prezzo (m) di sostegno support price

prezzo (m) di vendita selling price

prezzo (m) eccessivo overcharge (n)

prezzo (m) franco delivered price

prezzo (m) intero full price

prezzo (m) massimo maximum price *or* ceiling price

prezzo (m) medio average price

prezzo (m) minimo reserve price

prezzo (m) netto net price

prezzo (m) per contanti cash price

prezzo (m) per merce pronta spot price

prezzo (m) ridottissimo rock-bottom prices

prezzo (m) ridotto cut price (n)

prezzo ridotto: a prezzo ridotto cut-price (adj)

prezzo (m) scontato discount price

prezzo (m) sotto costo cost price

prezzo (m) stabile firm price

prezzo (m) stabilito set price

prezzo (m) tutto compreso all-in price

prezzo (m) unitario unit price

prima classe first class

prima: di prima classe first-class (adj) *or* A1

prima: di prima qualità prime *or* top grade

prima opzione (f) first option

primario primary

primato (m) record (n) *[better than before]*

primo first

primo *[di prima qualità]* prime

primo ad entrare primo ad uscire first in first out (FIFO)

primo giorno (m) del trimestre quarter day

primo trimestre (m) first quarter

principale principal (adj) *or* main *or* chief

principio (m) principle

privatizzare privatize

privatizzazione (f) privatization

privato private

privilegio (m) lien

privo di validità (inabile) invalid

privo di valore worthless

pro-capite per capita

probabile prospective

probatorio probationary

problema (m) problem

procacciare canvass

procedere proceed

procedimenti (mpl) legali judicial processes

procedimento (m) giudiziario prosecution *[legal action]*

procedura (f) procedure

procedura (f) di selezione selection procedure

processi (mpl) industriali industrial processes

processo (m) process (n)

processo (m) trial *[court case]*

processo (m) decisionale decision making

procura (f) power of attorney; proxy

procurarsi get

procurarsi fondi secure funds

procuratore (m) attorney

procuratore (m) legale solicitor

prodotti (mpl) agricoli agricultural produce

prodotti (mpl) che si fanno concorrenza competing products

prodotti (mpl) competitivi competitive products

prodotti (mpl) con etichetta propria own label goods

prodotti (mpl) con marchio proprio own brand goods

prodotti (mpl) di alta qualità high-quality goods

prodotti (mpl) di seconda qualità seconds

prodotti (mpl) essenziali staple product

prodotti (mpl) finiti finished goods

prodotti (mpl) semilavorati semi-finished products

prodotto (m) product *or* article

prodotto (m) derivato by-product

prodotto (m) di prestigio prestige product

prodotto (m) finito end product

prodotto (m) nazionale lordo (PNL) gross national product (GNP)

prodotto (m) per il mercato di massa mass market product

prodotto (m) sensibile ai cambiamenti di prezzo price-sensitive product

prodotto (m) interno lordo (PIL) gross domestic product (GDP)

prodotto-guida (m) del mercato market leader

produrre *[fabbricare]* produce (v) *or* manufacture *or* make

produrre *[presentare]* produce *or* show *or* bring out

produrre in eccesso overproduce

produrre in serie mass-produce

produrre automobili in serie
mass-produce cars

produttività (f) productivity

produttivo productive

produttore (m) *[fabbricante]* producer
or manufacturer

produzione (f) production *or* making *or*
output

produzione (f) in eccesso
overproduction

produzione (f) in serie mass production

produzione (f) totale total output

produzione (f) nazionale domestic
production

professionale professional *or*
occupational

professionista (m) *[esperto]*
professional (n) *or* expert

proficuo profitable

profitto (m) (utile) profit *or* earnings

proforma: fattura (f) proforma pro
forma (invoice)

progettare design (v)

progettare *[organizzare]* plan (v)

progettato projected

progettazione (f) *[design]* design (n)

progettazione (f) del prodotto product
design

progetto (m) *[piano]* project *or* plan

progetto (m) di legge bill (n) *[in
Parliament]*

progetto (m) edilizio di ricostruzione
redevelopment

progetto (m) pilota pilot scheme

progetto (m) redditizio
money-making plan

programma (m) programme *or*
timetable

programma (m) aziendale corporate
plan

programma (m) di computer
computer program

programma (m) di ricerca research
programme

programmare timetable (v)

programmare un computer program
a computer

programmatore (m) di computer
computer programmer

programmazione (f) aziendale
corporate planning

**programmazione (f) delle assunzioni
di manodopera** manpower planning

programmazione (f) di computer
computer programming

programmazione (f) economica
economic planning

progresso (m) *[sviluppo]* progress *or*
development

progresso: fare progressi progress (v)
or make progress

proibire forbid

proibitivo prohibitive

prolungamento (m) extension *[making
longer]*

prolungare extend *[make longer]*

promessa (f) promise (n)

promettere promise (v)

promozionale promotional

promozione (f) promotion *[better job,
publicity]*

promozione (f) delle vendite sales
promotion

promozione (f) di un prodotto
promotion of a product

promuovere promote *[give better job,
advertise]*

promuovere un'immagine aziendale
promote a corporate image

pronosticare tip (v) *[say what might
happen]*

pronta cassa (f) ready cash

pronto ready

pronunciarsi in una vertenza
adjudicate in a dispute

propaganda (f) canvassing

propagandista (m) canvasser

proporre propose *or* move *[a motion]*

proporre *[offrire]* offer (v) *[to buy]*

proporzionale proportional *or* pro rata

proporzione (f) proportion

proposito (m) *[scopo]* aim (n)

proposta (f) proposal *or* suggestion

proposta (f) *[di assicurazione]*
insurance proposal

proposta (f) unica di vendita unique
selling point *or* proposition (USP)

proprietà (f) ownership

proprietà (f) collettiva collective
ownership

proprietà (f) comune common
ownership

proprietà (f) immobiliare real estate

proprietà (f) multipla multiple ownership

proprietà (f) privata private property; private ownership

proprietaria (f) proprietress

proprietario (m) proprietor *or* owner

proprietario (m) legittimo rightful owner

prorata *[proporzionale]* pro rata

prosperare flourish *or* prosper

prospettive (fpl) prospects

prospetto (m) prospectus

prossimo early

protesta (f) *[reclamo]* protest *or* complaint

protesta (f) con occupazione sit-down protest

protestare *[reclamare]* complain (about)

protestare contro qualcosa protest (v) *[against something]*

protestare una cambiale protest a bill

protesto (m) *[per mancato pagamento]* protest (n) *[official document]*

protettivo protective

protezione (f) protection

protezione (f) *[barriera]* hedge (n)

protezione (f) del consumatore consumer protection

prova (f) test (n); protection; proof; trial

prova: in prova on approval

prova (f) documentata documentary proof

prova (f) gratuita free trial

provare test (v)

proventi (mpl) da partite invisibili invisible earnings

provvedere provide

provvedere a provide for; make provision for

provvedere di generi alimentari cater for

provvedimenti (mpl) fiscali fiscal measures

provvisorio provisional

provvista (f) supply (n) *or* stock of goods

prudente *[sicuro]* safe (adj)

pubblicazione (f) periodica periodical (n)

pubbliche relazioni (fpl) public relations (PR)

pubblicità (f) (reclame) publicity *or* advertising

pubblicità: fare pubblicità *[reclamizzare]* advertise

pubblicità (f) (spot) TV commercial

pubblicità (f) *[annuncio pubblicitario]* advertisement

pubblicità (f) a mezzo posta direct-mail advertising

pubblicità (f) di un prodotto product advertising

pubblicità (f) su tutto il territorio nazionale national advertising

pubblicizzare publicize

pubblicizzare un nuovo prodotto promote a new product

pubblico public (adj)

punto (m) point

punto (m) di pareggio fra costi e ricavi breakeven point

punto (m) di partenza starting point

punto (m) di riferimento benchmark

punto (m) di vendita point of sale (p.o.s. *or* POS)

punto (m) di vendita al dettaglio retail outlets

punto (m) di vendita diretta della fabbrica factory outlet

punto (m) di vendita elettronico electronic point of sale (EPOS)

punto (m) metallico staple (n)

punto (m) morto deadlock (n)

punto: essere a un punto morto be deadlocked

punto (m) per la dichiarazine doganale d'entrata customs entry point

punto (m) percentuale percentage point

puntuale on time

Qq

quadri (mpl) direttivi management team

quadri (mpl) intermedi middle management

quadro (m) generale survey (n) *or* general report

qualificarsi qualify as

qualificato *[abile]* qualified *or* skilled

qualifiche (fpl) professionali professional qualifications

qualità (f) quality

qualità (f) extra premium quality

qualità: di qualità inferiore low-grade *or* low-quality

qualità (f) scadente poor quality

qualità (f) superiore top quality

qualità superiore di qualità superiore high-quality

quantità (f) quantity

quartiere (m) *[zona]* area *or* quarter *or* district *[of town]*

quarto (m) quarter *[25%]*

quarto trimestre (m) fourth quarter

querelante (m) plaintiff

questione (f) *[argomento]* item *[on agenda]* *or* matter (n) *[to be discussed]*

quietanza (f) finale final discharge

quota (f) quota

quota (f) (tariffa) rate (n) *or* price

quota (f) d'ammortamento depreciation rate

quota (f) d'iscrizione admission fee

quota (f) di mercato market share

quotare quote (v) *[a reference number]*

quotare *[indicare un prezzo]* quote (v) *[estimate costs]*

quotazione (f) quotation *or* quote *[estimate of cost]*

quotidiano daily

Rr

raccogliere *[cogliere]* collect (v) *or* fetch

raccogliere fondi raise (v) *or* obtain money

raccoglitore (m) collector

raccomandare *[consigliare]* recommend *or* advise *[what should be done]*

raccomandata (f) registered letter

raccomandazione (f) recommendation

raddoppiare double (v)

raduno (m) dei venditori sales conference

rafforzarsi rally (v)

raggiungere reach *or* arrive at

raggiungere un obiettivo meet a target

raggruppare bracket together

ragione (f) sociale corporate name

ragioniere (m) *o* **ragioniera (f)** *[contabile]* accountant

ragioniere (m) iscritto all'albo *[revisore ufficiale dei conti]* certified accountant

rallentamento (m) slowdown

rallentare slow down

rammentare remind

rampa (f) di carico loading ramp

rapidamente *[velocemente]* fast (adv)

rapporto (m) report (n); ratio

rapporto (m) corso/utili price/earnings ratio (P/E ratio)

rapporto (m) di indebitamento gearing

rapporto (m) fra utile e dividendo dividend cover

rapporto (m) riservato confidential report

rappresentante (m) sales representative

rappresentante (m) *[agente]* agent *or* representative

rappresentante (m) commissionario commission rep

rappresentante (m) (di commercio) salesman *or* representative

rappresentante (m) esclusivo sole agent

rappresentanza (f) esclusiva sole agency

rappresentare represent

rappresentare qualcuno deputize for someone

rappresentativo representative (adj)

rata (f) instalment

ratifica (f) ratification

ratificare ratify

razionalizzare rationalize

razionalizzazione (f) rationalization

reale real

realizzabile viable

realizzare realize *or* sell for money

realizzare (attuare) implement (v) *or* put into practice

realizzare beni realize property

realizzare la penetrazione di un mercato penetrate a market

realizzare un piano *o* **un progetto** realize a plan

realizzazione (f) di cespiti realization of assets

reato (m) di omissione nonfeasance

reazione (f) response

recapito (m) *[indirizzo]* address (n)

recentissimo latest

recessione (f) recession

reciproco *[mutuo]* reciprocal *or* mutual

reclamare *[protestare]* complain (about)

reclame (f) *[pubblicità]* advertising

reclamizzare un nuovo prodotto advertise a new product

reclamo (m) *[domanda d'indennizzo]* claim (n)

reclamo (m) *[protesta]* complaint

recuperabile recoverable

recuperare collect (v) *[money]*

recuperare repossess

recuperare *[salvare]* salvage (v)

recuperare un debito collect a debt

recupero (m) collection *[of money]*; salvage *[of goods]*

recupero (m) dell'investimento payback

recupero (m) di crediti debt collection

redditività (f) profitability

redditività (f) dei costi cost-effectiveness

redditizio paying (adj); money-making *or* cost-effective

reddito (m) revenue *or* income

reddito (m) complessivo total revenue

reddito (m) da affittanze rental income

reddito (m) da dividendi dividend yield

reddito (m) da investimenti investment income

reddito (m) effettivo real income *or* real wages

reddito (m) fisso fixed income *or* regular income

reddito (m) imponibile taxable income

reddito (m) lordo gross income

reddito (m) netto net income *or* net salary

reddito (m) non imponibile non-taxable income

reddito (m) personale personal income

reddito (m) societario negativo negative cash flow

reddito (m) sugli investimenti return on investment (ROI)

reddito (m) totale total income

reddito (m) ufficiale official return

redigere *[abbozzare]* draw up *or* draft (v)

redimibile redeemable

referenze (fpl) *[attestato]* reference *[on person]*

regalare give (away) *[as gift]* *or* present (v)

regalo (m) gift *or* present (n)

regionale regional

regione (f) *[area]* region *or* area

registrare record (v) *or* write in

registrare chiamate log calls

registrare una voce *[contabile]* post an entry

registrato registered (adj)

registratore (f) di cassa cash register

registrazione (f) registration; registry

registrazione (f) *[prenotazione]* booking

registrazione (f) a credito credit entry

registrazione (f) a debito debit entry

registrazione (f) di storno contra entry

registrazione (f) sul computer computer listing

registro (m) register (n) *or* official list

registro (m) *[libro contabile]* register (n)

registro (m) degli amministratori register of directors

registro (m) degli azionisti *o* **registro (m) delle azioni** register of shareholders

registro (m) delle ordinazioni order book

registro (m) delle ricevute receipt book

Registro (m) delle SPA companies' register

regolamenti (mpl) *[disposizioni]* regulations

regolamento (m) regulation

regolamento (m) finanziario financial settlement

regolare (v) regulate *or* adjust

regolare *[normale]* regular *or* normal *or* ordinary

regolarizzare regulate *[by law]*

regolarmente *[dovutamente]* duly *[legally]*

regresso (m) downturn

reimportare reimport (v)

reimportazione (f) reimportation; reimport (n)

reinvestimento (m) reinvestment

reinvestire reinvest

relativo relevant

relativo a relating to

relazione (f) annuale al bilancio annual report

relazione (f) provvisoria interim report

relazione (f) sull'avanzamento progress report

relazioni (fpl) relations

relazioni (fpl) industriali industrial relations

remunerare (pagare) pay (v) *[worker]*

remunerativo *[redditizio]* profitable

remunerato *[pagato]* paid *[for work]*

rendere *[apportare]* bring in *or* yield

rendere *[fruttare]* produce (v) *[interest]*

rendere conto account for

rendere effettivo un accordo implement an agreement

rendere saturo il mercato saturate the market

rendersi conto di *[capire]* realize *[understand]*

rendiconti (mpl) annuali annual accounts

rendiconto (m) statement

rendiconto (m) del flusso di cassa cash flow statement

rendiconto (m) delle spese statement of expenses

rendimento (m) effettivo effective yield

rendimento (m) immediato current yield

rendimento (m) lordo gross yield

rendimento (m) netto net yield

rendita (f) yield (n) *[on investment]*

rendita (f) vitalizia *[usufrutto]* life interest

reparto (m) department *[in shop]*; division *[of company]*

reparto (m) esportazioni export department

reparto (m) marketing marketing division

reparto (m) contabilità accounts department

reperimento (m) retrieval

reperire retrieve

replica (f) repeat

rescindere rescind

rescindere *[invalidare]* void *or* invalidate

rescindere un accordo terminate an agreement

residente resident (adj)

residente (m) *[abitante]* resident (n) *or* inhabitant

residenza (f) residence

resoconto (m) dettagliato detailed
account

resoconto (m) mensile monthly
statement

resoconto (m) semestrale half-yearly
statement

respingere *[mandare indietro]* return
(v) *or* send back

respingere *[rifiutare]* reject (v)

responsabile (m) dei reclami claims
manager

responsabile (m) del mastro dei conti
dei creditori bought ledger clerk

responsabile (m) di un prodotto
product engineer

responsabile (m) di un ufficio acquisti
buyer *[for a store]*

responsabile di *o* per responsible *or*
liable (for)

responsabilità (f) responsibility *or*
responsibilties

responsabilità (f) *[obbligo]* liability

responsabilità (f) contrattuale
contractual liability

responsabilità (f) illimitata unlimited
liability

responsabilità (f) limitata limited
liability

restare remain

resti in linea per favore hold the line
please *or* please hold

restituibile returnable

restituire *[consegnare]* hand in *or*
deliver *or* consign

restringere tighten up on

restringimento (m) shrinkage

restrittivo restrictive

restrizione (f) restraint *or* restriction *or*
limitation

restrizione (f) endorsement *[on
insurance]*

restrizioni (fpl) alle importazioni
import restrictions

rete (f) network (n)

rete (f) di distribuzione distribution
network

reticolo (m) grid

retribuire remunerate

retribuzione (f) remuneration

retribuzione (f) *[stipendio]* pay (n) *or*
salary

retribuzione (f) a cottimo piece rate

retribuzione (f) a ore hourly rate

retribuzione (f) ferie holiday pay

retro (m) (dorso) back (n)

retroattivo retroactive

retrodatare antedate

rettifica (f) *[emendamento]*
rectification *or* amendment

revisionare service (v) *[a machine]*

revisione (f) *[manutenzione]* service
(n) *[of machine]*

revisione (f) contabile audit (n)

revisione (f) contabile periodica
general audit

revisione (f) dello stipendio salary
review

revisione (f) esterna external audit

revisione (f) interna internal audit

revisore (m) esterno external auditor

revisore (m) interno internal auditor

revisore (m) ufficiale dei conti auditor

revoca (f) di una nomina cancellation
of an appointment

revocare revoke

riacquistare buy back

riadattare readjust

riaddestramento (m) retraining

riaddestrare retrain

riassestamento (m) readjustment

riassicurare reinsure

riassicuratore (m) reinsurer

riassicurazione (f) reinsurance

riassumere *[una persona]* re-employ
[someone]

riassunzione (f) re-employment

ribassista (m) bear (n) *[on Stock
Exchange]*

ribasso (m) *[caduta]* reduction *or* drop
(n)

ribasso: in ribasso falling

ribasso (m) delle vendite drop in sales

ricambio (m) turnover *[of staff]*

ricavare al netto net (v)

ricavi (mpl) netti net sales

ricavo (m) dalla pubblicità revenue
from advertising

ricavo (m) nullo nil return

ricerca (f) research (n)

ricerca: fare ricerche do research *or*
research (v)

ricerca (f) **automatica dell'informazione** data retrieval

ricerca (f) di mercato market research

ricerca (f) e sviluppo (RS) research and development (R & D)

ricercatore (m), ricercatrice (f) research worker *or* researcher

ricettività (f) alberghi hotel accommodation

ricevente receiving

ricevere receive

ricevimento (m) receipt *[receiving]*

ricevuta (f) receipt *[piece of paper]*

ricevuta (f) (di vendita) sales receipt

ricevuta (f) in duplicato duplicate receipt *or* duplicate of a receipt

richiamo (m) appeal (n) *or* attraction

richiamo (m) per i clienti customer appeal

richiedere *[domandare]* demand *or* request (v)

richiedere *[volere]* take (v) *or* need

richiesta (f) request (n); inquiry

richiesta: su richiesta on request

richiesta (f) *[domanda]* demand (n) *[for payment]*

richiesta (f) di indennizzo assicurativo insurance claim

richiesta (f) di informazioni enquiry

richiesta (f) di iscrizione letter of application

richiesta (f) di pagamento call (n) *[for money]*

richiesta (f) stagionale seasonal demand

richieste (fpl) requirements

riciclare recycle; launder *[money]*

ricollocamento (m) reappointment

ricollocare reappoint

ricompensa (f) *[compenso]* compensation

riconciliare reconcile

riconciliazione (f) reconciliation

riconciliazione (f) dei conti reconciliation of accounts

riconoscere un sindacato recognize a union

riconoscimento (m) recognition

riconoscimento (m) scritto di un debito *[pagherò]* IOU (= I owe you)

riconoscimento (m) sindacale union recognition

ricorrente recurrent

ricorrere a consulenza legale take legal advice

ricorrere in appello *[appellare]* appeal (v) *[against a decision]*

ricorso (m) *[appello]* appeal (n) *[against a decision]*

ricuperare recover *or* get something back

ricuperare mediante tassazione clawback

ricupero (m) recovery *[getting something back]*

ridistribuire redistribute

ridurre *[abbassare]* reduce *or* knock down (v) *[price]*

ridurre il valore write down *[assets]*

ridurre le spese reduce expenditure

ridurre un prezzo reduce a price

riduzione (f) *[sconto]* rebate *or* price reduction

riduzione (f) d'imposta tax allowance

riduzione (f) dei costi cost-cutting

riduzione (f) delle spese retrenchment

riduzione (f) di posti lavorativi job cuts

riduzione (f) di prezzi knockdown prices

riduzioni (fpl) d'imposta tax reductions

rieleggere re-elect

rielezione (f) re-election

riesaminare revise

riesportare re-export (v)

riesportazione (f) re-export (n)

rifarsi delle perdite recoup one's losses

riferimento (m) reference *[dealing with]*

riferimento: fare riferimento a refer *[to item]*

riferire report (v)

riferirsi (fare riferimento a) refer (to)

rifinanziamento (m) di un prestito refinancing *or* restructuring of a loan

rifiutare fall *or* decline (v)

rifiutare *[respingere]* refuse *or* reject (v) *or* turn down

rifiutare un accordo repudiate an agreement

rifiuto (m) refusal or rejection

rifornimento (m) restocking

rifornire restock

rifugio (m) fiscale tax haven

riguardante regarding

riguardare apply to or affect

rilasciare release (v) *[make public]*

rilascio (m) release (n) or issue *[of shares]*

rilevamento (m) takeover

rimandare *[aggiornare]* adjourn

rimandare una lettera al mittente return a letter to sender

rimanenze (fpl) iniziali opening stock

rimanere indietro fall behind *[be in a worse position]*

rimborsabile refundable

rimborsabile repayable or repayable

rimborsare pay back

rimborsare un'obbligazione redeem a bond

rimborso (m) reimbursement or refund or repayment

rimborso (m) delle spese reimbursement of expenses

rimborso (m) totale full refund

rimessa (f) remittance

rimetterci out of pocket

rimettere remit (v)

rimuovere remove

ringraziamento (m) vote of thanks

rinnovare renew

rinnovare un abbonamento renew a subscription

rinnovare un contratto d'affitto renew a lease

rinnovare una cambiale renew a bill of exchange

rinnovo (m) renewal

rinnovo (m) di un contratto d'affitto renewal of a lease

rinnovo (m) di un abbonamento renewal of a subscription

rinnovo (m) di una cambiale renewal of a bill

rinuncia (f) renunciation; waiver *[of right]*

rinunciare waive

rinunciare ad un pagamento waive a payment

rinunciare ad un'azione (f) abandon an action

rinviare *[differire]* postpone

rinvio (m) return (n); deferment or postponement

rinvio (m) di pagamento deferment of payment

riordinare reorder (v)

riorganizzare reorganize

riorganizzazione (f) reorganization

riorganizzazione (f) di una società restructuring of the company

ripagare repay

riparare *[aggiustare]* repair (v) or fix or mend

riparazione (m) repair (n)

riparo (m) shelter

ripartire un rischio spread a risk

ripartizione (f) breakdown (n) *[of items]*

ripetere un'ordinazione repeat an order

riportare a nuovo carry forward

riportare un pareggio carry over a balance

riprendere resume

riprendere le trattative resume negotiations

riprendersi recover or get better or stage a recovery

ripresa (f) recovery or getting better; rally

riprodurre *[copiare]* copy (v)

ripudiare repudiate

risarcimento (m) di danni damages or compensation for damage

risarcire *[indennizzare]* indemnify

risarcire qualcuno per una perdita indemnify someone for a loss

riscattare surrender (v) *[an insurance]*

riscattare un pegno redeem a pledge

riscattare una polizza surrender a policy

riscatto (m) surrender (n) *[of an insurance policy]*

riscatto (m) *[di un prestito]* redemption *[of a loan]*

rischiare risk (v) *[money]*

rischio (m) risk (n)

rischio (m) d'incendio fire risk

rischio (m) finanziario financial risk *or* exposure

rischioso risky

riscossione (f) delle imposte tax collection

riserva (f) store *[of items kept] or* reserve *[of supplies]*

riserva (f) *[accantonamento]* reserve *or* provision *[money put aside]*

riserva: di riserva backup (adj) *[copy]*

riserva (f) di cassa cash reserves

riserva (f) di materia prima stock of raw materials

riservare reserve (v)

riservatezza (f) confidentiality

riservato confidential

riserve (fpl) reserves

riserve: con riserve *[condizionato]* with reservations

riserve (fpl) d'emergenza emergency reserves

riserve (fpl) occulte hidden reserves

riserve (fpl) valutarie currency reserves

risoluzione (f) resolution

risoluzione (f) di problemi problem solving

risolvere un problema solve a problem

risorse (fpl) resources

risorse (fpl) finanziarie financial resources

risorse (fpl) naturali natural resources

risparmi (mpl) savings

risparmiare *[economizzare]* save (v)

risparmiare: che risparmia energia energy-saving (adj)

rispettare respect (v)

rispettare una scadenza (f) meet a deadline

rispondere answer (v) *or* reply (v)

rispondere: dover rispondere a qualcuno report to someone

rispondere: che deve rispondere a qualcuno responsible to someone

rispondere a una lettera answer a letter

rispondere al telefono answer the telephone

risposta (f) answer (n) *or* reply (n)

ristagno (m) stagnation

ristrutturare restructure

ristrutturazione (f) restructuring

risultati (mpl) results *[company's profit or loss]*

risultato (m) result *[in general]*

risultato: avere come risultato result in

ritaglio (m) (di campioni) swatch

ritardare delay (v)

ritardo (m) delay (n) *or* hold-up (n)

ritardo: in ritardo late (adv)

ritardo: essere in ritardo *[nel fare una cosa]* fall behind *or* be late *[in doing something]*

ritelefonare phone back

ritenuta (f) d'acconto withholding tax

ritirare withdraw *[an offer]*

ritirare la propria candidatura stand down

ritiro (m) collection *[of goods]; withdrawal [of money]*

ritorno (m) return (n) *or* going back

ritrattare un'offerta di rilevamento withdraw a takeover bid

riunione (f) meeting; conference

riunione (f) del consiglio di amministrazione board meeting

riuscire *[avere successo]* succeed *or* do well

riuscire a manage to

riuscire: non riuscire fail *[not to do something]*

rivalutare revalue (v)

rivalutazione (f) revaluation; appreciation *[in value]*

rivelare (divulgare) reveal *or* disclose

rivelazione (f) *[divulgazione]* revelation *or* disclosure

rivendicare claim (v) *[insurance]*

rivendicazione (f) salariale wage claim

rivendita (f) resale

rivenditore (m) stockist

rivista (f) (periodico) magazine *or* journal

rivista (f) aziendale house magazine

rivista (f) di categoria trade magazine

rivolgere la parola a qualcuno address (v) *or* speak to someone

rivolto a una fascia alta del mercato up-market

roll on/roll off *[traghetto per automezzi]* roll on/roll off ferry

rompere break (v) *[a contract]*

rompersi break down (v) *[of machine]*

rotazione (f) turnround *[goods sold]*

rotazione (f) delle scorte stock turnover

rottura (f) breakdown (n) *[of talks]*

rotture (fpl) *[danni]* breakages

routine (f) *[ordinaria amministrazione]* routine (n)

rovinare (viziare) spoil

RS (ricerca e sviluppo) R&D (= research and development)

Ss

sacchetto (m) di carta paper bag

saggio (m) *[campione]* sample (n)

sala (f) di esposizione showroom

sala (f) di vendita all'asta auction rooms

sala (f) esposizioni exhibition hall

sala (f) per VIP VIP lounge

sala (f) riunioni boardroom; conference room

sala (f) transiti transit lounge

salario (m) wage

salario (m) minimo minimum wage

salario (m) minimo garantito guaranteed minimum wage

salario (m) orario hourly wage

saldare *[pagare]* pay (v) *or* settle *[bill]*

saldare un conto settle an account

saldezza (f) steadiness

saldi (mpl) per inventario stocktaking sale

saldo (m) sale (n) *[at a low price]*

saldo (m) a metà prezzo half-price sale

saldo (m) da riportare balance brought down *or* brought forward

saldo (m) debitore debit balance

saldo (m) di cassa cash balance

saldo (m) di un debito clearing *or* paying *[of a debt]*

saldo (m) dovuto balance due to us

saldo (m) in banca bank balance

saldo (m) riportato balance carried down *or* carrried forward

salire *[ascendere]* climb

salire alle stelle soar

salone (m) delle partenze departure lounge

salvaguardia (f) safeguard

salvare *[su disco]* save (v) *[on computer]*

salvare *[recuperare]* salvage (v)

salvo errori e omissioni (S.E. & O) errors and omissions excepted (e. & o.e.)

salvo vista e verifica on approval

saturare saturate *or* glut (v)

saturare di prodotti overstock (v)

saturazione (f) saturation *or* glut

sbagliato wrong

sbarcare land (v) *[passengers, cargo]*

sbarrare un assegno cross a cheque

sbocco (m) outlet

sborsare pay out

scadente *[basso]* low (adj)

scadenza (f) *[fine]* expiry

scadere *[terminare]* expire *or* mature *or* lapse

scaduto overdue

scaffalatura (f) shelving *or* shelves

scaffale (m) shelf

scaglionare stagger

scala (f) scale *[system]*

scala: in scala naturale full-scale (adj) *or* full-size

scala: in scala ridotta small-scale

scala (f) *[variazioni]* range (n) *or* variation

scala (f) incrementale incremental scale

scala (f) retributiva wage scale

scala (f) temporale time scale

scalo (m) merci freight depot

scalo (m) per container container port

scambiabile exchangeable

scambiare swap (v) *or* exchange

scambiare con exchange (v) *[one thing for another]*

scambio (m) swap (n) *or* exchange

scambio (m) *[baratto]* barter (n)

scambio (m) di merci e prodotti bartering

scappatoia (f) fiscale tax shelter

scaricare unload *[goods]*

scaricare merce in un porto land goods at a port

scaricatore (m) (di porto) *[stivatore]* stevedore

scarsità (f) shortage

scarto (m) reject (n)

scatola (f) di cartone cardboard box

scatola (f) per la piccola cassa petty cash box

scegliere choose

scegliere la strada più facile take the soft option

scelta (f) choice (n)

scelta (f) del momento opportuno timing

scendere *[diminuire]* fall off

scheda (f) filing card *or* index card

schedare card-index (v)

schedario (m) card index; filing cabinet

schedatura (f) filing *[action]*; card-indexing

schema (m) del ciclo flow chart

scienze (fpl) economiche *[economia]* economics *[study]*

sciogliere una società di persone dissolve a partnership

scioglimento (m) *[liquidazione]* winding up

sciolto loose

scioperante (m) striker

scioperare strike (v)

sciopero (m) strike (n)

sciopero (m) bianco go-slow *or* work-to-rule

sciopero (m) con occupazione sit-down strike

sciopero (m) di protesta protest strike

sciopero (m) di solidarietà sympathy strike

sciopero (m) generale general strike

sciopero (m) selvaggio wildcat strike

scontabile discountable

sconti (mpl) al rivenditore trade terms

scontista (m) discounter

sconto (m) *[riduzione]* discount *or* rebate *or* price reduction

sconto: con sconto di off *[reduced by]*

sconto: fare uno sconto di take off *or* deduct

sconto (m) ai rivenditori trade discount

sconto (m) all'ingrosso wholesale discount

sconto (m) cassa cash discount

sconto (m) del valore attuale discounted cash flow (DCF)

sconto (m) di base basic discount

sconto (m) percentuale percentage discount

sconto (m) per pagamento in contanti cash discount

sconto (m) sul quantitativo quantity discount *or* volume discount

scontrarsi con crash (v) into

scoperto (di c/c) overdraft

scopo (m) *[proposito]* aim (n)

scopo: avere lo scopo di aim (v)

scorrettamente incorrectly

scorretto incorrect

scorta (f) *[di materie prime]* stockpile (n)

scorte (fpl) stock (n) *or* goods *or* inventory (n)

scritto a mano handwritten

scrittura (f) writing

scrittura (f) contabile entry *[writing]*

scrivania (f) desk

scrivere write

scuola (f) per segretarie d'azienda secretarial college

scuola (m) superiore di commercio commercial college

scusa (f) apology

scusarsi apologize

S. E. & O. (salvo errori e omissioni) e. & o.e. (errors and omissions excepted)

seconda categoria *o* **seconda classe** second-class

seconda mano: di seconda mano secondhand

secondo second (adj)

secondo: a secondo di according to *or* under

secondo i termini convenuti according to the terms agreed; on agreed terms

secondo trimestre (m) second quarter

sede (f) head office

sede (f) legale registered office

sede (f) centrale headquarters (HQ); main office

segnale (m) di linea libera dialling tone

segnale (m) di linea occupata engaged tone

segno (m) place (n) *[in a text]*

segretaria (f), segretario (m) secretary

segretaria (f) personale personal assistant (PA)

segretaria (f) temporanea temp (n)

segretario (m) del consiglio d'amministrazione company secretary

segreteria (f) telefonica answering machine

segreto secret (adj)

segreto (m) secret (n)

seguire follow

seguito: fare seguito follow

seguito: in seguito a further to

selezionare candidati screen candidates

selezione (f) selection

sembrare appear

semestre (m) half-year

senza scalo *[ininterrotto]* non-stop

senza scopo di lucro non profit-making

senza sovvenzioni unsubsidized

senza spese *[franco]* franco

senza tener conto di regardless of

separare separate (v)

separato separate (adj)

sequela (f) *[serie]* run (n) *[work routine]*

sequestrare sequester *or* sequestrate *or* seize

sequestratario (m) sequestrator

sequestro (m) sequestration *or* seizure

serie (f) set (n); run (n)

serratura (f) lock (n)

servire serve

servire un cliente serve a customer

servizi (mpl) facilities

servizi (mpl) di elaborazione elettronica computer services

servizi (mpl) di trasporto transport facilities

servizio (m) service (n)

servizio (m) di marketing marketing department

servizio (m) in camera room service

servizio (m) pacchi postali parcel post

servizio (m) postale postal service

servizio (m) scadente poor service

servizio (m) segreteria telefonica answering service

servizio (m) sollecito prompt service

servizio (m) spedizioni dispatch department

servizio (m) stralci giornalistici clipping service

servizio (m) telefonico gratuito toll free number *or* 0800 number

settimana (f) week

settimanale weekly

settore (m) sector *or* branch

settore (m) privato private sector

settore (m) pubblico public sector

settore (m) terziario tertiary sector

sezione (f) *[reparto]* department *[in office]*

sfavorevole unfavourable

sforzo (m) effort

sfruttare exploit

sgravio (m) per doppia tassazione double taxation agreement

sicurezza (f) security *or* safety

sicurezza (f) del posto di lavoro job security

sicurezza (f) dell'impiego security of employment

sicurezza (f) di possesso security of tenure

sicuro (prudente) safe (adj)

sigillare seal (v) *[attach a seal]*

sigillo (m) seal (n)

sigillo (m) doganale customs seal

siglare initial (v)

silo (m) grain elevator

simbolo (m) token

simbolo (m) di successo status symbol

sindacalista (m) trade unionist

sindacato (m) (trade) union

sindacato (m) degli inquilini rent tribunal

sindrome (f) della fenice phoenix syndrome

sinergia (f) synergy

singolo single

sinistro left *[not right]*

sistema (m) system

sistema (m) *[rete]* network (n)

sistema (m) di acquisti a rate hire purchase (HP)

sistema (m) di controllo control systems

sistema (m) di recupero delle informazioni retrieval system

sistema (m) di sorveglianza dell'ufficio office security

sistema (m) elettronico di elaborazione computer system

sistema (m) in tempo reale real-time system

Sistema (m) Monetario Europeo (SME) European Monetary System (EMS)

sistema (m) operativo operating system

sistema (m) tributario tax system

sistemare settle *or* arrange things

sistemare (disporre) arrange *or* set out

sistemazione (f) *[disposizione]* system *or* arrangement

situato situated

situazione (f) *[posizione]* situation *or* position *or* state of affairs

situazione (f) contrattuale bargaining position

SME (Sistema Monetario Europeo) EMS (= European Monetary System)

smentita (f) disclaimer

sociale social

società (f) society *[in general]*

società (f) a responsabilità limitata (Srl) private limited company

società (f) collegata (f) associate company

società (f) commerciale trading company

società (f) controllante parent company; holding company

società (f) cooperativa cooperative society

società (f) (di capitali) company

società (f) di capitali a responsabilità limitata limited (liability) company (Ltd)

società (f) di capitali a sottoscrizione pubblica (SpA) Public Limited Company (Plc)

società (f) di factoring factor (n) *[company]*

società (f) di medie dimensioni middle-sized company

società (f) di navigazione shipping company

società (f) di persone partnership

società (f) di servizi service (n) (business)

società (f) di vendita per corrispondenza mail-order business *or* mail-order firm

società (f) esistente solo di nome shell company

società (f) fiduciaria trust company

società (f) finanziaria finance company

società (f) in accomandita semplice limited partnership

società (f) mutua (di assicurazioni) mutual (insurance) company

società (f) orientata al profitto profit-oriented company

società (f) quotata in Borsa quoted company

società (f) rivale rival company

società (f) sorella sister company

socio (m) member *[of a group]*

socio (m) *[compagno]* partner

socio (m) *[associato]* associate (n)

socio (m) accomandante sleeping partner

socio (m) anziano senior partner

soddisfacente *[accettabile]* satisfactory *or* acceptable

soddisfare satisfy *[customer]*; meet *[a need]*

soddisfare una richiesta satisfy a demand

soddisfazione (f) satisfaction

soddisfazione (f) dei clienti customer satisfaction

soddisfazione (f) sul lavoro job satisfaction

software (m) software

soggetto a subject to

soggetto a condizioni conditional

soglia (f) threshold

soldi (mpl) in anticipo money up front

solido *[stabile]* solid *or* firm (adj)

solito *[abituale]* usual *or* normal

sollecitare ordinazioni solicit orders

sollecito prompt

sollecito (m) reminder *or* follow-up

sollevare raise (v) *[a question]*

solo *[unico]* sole

soluzione (f) solution

solvente solvent (adj)

solvibile credit-worthy

solvibilità (f) solvency

somma (f) sum *[of money]*

somma (f) *[addizione]* sum *or* addition *[calculation]*

sommare *[aggiungere]* add

sommare una colonna di cifre add up a column of figures

sondaggio (m) random check

sondaggio: fare un sondaggio sample (v) *or* ask questions

sondaggio (m) d'opinione opinion poll

soprattassa (f) di importazione import surcharge

sopravvalutare overvalue *or* overestimate (v)

sorpassare *[superare]* exceed *or* go higher than

sorvegliare supervise

sospendere suspend

sospendere i pagamenti stop payments

sospendere le trattative break off negotiations

sospendere un'attività *[chiudere]* close down

sospensione (f) suspension *or* stoppage

sospensione (f) dei pagamenti suspension of payments

sospensiva (f) stay of execution

sostegno (m) *[contenitore]* holder *[thing]*

sostegno (copia) backup copy

sostenere bear (v) *or* pay for

sostenere le spese di qualcuno defray someone's expenses

sostenere spese incur *[costs]*

sostenitore (m) *[avallante]* backer

sostituire replace

sostituto (m) *[delegato]* replacement *or* deputy

sostituto *[facente funzione di]* acting

sostituzione (f) replacement *[of an item]*

sotterfugio (m) fiscale tax loophole

sotto contratto under contract

sotto controllo under control

sotto nuova gestione under new management

sottoporre refer *or* pass to someone

sottoprodotto (m) spinoff

sottoscritto undersigned

sottoscrittore (m) contributor

sottoscrivere una polizza take out a policy

sottrarsi al pagamento delle tasse evade tax

sovraccarico (m) di scorte overstocks

sovrappiù (m) *[surplus]* surplus

sovrapprezzo (m) surcharge

sovrapprofitti (mpl) excess profits

sovvenzionare subsidize

sovvenzione (f) *[sussidio]* subvention *or* subsidy

spaiato odd *[not a pair]*

spartire *[dividere]* share (v) *or* divide among

spartire un ufficio share an office

spazio (m) space *or* room

spazio (m) *[vuoto]* blank (n)

spazio (m) pubblicitario advertising space

speciale special

specialista (m) specialist

specializzato skilled

specializzato: essere specializzato specialize in

specializzato: non specializzato unskilled

specializzazione (f) specialization

specifica (f) specification

specificare specify

specificare *[dettagliare]* itemize

specificazione (f) delle mansioni job specification

speculatore al rialzo bull *[on stock exchange]*

spedire dispatch (v) *or* send *or* forward *or* ship (v)

spedire merce in container ship in containers

spedire per espresso express (v) *or* send fast

spedire per posta post (v) *or* mail (v)

spedire per posta aerea airmail (v)

spedire un pacco per posta ordinaria send a package by surface mail

spedire un pacco per via aerea send a package by airmail

spedire una fattura (per posta) send an invoice by post

spedizione (f) dispatch (n) *or* sending

spedizione (f) consolidata consolidated shipment

spedizione (f) in massa bulk shipments

spedizione (f) marittima shipping

spedizione (f) per espresso express delivery

spedizioniere (m) (per via terra) forwarding agent

spedizioniere (m) marittimo shipper *or* shipping agent

spendere spend *[money]*

spendere meno underspend

spendere oltre il proprio budget overspend one's budget

spendere oltre le proprie possibilità overspend

spesa (f) shopping

spesa (f) (conto) expense

spesa (f) compresa inclusive charge

spesa (f) non autorizzata unauthorized expenditure

spesa (f) postale postage

spesa (f) totale total expenditure

spese (fpl) expenditure *or* expenses *or* outgoings

spese (fpl) bancarie bank charges

spese (fpl) conto capitali capital expenditure

spese (fpl) d'ammissione *o* **spese (fpl) d'entrata** admission charge *or* entrance charge

spese (fpl) d'esercizio running costs *or* running expenses *or* operating costs *or* operating expenses

spese (fpl) d'imballo packing charges

spese (fpl) d'incasso collection charges *or* collection rates

spese (fpl) di amministrazione administrative expenses

spese (fpl) di avviamento start-up costs

spese (fpl) di confezione *o* **spedizione** handling charges

spese (fpl) di consumo consumer spending

spese (fpl) di immagazzinamento storage cost

spese (fpl) di scarico (da nave) landing charges

spese (fpl) di trasporto freight costs

spese (fpl) extra extra charges

spese (fpl) generali overhead costs *or* overheads

spese (fpl) generali di produzione manufacturing overheads

spese (fpl) impreviste incidental expenses

spese (fpl) legali legal costs *or* legal charges *or* legal expenses

spese (fpl) postali postal charges *or* postal rates

spese (fpl) postali e imballo postage and packing (p & p)

spese (fpl) pubblicitarie publicity expenditure

spese (fpl) straordinarie below-the-line expenditure

spese (fpl) supplementari additional charges *or* extras

spese (fpl) trasporto merci via aerea air freight charges *or* rates

spiccioli (mpl) change (n) *or* cash

spiegare explain

spiegazione (f) explanation

spina (f) elettrica electric plug

spinta (f) boost (n)

spionaggio (m) industriale industrial espionage

sponsor (m) *[garante]* sponsor (n)

sponsorizzare *[patrocinare]* sponsor (v)

sponsorizzato dal governo government-sponsored

sponsorizzazione (f) *[avallo]* sponsorship

sportellista (m) teller

sportello (m) di cassa cash desk

spot (m) *[pubblicità]* TV commercial (n)

sprecare waste (v) (use too much)

spreco (m) waste (n) or wastage

stabile *[solido]* firm (adj) or stable

stabilimento (m) *[fabbrica]* plant (n) or factory

stabilire *[istituire]* establish

stabilire *[organizzare]* arrange *[meeting]*

stabilire come obiettivo target (v)

stabilire il prezzo price (v) or fix a price

stabilire il valore *[accertare]* assess

stabilità (f) stability

stabilità (f) dei prezzi price stability

stabilizzare stabilize

stabilizzarsi level off or level out

stabilizzazione (f) stabilization

stadio (m) stage (n)

stagionale *[periodico]* seasonal

stagione (f) season

stagnante stagnant

stampa (f) press

stampante (f) printer *[machine]*

stampante (f) a matrice d'aghi dot-matrix printer

stampante (f) con testina a margherita daisy-wheel printer

stampante (f) laser laser printer

stampante (f) lineare line printer or computer printer

stampare print out

stampato (m) printout

stand (m) stand (n) *[at exhibition]*

standard standard (adj) or stock (adj) or normal

standard (mpl) di produzione production standards

standardizzare standardize

standardizzazione (f) standardization

standista (m) *[espositore]* exhibitor

stanziamento (m) promozionale promotional budget

stanziare allocate

star del credere del credere

stare al passo con la richiesta keep up with the demand

statistica (f) statistics

statistico statistical

stato (m) *[nazione]* state (n) or country

stato (m) *[condizione]* state (n) or condition

stato (m) giuridico legal status

stato (m) ordinato: essere stato ordinato on order

statutario statutory

statuto (m) societario articles of association

stazione (f) ferroviaria railway station

sterlina (f) pound sterling

stima: fare una nuova stima reassess

stimare *[valutare]* estimate (v) or value (v)

stimatore (m) valuer

stimolare l'economia stimulate the economy

stimolo (m) stimulus

stipendiato salaried

stipendio (m) salary

stipendio (m) iniziale starting salary

stipendio (m) interessante attractive salary

stipendio (m) lordo gross salary

stipula (f) stipulation

stipulare stipulate

stipulare un contratto draw up a contract

stiva (f) hold (n) *[of ship]*

stivatore (m) *[scaricatore di porto]* stevedore

stoccare *[costruire riserve]* stockpile (v)

stock (m) *[scorte]* stock (n) *[goods]*

stop (m) *[fine]* stop (n)

stornare una registrazione contra an entry

strada (f) road

straniero *[estero]* foreign or external

straordinario extraordinary; outstanding or unusual

strategia (f) strategy

strategia (f) commerciale business strategy

strategia (f) di marketing marketing strategy

strategico strategic

strozzatura (f) *[nel processo aziendale]* bottleneck

strumenti (mpl) *[mezzi]* ways or means

strumenti (mpl) scontabili *[effetti bancabili]* bankable paper

strumento (m) instrument or implement (n)

strumento (m) *[documento]* instrument *[document]*

strumento (m) negoziabile negotiable instrument

strumento (m) non negoziabile non-negotiable instrument

struttura (f) structure (n)

struttura a rete grid structure

strutturale structural

strutturare structure (v) *or* arrange

studiare study (v)

studio (m) study (n)

studio (m) dei tempi e dei movimenti time and motion study

studio (m) della fattibilità feasibility report

su richiesta on request

subaffittante (m) sublessor

subaffittare sublease (v) *or* sublet

subaffitto (m) sublease (n)

subaffittuario (m) sublessee

subappaltatore (m) subcontractor

subappalto (m) subcontract (n)

subire un danno suffer damage

subire una forte flessione slump (v)

succedere succeed *or* take over *[from someone else]*

successo (m) success

successo: avere successo *[riuscire]* succeed *[do well]*

successo: che non ha successo unsuccessful

successo: di successo successful

sufficiente sufficient; adequate

superare (sorpassare) exceed *or* go higher than

superficie (f) area *[surface]*

superficie (f) di pavimento floor space

superiore superior (adj) *[better quality]*

superiore (m) superior (n) *[person]*

supermercato (m) supermarket

supermercato (m) all'ingrosso cash and carry

supervisione (f) *[vigilanza]* supervision

supervisione: di supervisione supervisory

supervisore (m) supervisor

supplementare supplementary; additional

surplus (m) *[sovrappiù]* surplus

sussidiario subsidiary (adj)

sussidio (m) *[sovvenzione]* subsidy

sussidio (m) di disoccupazione unemployment pay

svalutare devalue *or* depreciate *or* lose value

svalutazione (f) devaluation *or* depreciation *or* loss of value

svendere sell off

svendere merci sul mercato dump goods on a market

svendita (f) per chiusura d'esercizio closing-down sale

svendite (fpl) di fine stagione end of season sales

sviluppare develop *or* plan

sviluppare *[costruire]* develop *or* build

sviluppo (m) *[progresso]* development

sviluppo (m) del prodotto product development

sviluppo (m) economico economic development

svincolo (m) doganale customs clearance

svolgere esercizio d'impresa carry on a business

Tt

tabella (f) fissa dei prezzi fixed scale of charges

tabellone (m) hoarding *[for posters]*

tabulare tabulate

tabulato (m) computer printout

tabulatore (m) tabulator

tabulazione (f) tabulation

taccheggiare shoplifting

taccheggiatore (m) shoplifter

tachigrafo (m) tachograph

tacito consenso (m) tacit approval

taglia (f) size

taglia (f) standard stock size

taglia: di taglia forte outsize (OS)

tagliare cut (v)

tagliare i prezzi *o* **le condizioni di credito** slash prices *or* credit terms

taglio (m) cut (n)

tangente (f) *[bustarella]* bribe (n)

tangibile tangible

tappare plug (v) *or* block

tara (f) tare

tardi *[in ritardo]* late (adv)

tariffa (f) tariff; fare; scale of charges *or* rate

tariffa (f) a tempo time rate

tariffa (f) doganale customs tariff

tariffa (f) in vigore going rate

tariffa (f) notturna night rate

tariffa (f) protezionistica protective tariff

tariffa (f) ridotta cheap rate

tariffe (fpl) delle inserzioni pubblicitarie advertising rates

tariffe (fpl) di assicurazione insurance rates

tariffe (fpl) di nolo freight rates

tariffe (fpl) differenziali differential tariffs

tariffe (fpl) pubblicitarie differenziali graded advertising rates

tasca (f) pocket (n)

tassa (f) (imposta) tax (n)

tassa (f) ad valorem ad valorem tax

tassa (f) di base basic tax

tassa (f) di circolazione road tax

tassa (f) di registrazione registration fee

tassa (f) esclusa exclusive of tax

tassabile taxable

tassare *[gravare d'imposta]* tax (v)

tassazione (f) taxation

tassazione (f) alta high taxation

tassazione (f) diretta direct taxation

tassazione (f) indiretta indirect taxation

tasse (fpl) aeroportuali airport tax

tassi (mpl) monetari money rates

tasso (m) rate (n) *or* amount

tasso (m) d'inflazione rate of inflation

tasso (m) d'interesse interest rate

tasso (m) di base prime rate

tasso (m) di cambio exchange rate *or* rate of exchange

tasso (m) di cambio corrente current rate of exchange

tasso (m) di cambio sfavorevole unfavourable exchange rate

tasso (m) di cambio stabile stable exchange rate

tasso (m) di conversione conversion price *or* conversion rate

tasso (m) di produzione rate of production

tasso (m) di sconto discount rate

tasso (m) fisso di cambio fixed exchange rate

tasso (m) fluttuante di cambio floating exchange rates

tasso (m) ridotto reduced rate

tasso (m) su prestiti a breve call rate

tasso (m) ufficiale di sconto bank base rate

tastiera (f) keyboard (n)

tastierino (m) numerico numeric keypad

tasto (m) key *[on keyboard]*

tasto (m) delle maiuscole shift key

tasto (m) di comando control key

tavole (fpl) attuariali actuarial tables

tecnica (f) di vendita selling technique

tecniche (fpl) di marketing marketing techniques

tecniche (fpl) di propaganda canvassing techniques

tecniche (fpl) gestionali management techniques

telecomando (m) remote control

telefonare phone (v) *or* telephone (v)

telefonata (f) a carico del ricevente reverse charge call *or* collect call *[US]*

telefonata (f) d'affari business call

telefonata (f) di routine routine call

telefonata (f) in arrivo incoming call

telefonata (f) internazionale international call

telefonata (f) urbana local call

telefonista (mf) telephonist

telefono (m) phone (n) *or* telephone (n)

telefono (m) a gettoni pay phone

telefono (m) a schede card phone

telefono (m) cellulare cellular phone

telefono (m) interno internal telephone

telefono (m) per conferenze conference phone

telescrivente (f) *[telex]* telex (n)

teleselezione (f) dial direct

teleselezione (f) internazionale international direct dialling

telex (m) telex (n)

tempo (m) di elaborazione computer time

tempo (m) improduttivo down time

tempo (m) libero spare time

tendenza (f) al rialzo upward trend

tendenza (f) di mercato market trends

tenere hold (v) *or* keep; stock *[goods]*

tenere in affitto *[affittare]* lease (v) *[of tenant]*

tenere in efficienza maintain *or* keep going

tenere su keep up

tenere una seduta hold a meeting *or* a discussion

terminal (m) airport terminal

terminal (m) della compagnia aerea air terminal

terminal (m) per container container terminal

terminale terminal (adj) *[at the end]*

terminale (m) di computer computer terminal

terminare *[scadere]* terminate; expire

termine (m) termination; expiration

termine (m) *[chiusura]* closure

termine (m) *[fine]* end (n)

termine (m) ultimo *[data di chiusura]* closing date *or* time limit

termine (m) ultimo *[data di scadenza]* deadline

termini (mpl) stabiliti terms of reference

terra (f) *o* **terreno (m)** land (n)

territorio (m) territory *[of salesman]*

terza persona (f) third party

terzo trimestre (m) third quarter

tesoreria (f) treasury

tessera (f) card

tessera (f) *[di abbonamento ferroviario]* season ticket

tessera (f) prelievo contanti cash card

testa: che è in testa alle vendite top-selling

testimone (m) witness (n)

tetto (m) dei prezzi price ceiling

tetto (m) salariale credit ceiling

timbrare stamp (v) *[mark]*

timbro (m) stamp (n) *[device]*

tipografia (f) printer *or* printing company

tirare sul prezzo *[contrattare]* bargain (v)

tiratura (f) circulation *[of newspaper]*

tirocinante (m) trainee

titolare (m) holder *[person]*

titoli (mpl) securities

titoli (mpl) di prim'ordine gilt-edged securities *or* gilts

titoli (mpl) di stato government stock *or* government bonds

titolo (m) di prim'ordine blue chip

togliere lift (v) *or* remove

togliere l'embargo lift an embargo

togliere la seduta close a meeting

tonnellaggio (m) tonnage

tonnellaggio (m) lordo gross tonnage

tonnellata (f) ton *or* tonne

totale total (adj) *or* overall

totale (m) total (n) *or* sum

totale (m) corrente running total

totale (m) delle attività total assets

totale (m) generale grand total

totale (m) parziale subtotal

totale *[globale]* total (adj) *or* all-in

tradurre translate

traduttore (m), traduttrice (f) translator

traduzione (f) translation

traente (m) drawer

trafficare *[commerciare]* trade (v)

trafficare in *[commerciare in]* trade in *[buy and sell]*

traghetto (m) ferry

traghetto (m) per automezzi car ferry *or* roll on/roll off ferry

tramite (via) via

tranne (eccetto) except

transazione (f) transaction

transazione (f) a pronti spot purchase

transazione (f) commerciale business transaction

transazione (f) sul disponibile cash transaction *or* cash deal

transazioni (fpl) *[operazioni]* stock exchange dealing

transito (m) transit

trarre vantaggio da benefit from (v) *or* capitalize on

trascurabile negligible

trascurare *[omettere]* omit

trasferibile transferable

trasferimento (m) transfer (n) *or* assignment *or* cession

trasferimento (m) di capitali transfer of funds

trasferire transfer (v)

traslocare move *[house, office]*

trasloco (m) move *[to new house]*

trasmissione (f) conveyance; drive (n) *[part of machine]*

trasportare transport (v) *or* ship (v)

trasportare *[portare]* carry

trasportare a mezzo di palette palletize

trasportare merci via aerea airfreight (v)

trasportatore (m) haulage contractor

trasportatore (m) su strada road haulier

trasporti (mpl) pubblici public transport

trasporto (m) transport (n); carriage *or* freight

trasporto (m) di merci freightage

trasporto (m) di ritorno homeward freight

trasporto (m) ferroviario rail transport

trasporto (m) in container containerization *or* shipping in containers

trasporto (m) in superficie surface transport

trasporto (m) marittimo shipment

trasporto (m) mediante autocarro trucking

trasporto (m) merci via aerea air freight

trasporto (m) su strada road transport *or* road haulage

Trasporto Internazionale su Strada Transports Internationaux Routiers (TIR)

tratta (f) (bank) draft (n)

tratta (f) a vista sight draft

trattabile *[controllabile]* manageable

trattabile *[negoziabile]* negotiable

trattamento (m) equo fair dealing

trattare process (v) *or* deal with *or* negotiate

trattare *[lavorare]* process (v) *[raw materials]*

trattare con qualcuno deal with someone

trattario (m) drawee

trattativa (f) negotiation

trattative (fpl) difficile hard bargaining

trattato (m) commerciale trade agreement

trattenere hold up (v) *or* delay *or* keep back

tredicesima (f) *[gratifica natalizia]* Christmas bonus

treno (m) train (n)

treno (m) merci goods train *or* freight train

tribunale (m) law courts

tribunale (m) arbitrale arbitration board *or* arbitration tribunal

tribunale (m) del lavoro industrial tribunal

tribunale (m) di arbitrato adjudication tribunal

tribunale (m) di arbitrato industriale industrial arbitration tribunal

trimestrale quarterly (adj)

trimestralmente quarterly (adv)

trimestre quarter *[three months]*

triplicare triple (v)

triplice: in triplice copia in triplicate

triplo triple (adj)

truffa (f) *[imbroglio]* fiddle (n)

turno (m) *[di lavoro]* shift (n) *[team of workers]*

turno (m) di giorno day shift

turno (m) di notte night shift

tutte le spese pagate all expenses paid

Uu

UE (Unione Europea) EU (European Union)

ufficiale official (adj)

ufficiale: non ufficiale unofficial

ufficiale (m) di dogana customs official

ufficiale (m) di stato civile registrar

ufficio (m) office

ufficio: d'ufficio clerical

ufficio (m) a pianta aperta open-plan office

ufficio (m) acquisti buying department *or* purchasing department

ufficio (m) addetto alla fatturazione invoicing department

ufficio (m) assistenza service department

ufficio (m) assistenza ai clienti customer service department

ufficio (m) cambio bureau de change

ufficio (m) computer computer department

Ufficio (m) Dazio e Dogana Customs and Excise Department

ufficio (m) del personale personnel department

ufficio (m) della pubblicità publicity department

ufficio (m) delle pubbliche relazioni public relations department

ufficio (m) deposito bagagli left luggage office

ufficio (m) design design department

ufficio (m) di rappresentanza representative company

ufficio (m) indennità claims department

ufficio (m) informazioni information bureau

ufficio (m) legale legal department

ufficio (m) prenotazioni booking office

ufficio (m) produzioni production department

ufficio (m) pubblico general office

ufficio (m) reclami complaints department

ufficio (m) traduzioni translation bureau

ufficio (m) vendite sales department

ufficiosamente off the record

ufficioso *[non ufficiale]* unofficial

uguagliare equal (v)

uguale equal (adj)

ultima offerta (f) *[di licitazione]* closing bid

ultimo a entrare, primo a uscire last in first out (LIFO)

ultimo trimestre (m) last quarter

unico one-off *or* unique

unico proprietario (m) sole owner

uniforme *[indiscriminato]* general *or* across-the-board

unilaterale unilateral

unione (f) doganale customs union

Unione (f) Europea (UE) European Union (EU)

unire join

unire *[attaccare]* attach *or* join

unità (f) unit *or* item

unità (f) a dischi magnetici disk drive

unità (f) monetaria monetary unit

unito *[congiunto]* joint; united

uomo (m) man (n)

uomo (m) d'affari businessman

uomo (m) delle consegne deliveryman

uomo (m) di fiducia right-hand man

urgente urgent

usare use (v)

usato *[di seconda mano]* secondhand

uscente retiring

uscita (f) exit

uscita: in uscita outgoing

uso (m) use (n)

usuale *[comune]* common *or* frequent

usuale *[standard]* stock (adj) *or* normal

usufrutto (m) *[rendita vitalizia]* life interest

usurpare un brevetto infringe a patent

usurpazione (f) di brevetto infringement of patent

utente (m) user

utente (m) finale end user

utile useful

utile (m) *[profitto]* profit

utile (m) al lordo delle imposte pretax profit *or* profit before tax

utile (m) al netto delle imposte profit after tax

utile (m) d'esercizio operating profit *or* trading profit

utile (m) in aumento increasing profits

utile (m) lordo gross profit

utile (m) netto net profit

utile (m) per azione earnings per share *or* earnings yield

utili (mpl) distribuibili distributable profit

utili (mpl) ipotetici paper profit

utili (mpl) netti net earnings *or* net income

utili (mpl) record record profits

utili (mpl) societari corporate profits

utilità (f) *[beneficio]* usefulness *or* benefit (n)

utilizzazione (f) utilization

utilizzo (m) della capacità produttiva capacity utilization

Vv

vacante vacant

vaglia (m) *[mandato di pagamento]* money order

vaglia (m) postale postal order

valere be worth

validità (f) validity

valido valid

valido: essere valido be valid *or* be in force

valigia (f) case *or* suitcase

valore (m) value (n) *or* worth

valore: in base al valore di ad valorem

valore (m) attuale present value

valore (m) contabile book value

valore (m) di mercato market value

valore (m) di riscatto surrender value

valore (m) di sostituzione replacement value

valore (m) dichiarato declared value

valore (m) massimo peak (n)

valore (m) mediano median

valore (m) nominale nominal value *or* face value *or* par value

valore (m) patrimoniale asset value

valore (m) patrimoniale netto net assets *or* net worth

valore (m) totale della fattura total invoice value

valorem: ad valorem ad valorem

valuta (f) currency

valuta

(f) bloccata blocked currency

valuta (f) convertibile convertible currency

valuta (f) debole soft currency

valuta (f) di riserva reserve currency

valuta (f) estera foreign exchange *[currency]*

valuta (f) solida hard currency

valutare value (v) *or* evaluate

valutare *[stimare]* estimate (v)

valutare i costi evaluate costs

valutato estimated

valutazione (f) valuation; evaluation; estimate

valutazione (f) approssimativa rough estimate

valutazione (f) dei costi costing

valutazione (f) del mercato azionario stock market valuation

valutazione (f) della prestazione performance rating

valutazione (f) delle scorte stock valuation

vantaggioso economic *or* profitable

variare *[estendersi]* vary; range (v)

variazione (f) variation; variance

variazioni (fpl) *[scala]* range (n) *or* variation

variazioni (fpl) stagionali seasonal variations

vario *[miscellaneo]* various *or* miscellaneous

vecchio old

vecchio: di vecchia data long-standing

vecchio: di vecchia istituzione old-established

vecchio: più vecchio senior

veicolo (m) vehicle

veicolo (m) per merci pesanti heavy goods vehicle (HGV)

veicolo (m) articolato articulated vehicle

veloce fast (adj)

velocemente *[rapidamente]* fast (adv) *or* rapidly

vendere sell

vendere *[commercializzare]* market (v) *or* put on the market

vendere a minor prezzo di un concorrente undercut a rival

vendere a termine sell forward

vendere al dettaglio retail (v) *[goods]*

vendere all'asta auction (v)

vendere sotto costo discount (v); undersell

vendere tutto *[esaurire]* sell out *[all stock]*

vendersi be sold; move

vendersi a retail for (v) *or* sell for a price

vendibile saleable

vendibilità (f) saleability

vendita (f) sale (n) *or* selling

vendita: in vendita for sale

vendita (f) a domicilio house-to-house selling

vendita (f) al dettaglio retailing

vendita (f) all'asta sale by auction

vendita (f) coatta forced sale

vendita (f) con carta di credito credit card sale

vendita (f) con possibilità di resa see-safe

vendita (f) di merce sotto costo distress sale

vendita (f) di realizzo bargain made (n) *[on stock exchange]*

vendita (f) diretta direct selling

vendita (f) diretta tramite corrispondenza direct mail

vendita (f) per contanti cash sale

vendita (f) porta a porta door-to-door selling

vendite (fpl) *[fatturato]* sales

vendite (fpl) a termine forward sales

vendite (fpl) basse low sales

vendite (fpl) interne domestic sales

vendite (fpl) nazionali *o* **vendite sul mercato interno** home sales

vendite (fpl) per telefono telesales

vendite (fpl) presunte estimated sales

vendite (fpl) previste projected sales

vendite (fpl) record record sales

vendite (fpl) registrate book sales

venditore (m) salesman; seller *or* vendor

venditore (m) a domicilio door-to-door salesman

venditore (m) di assicurazioni insurance salesman

venditori (mpl) sales people

venduto: essere venduto be sold *or* change hands

venduto con possibilità di resa sale or return

venire a un compromesso compromise (v)

ventiquattrore (f) personalizzata personalized briefcase

verbale verbal

verbale (m) *[di assemblea]* minutes (n) *[of meeting]*

verbalizzare *[mettere a verbale]* minute (v)

verde: al verde broke (informal)

verdetto (m) *[decisione]* judgement *or* judgment; verdict

verifica (f) *[controllo]* verification; control (n) *or* check

verificare verify; audit (v)

verificare i conti audit the accounts

verificato: non verificato unaudited

vero *[autentico]* genuine *or* true

versamento (m) d'acconto down payment

versare denaro deposit (v)

vertenza (f) di lavoro labour disputes

vertenza (f) operaia industrial disputes

veto (m) veto (n)

veto: porre il veto a una decisione
veto (v) a decision

vetrina (f) shop window

vetrinetta (f) display case

vetta (f) (cima) top (n) *or* highest point

vettore (m) common carrier

via (tramite) via

viaggio (m) d'affari business trip

viaggio (m) di ritorno homeward
journey

vice amministratore (m) delegato
deputy managing director

vice direttore (m) assistant manager *or*
deputy manager

vicino a close to

videoscrittura (f) word-processing

video-unità (f) display unit

vie (fpl) legali legal proceedings

vietare *[interdire]* ban (v)

vigilanza (f) *[supervisione]* supervision

vigore: essere in vigore rule (v) *or* be
in force

vincere un contratto win a contract

vincolante binding

violare la legge break the law

violazione (f) dei regolamenti doganali
infringement of customs regulations

violazione (f) di garanzia breach of
warranty

virgola (f) decimale decimal point

visita (f) visit *or* call (n)

visita (f) a freddo cold call

vista (f) sight

vista: tratta a vista sight draft

visto (m) consolare visa

visto (m) consolare di transito transit
visa

visto (m) consolare multiplo multiple
entry visa

visto (m) d'ingresso entry visa

vita (f) ciclica di un prodotto product
cycle

viziare *[rovinare]* spoil

viziato *[privo di validità]* defective *or*
not valid

voce (f) item *[of information]*

voci (fpl) straordinarie extraordinary
items *or* exceptional items

volantino (m) leaflet

volere *[richiedere]* take (v) *or* need

volo (m) flight *[of plane]*

volo (m) a lunga percorrenza
long-distance flight

volo (m) a lungo raggio long-haul
flight

volo (m) charter charter flight

volo (m) di coincidenza connecting
flight

volo (m) di linea scheduled flight

volume (m) volume

volume (m) *[grande quantità]* bulk *or*
mass

volume (m) d'affari sales figures *or*
turnover

volume (m) degli scambi commerciali
volume of trade *or* volume of business

volume (m) delle vendite sales
volume *or* volume of sales

voluminoso bulky

voto (m) decisivo casting vote

voto (m) per delega proxy vote

vuotare empty (v)

vuoti (mpl) a rendere returned empties

vuoto empty (adj)

vuoto (m) *[spazio]* blank (n)

vuoto *[in bianco]* blank (adj)

Zz

zero (m) *[nulla]* zero *or* nil

zona (f) *[quartiere]* zone; area *or*
district *[of town]*

zona (f) commerciale shopping
precinct

zona (f) di libero scambio free trade area

zona (f) di libero scambio free trade zone

zona (f) franca free zone

zona (f) industriale industrial estate

BILINGUAL DICTIONARIES

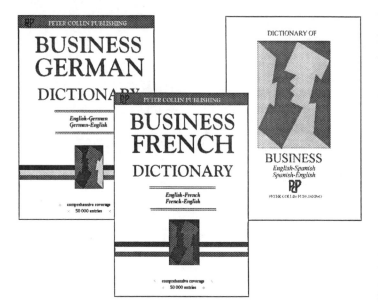

A range of comprehensive, up-to-date fully bilingual business dictionaries. The dictionaries cover all aspects of business usage: buying and selling, office practice, banking, insurance, finance, stock exchange, warehousing and distribution.

Each dictionary includes over 50,000 entries

example sentences	grammar notes
clear and accurate translations	part of speech

Ideal for any business person, teacher, or student

Business French	*ISBN 0-948549-64-5*	*600pp*	*h/b*
Business German	*ISBN 0-948549-50-5*	*650pp*	*h/b*
Business Spanish	*ISBN 0-948549-30-0*	*736pp*	*h/b*
Business Chinese	*ISBN 0-948549-63-7*	*534pp*	*h/b*
Business Swedish	*ISBN 0-948549-14-9*	*420pp*	*h/b*

Available from all good bookshops
or contact: Peter Collin Publishing
1 Cambridge Road, Teddington, Middx. TW11 8DT
tel: 0181 943 3386   fax: 0181 943 1673